Imperialism

IMPERIALISM

*The Idea and Reality of
British and French
Colonial Expansion,
1880–1914*

by
WINFRIED BAUMGART

**TRANSLATED BY THE AUTHOR
WITH THE ASSISTANCE OF
BEN V. MAST**

**With a preface by
Henri Brunschwig**

**OXFORD UNIVERSITY PRESS
1982**

Oxford University Press, Walton Street, Oxford OX2 6DP

London Glasgow New York Toronto
Delhi Bombay Calcutta Madras Karachi
Kuala Lumpur Singapore Hong Kong Tokyo
Nairobi Dar es Salaam Cape Town
Melbourne Auckland

and associate companies in
Beirut Berlin Ibadan Mexico City

Revised Edition.
Originally published in German
under the title of
Der Imperialismus. Idee und
Wirklichkeit der englischen
und französischen Kolonial-
expansion 1880–1914.
Wiesbaden, 1975
© France Steiner Verlag 1975

Published in the United States by
Oxford University Press, New York

British Library Cataloguing in Publication Data
Baumgart, Winfried
Imperialism: the idea and reality of British and
French colonial expansion, 1880–1914.
1. Imperialism   2. Great Britain—Foreign relations
—1837–1901   3. Great Britain—Foreign relations—
20th century   4. France—Foreign relations—1870–
1940
I. Title   II. Der Imperialismus. English
325'.32'0941   JV1017
ISBN 0–19–873040–3
ISBN 0–19–873041–1   Pbk

Library of Congress Cataloging in Publication Data
Baumgart, Winfried.
Imperialism: the idea and reality of British and
French colonial expansion, 1880—1914.
Translation of: Der Imperialismus.
Bibliography: p.
Includes index.
1.—Great Britain Colonies. 2.—France Colonies.
3.—Imperialism. I. Title.
JV1017.B3813   325'.32'09   81-22434
ISBN 0–19–873041–1   AACR2
ISBN 0–19–873040–3 (pbk.)

Typeset by Hope Services
Printed and Bound by
Mackays of Chatham Ltd
Lordswood, Chatham

Preface

The word imperialism, like all political terms, has assumed a great number of meanings. It was first used on the international scene about 1880 to describe the effort of a state or a people to impose rule (*imperium*) on others. As the nations of Europe took on the mission of spreading their civilization and culture across the world, thereby enhancing their prestige, the purely political and legal definition of imperialism was broadened to include psychological and moral considerations. Still later, the term gained an economic connotation when the European powers tried to secure for themselves access to the raw materials and markets indispensable for their development. (This control, incidentally, could be exercised without the establishment of formal rule.) Finally, imperialism assumed a social meaning when the domestic tensions spawned by the industrial revolution were eclipsed by nationalist passions and rivalry among states for world domination. International relations, colonial expansion, and domestic policy converged on the dynamics of imperialism from 1880 to 1914 and were the subjects of a multiplicity of theories.

In an excellent book entitled *Germany in the Age of Imperialism* (1st edition, 1972, 3rd edition, 1979), Professor Baumgart has provided an admirable analysis of the various motives leading the Second *Reich* initially to colonial expansion and then to *Weltpolitik*. He now continues his inquiry with a study of British and French colonial expansion. His account is mercifully devoid of abstractions and cant. Both scholars and the general public are thus allowed unencumbered access to the theories which justified colonial conquests, and will appreciate the soundness, clarity, and objectivity of his analysis.

Historians who continue to investigate the phenomenon of imperialism have sometimes insisted that, despite the diversity of the theories, the representatives of the imperialist powers in actual practice displayed a similar behaviour towards the

natives. Between British 'indirect rule' and the French protectorate, for example, there allegedly was often hardly any
difference. However, when one attempts to learn how these
theories — all originating in the West — were met with by
conquered peoples, certain distinctions must be made. In
contrast to the British, the French long believed in the feasibility of assimilating colonized peoples and of amalgamating
them with the metropolis into a multiracial empire. Following
the abolition of slavery in 1848, they granted French citizen-
ship to Negroes. Subsequently and well beyond 1914 they
welcomed in their parliaments and governments, either
explicitly or implicitly, coloured deputies and ministers.
They did so with more reservations as time went on but without closing the door altogether. This explains the attachment
shown by a number of colonized subjects to the French
'Mother Country', especially in Black Africa. The idea of
'assimilation' was put forward by the *jeunesses ('young')*
Senegalese and Dahomans in 1914-18, then by the *Evolués*
(the native elite) at the time of the Brazzaville conference of
1943, especially by Ferhat Abbas in Algeria before the failure
of the Blum-Violette Bill of 1937, and by other important
persons of the calibre of Blaise Diagne. To all of them, assimilation seemed for a long time to result naturally from colonization. As it later turned out, France, no longer desiring
assimilation, preferred rather to grant independence to her
Black African colonies; the leaders of these colonies, however,
did not desire independence and would have preferred
assimilation.

The history of decolonization remains to be written and
will certainly be interpreted in many different ways in the
light of still inaccessible archival material. However, in order
to understand the problems associated with decolonization
and the evolution of the modern world, sound information is
necessary on the theoretical and psychological approaches to
the events and the theories of the colonial period. Professor
Baumgart's books, which are readily available, provide just
that information.

Henri Brunschwig, Paris, 1981.

Acknowledgement

It is a pleasure for the author to thank Mr Ben V. Mast of Washington, DC, who took great pains in revising and polishing the author's translation of this book. Thanks are also due to his wife Ingrid who retyped the manuscript and helped in various ways to get it finished. Without their help no editor would have accepted the text.

Contents

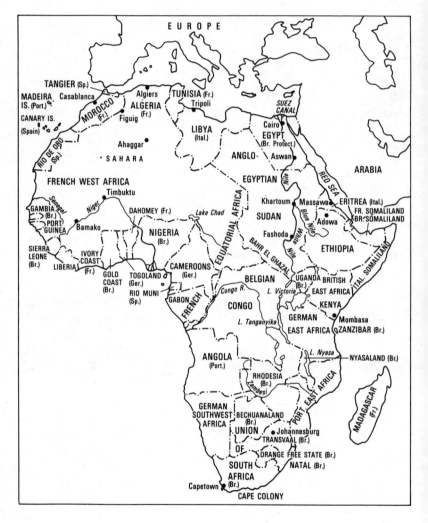

Africa, 1914

I. Imperialism: a Definition of the Term

1. THE ORIGIN

Imperialism is a vague and imprecise catchword. It is well-worn like an old coin, but, in contrast to a coin, it has more than two sides. It is as many-faceted as a crystal, but lacks the crystal's transparency and clearly defined lines. Imperialism is a hybrid term, much like a fabulous creature wrought from several entities. Broadly speaking, imperialism may be defined as the domination or control of one group over another group. There are widely varying relationships involving such domination and dependence. They may be planned or unplanned, conscious, half-conscious, or unconscious, direct or indirect, physical or psychological, open or concealed. One could speak of a cultural imperialism, a religious imperialism, a tariff, finance, dollar, or Deutsche-Mark imperialism.

These sweeping generalizations are of little value in seeking a precise definition, nor are they likely to clarify the phenomenon on a historical basis. If imperialism is narrowly construed according to the etymology of the word, that is, as the formation of an empire, it can be applied to all periods of history in which one nation has extended its domination over one or several neighbouring nations. Thus, as examples, imperialism existed when the Egyptians expelled the Hyksos and extended their 'new empire' to the south and east; when the Greeks and Romans ruled over several continents; when the Franks of the Middle Ages under Clovis I subjugated tribe after tribe; when the Ottomans, after having conquered Constantinople, extended their power in all directions; when the Muscovites collected one stretch of 'Russian soil' after the other; when the French under Napoleon I amassed the great Empire; when the British extended their dominion around the world; when the Germans under Hitler established the *Grossdeutsches Reich*; when the Russians under Lenin and Stalin forged the Soviet empire. It is common in historiography to apply the term imperialism to the formation of such empires. And this seems reasonable.

When the term imperialism gained coinage in the second half of the nineteenth century, it did not yet connote a policy of territorial expansion.[1] Initially it was descriptive of the government and policies of Napoleon III. In the 1870s it was used in the disputes of the two political parties in Britain. The Liberals spoke of 'Beaconsfieldian Imperialism' in their attempt to criticize the greater activity of the Conservatives in European policy, and especially Disraeli's growing interest in India.

Afterwards 'imperialism' took on still more meanings. It was used to refer to the expansion of the European industrial powers, of the United States, of Japan beyond their own borders; it also stamped foreign policy in general if it evinced expansionist tendencies of a military, political, territorial, or economic nature. Depending on the context, imperialism now meant France's colonial policy *and* her chauvinism towards Germany or Britain; Britain's empire policy *and* her jingoism or navalism towards the Continental powers of Europe, Germany's colonial policy *and* Prussian militarism; and Russia's expansion into the Balkans and Asia *and* her Pan-Slavism.

This expanded definition of imperialism came around the turn of the century. Further inflation of the term was contributed to by Socialist and Marxist critics, who also narrowed its application when discussing the contemporary social and economic situation and tying it to a certain stage in the development of the capitalist economy and society. Their best-known representative was Lenin. He was well aware of the various meanings of the term[2] when he equated France's export of capital with 'usury imperialism'; or when he associated the rule of seventy million Great Russians over one hundred million non-Russians in the Tsarist empire with 'militarism' or 'feudal imperialism'. According to the Marxist interpretation of history, imperialism had already reached its highest stage of development and would now begin its self-destruction. This Lenin called 'capitalist imperialism'. Because of its inherent over-production and formation of surplus capital, he wrote, it must push towards new markets and investment areas lest it should get bogged down in its own excess. This form of imperialism he saw affecting both the ties between the industrialized countries and their African and Asian colonies, as well as their relations among themselves. When the First World War erupted, Lenin thought that the centre of gravity of imperialism had shifted from the colonies to Europe itself, where he believed the struggle was on for the redistribution of territories.

2. THE CHRONOLOGICAL BOUNDARIES

The expansionist policies which modern industrial powers pursued after the last two decades of the nineteenth century may be called classical imperialism in order to distinguish them from the imperialism of other periods and to point out that they were the main characteristic of that epoch.[3] The chronological framework of this classical imperialism depends on what characteristics are ascribed to it. There has been general agreement that the age of classical or modern imperialism began around 1880.

At the time, however, the year 1885 was regarded as the starting-point. That was the year the Berlin Congo Conference ended, and the 'scramble for Africa' supposedly got under way. For example, the British Prime Minister Salisbury said in an 1891 speech: 'When I left the Foreign Office in 1880, nobody thought about Africa. When I returned to it in 1885, the nations of Europe were almost quarrelling with each other as to the various portions of Africa which they should obtain.'[4] The notion is still entertained that the partitioning of Africa and the annexation of the islands in the Pacific — the most conspicuous events of imperialism — were triggered by the Berlin Conference of 1885. Thus the former president of Ghana, Kwame Nkrumah, wrote some years ago that 'the original carve-up of Africa [was] arranged at the Berlin Conference of 1884'.[5]

Historians today have concluded that this notion is incorrect. At first they set the year 1882 as the starting-point of the scramble, citing the occupation of Egypt in July of that year, and the ratification of the Brazza–Makoko treaty by France in November of the same year, which touched off the struggle for the Congo. More recently the date has been revised backward by another three years to 1879 when the rivalry between Britain and France became especially intense in West

Africa.[6] Even those historians who see imperialism rooted in economic and social causes will agree on the years 1879–82 as the *terminus a quo*, because that was when they believed the European powers felt compelled to acquire colonies as an antidote for domestic and economic problems.

The point at which the age of classical imperialism is supposed to have come to an end may be more debatable. If imperialism is defined as the political and territorial domination by the industrial powers over the colonial and semi-colonial regions of the earth, then the First World War may be regarded as the time of its demise. Because of the universal consequences of this war imperialism lost its quality as the main characteristic of the age. This does not mean that imperialism, even when it is only associated with colonialism, completely ceased to exist at the end of the First World War. On the contrary, the British and French colonial empires actually increased in size after the war. Only then did the idea of the *Empire français* become popular in France, whose colonies finally began to pay long-awaited dividends. The Italian colonial empire reached its zenith still later under Mussolini. On the other hand, the British Empire began its transformation into the Commonwealth of Nations during the interwar period. This decolonization of the British colonies in Africa and Asia was accelerated after 1945. Beyond the date the last vestiges of classical imperialism rapidly disappeared.

Imperialism in the general sense of empire-building, of the expansion of powerful states over weaker neighbours, has remained a characteristic of the years since the First World War. Thus when Lenin consolidated Soviet power inside Russia, the Soviet empire expanded at the cost of the neighbouring states, and later on at the cost of the Third Reich and of the peoples of eastern Europe subjugated for a short period by Hitler.

According to the Marxist–Leninist interpretation, imperialism reached its climax during the First World War, not its end. The First World War, during which the antagonism of the Great Powers came to a violent clash, was seen by Lenin as the struggle for the redistribution of the regions of the world; it was the inevitable result of crisis-ridden capitalism, and it would end with the self-annihilation of imperialism and the victory of the proletarian revolution. Imperialism, however, did not collapse after the war and it was necessary for Stalin and Bukharin to proclaim the theory of the inevitability of wars as the dooming factor. With capitalist imperialism still alive even after the Second World War, Krushchev invented the thesis of peaceful coexistence between the Socialist and capitalist camps: capitalist imperialism would eventually be 'buried' by the steadily increasing power of the Socialist economic system and the appeal of the Communist social system. Despite major modifications of Lenin's theory, imperialism survives, so Marxists believe, because of the continued existence of the capitalist camp.

3.   'INFORMAL' IMPERIALISM

In recent years the starting-point of classical imperialism has again been questioned by the reintroduction and acceptance of the term 'informal' imperialism. This term was first used by Charles Ryle Fay in 1934 in a casual dissent[7] against established historical works of the twenties and thirties dealing with the British empire. According to the view held in these years, Britain during the early and middle Victorian age had regarded the colonial empire inherited from the eighteenth century and from the Napoleonic wars with indifference and even opposition. Contemporary theorists favouring political liberalism as well as the advocates of free trade thought it superfluous and even undesirable to maintain bonds between the mother country and the colonies beyond a minimally necessary limit. By granting 'responsible government' to the white settlement colonies, the gradual secession of those colonies from the mother country was deliberately prepared. Successful relations with the other colonies had worked almost automatically by applying the principle of free trade so that the government of the mother country intervened only when asked to do so by the local authorities.

Fay's criticism of these views was espoused by John Gallagher and Ronald Robinson in the now famous essay they published in 1953.[8] They described the empire policy of the early and middle Victorian age both as formal imperialism, directed at annexing and controlling colonial territories, and informal imperialism, aimed at spreading influence by economic means in regions where direct political predominance seemed unnecessary. According to their reasoning, the usual summing-up of a free-trade empire policy as 'trade not rule' should read 'trade with informal control if possible; trade with rule when necessary'. If formal and informal (free-trade) imperialism was the main characteristic of British empire policy throughout the nineteenth century, the year 1880 cannot be regarded as a genuine dividing-line between an era erroneously described as an anti-imperialist age and the age of expansionist imperialism.

This theory categorically rejects the idea of a break in Britain's empire policy and instead emphasizes its continuity. The Gallagher–Robinson essay sparked a lively debate which continues to this day. Their thesis is both approved and rejected.[9] It seems that usage of the term 'informal imperialism' creates more problems than it solves. If subjected to logic it permits of no clear borderlines. It is synonymous with any form of dependence and is therefore unacceptably vague. David Landes, who seems basically to agree with Gallagher and Robinson, believes that imperialism arises whenever there is an imbalance of power between two social groups which the stronger one tries to exploit to the detriment of the weaker.[10] Using this definition, the term imperialism can be equally applied to the following instances: the personal relationship between a medieval feudal lord and his vassal; the economic and legal relations between the Ottoman empire and the European powers, regulated since the sixteenth century by the so-called capitulations which increasingly worked to Turkey's disadvantage; and the economic, technological, and cultural relations between modern industrial nations and the less developed countries.

The latter application of Landes's definition would seem to approximate to the Marxist interpretation of imperialism. Those who use the term in an all-embracing fashion say their interpretation is restricted to the relations between two unequal groups, with the stronger exploiting and dominating the weaker; such an interpretation cannot, for example, be applied to relations based on partnership. This dividing-line, however, is arbitrary and increases the vagueness of the term. The export of British capital to the United States, Britain's foremost debtor country, at the beginning of this century was aimed at profit-making. Did, therefore, industrialized Britain pursue imperialism towards the industrialized United States? More recently, do the Arab oil-producing countries pursue imperialism towards dependent European countries because they are exploiting their dominant position in the oil market for ever larger profits and even for massive political pressure?

Although the vague term informal imperialism is widely and more or less arbitrarily used today, its earlier advocates, Robinson and Gallagher, indirectly discarded it[11] in their 1961 book, *Africa and the Victorians*, and have adopted a concept of imperialism defined mainly in political terms.[12] I prefer a definition restricted to political and territorial domination to the more flexible but less precise term informal imperialism.

My position is supported by commentaries from the age of imperialism when people became conscious of imperialism as an international phenomenon and when the term was no longer paraphrased with nationally limited auxiliary terms such as *deutsche Weltpolitik* or Russian expansionism. In his book entitled *World Politics*, published in 1900, the US political scientist Paul Samuel Reinsch described imperialism 'as a desire to control as large a portion of the earth's surface as their [the nation's] energy and opportunities will permit'.[13] In a similar way, the German liberal pacifist Friedrich Wilhelm Foerster in 1901 summed up imperialism as the political doctrine 'which aims at the acquisition of new areas of exploitation for the accumulated energies of big industry by forcibly conquering new lands and doing violence to weaker races, and which for this purpose pushes the nations to use as many of their military resources as they can so that they won't arrive late in the process of redistributing the earth's surface'. The British liberal historian George Peabody Gooch pointed out in a simultaneously published essay that imperialism involves more than merely dominating other nations; there must also be annexation of colonial territory, of 'tropical territory'.[14]

4. SPECIAL AND BORDERLINE CASES OF IMPERIALISM

It could be argued that limiting the definition of imperialism to formal annexation of colonial territories as suggested by Gooch is as arbitrary as riveting imperialism to a certain stage of development of the capitalist economy in the Marxist doctrine. This argument is justified. As is the case with every definition of an 'ism', the borderlines with neighbouring phenomena fluctuate. But in order not to let them melt away, the criterion of effective long-term political and territorial domination of larger groups over others should be deemed necessary when defining the general species of imperialism. Similarly, when defining classical imperialism, the criterion of effective long-term political and territorial domination of the technologically superior nations over technologically inferior nations — as colonies and semi-colonies — should be regarded as necessary.

Both forms of imperialism existed between 1880 and the war years 1914–18. The first (domination by social groups) became especially manifest in the extreme war aims of both belligerent camps between 1914 and 1918. The second refers to the annexation of colonies by the European powers as well as by the United States and Japan, but it also comprises special forms and variants such as the occupation and annexation of Bosnia by Austria–Hungary, the French protectorate (legally speaking, not a formal domination) over Tunisia, the one-man or private imperialism of King Leopold II in the Congo basin, as well as the extension of Ethiopia over neighbouring territories several times its own size.

A borderline case in this definition of imperialism is the complex dependence of Turkey (also of Persia and China) on the European powers. The carving-out of peripherally located regions (Tunisia, Egypt, Tripoli, Bosnia, regions in the Caucasus) from the Ottoman Empire definitely is imperialism, or at least 'partial' imperialism; but the cultural, technological, and financial dependence of the Turkish mainland proper on the European powers was not imperialism, though it could become so (witness the various partition plans from the eighteenth century to the Sykes–Picot agreement of 1915). These cases, where an imbalance of power was exploited, may be regarded as preliminary steps possibly, but not necessarily, leading to imperialism.

When trying to compile and sum up the numerous theories of imperialism which have been worked out by contemporary critics, politicians, and scholars, one gains the impression that there are more people who have written on imperialism than people who have acted on it or fought for it. The number of studies that have been written on classical imperialism alone cannot be counted.

For the sake of clarity the various explanations of imperialism can be grouped together under four headings:[15] 1. the political-historical group; 2. the social-psychological group; 3. the economic group; and 4. the social-economic group. The first two are a compilation of a great number of empirically rather easily verifiable causes and motives. The third and fourth suggest a more theoretical and structural approach which can only be partially verified through history. Nevertheless, they are indispensable planks of the whole phenomenon and they are of great value for finding out the truth. All four groups interlock and overlap constantly so that their separation and separate listing seem justified only in analytical research which does not necessarily coincide with historical reality.

II. The Political and Historical Attempt at a Definition

1. THE UNITY OF EUROPEAN COLONIAL HISTORY

The term 'informal imperialism' introduced by Fay, Robinson, and Gallagher for characterizing British (but not French, etc.) colonial policy between 1815 and the outbreak of the First World War has the advantage that it points to the important factor of continuity in European colonial history. Since the discovery of new continents in the fifteenth century, European powers had acquired and found colonies again and again. The period between the acquisition of colonies in the fifteenth century until the decolonization in the twentieth century may therefore be regarded as one process in which the year 1880 is only one turning-point among others. This process is, broadly speaking, identical with the transfer of European civilization and culture across the earth.

From an over-all historical perspective the Europeanization of the globe is a typical case of the contact and conflict between two civilizations, and it came about in three big waves. First was the age of discovery during the fifteenth and sixteenth centuries. This was, for the first time, a global phenomenon; its main features were a spirit of exploration and adventure, the search for precious metals and for spices, a missionary urge, and the desire to escape religious persecution. Next came the age of mercantilism during the seventeenth and eighteenth centuries, which witnessed many colonial wars amongst the European powers and the prime motive of which was the accumulation of material riches. Finally, there was the age of imperialism, during which both economic and non-economic motives became inextricably intertwined.

The broad bases of the world economy of the nineteenth and twentieth centuries were already laid at the very beginning of this over-all process. However, much as the economic system of the occidental world may have changed since the fifteenth and sixteenth centuries, above all through the various phases of industrialization, the development of modern capitalism in

Europe and its spread across the globe are inconceivable without the two preceding waves.

Those who promoted this planetary expansion were not, as the Swiss historian Herbert Lüthy cogently pointed out,[16] the governments and the states, but rather those hundreds of thousands of colonists, merchants, pioneers, and adventurers who, as 'the surplus energies' of Europe, permeated the primitive civilizations in the extra-European world like leaven. According to Lüthy, it is indisputable that after 1880, compared to the preceding waves of colonization, the role of the state increased. This must be attributed, among many other reasons, to the necessity of curbing the various irregularities of colonization, of pursuing it according to rational principles which considered the interests both of the colonizers and of the colonized — if, that is, these interests were to the advantage of the colonizers.

2. ANTI-SLAVERY AND THE FOUNDING OF COLONIES

The taming of selfishly pursued commercial and adventurer imperialism came with the take-over of various colonial charter companies after 1880 by their corresponding European governments. For example, the Imperial British East Africa Company and the Royal Niger Company were taken possession of by the British government, and the German Company for South West Africa and the German East Africa Company were absorbed by the German government. Actually, however, the process started decades before 1880 through the abolition of slavery which was demanded by a broad humanitarian movement and sanctioned by the Congress of Vienna at Britain's request.

While the struggle against illicit slave-trading did not lead to a wholesale acquisition of colonies as was the case when bankrupt trading companies were supported or taken possession of, it did lead to the establishment of military bases along the African coast from which the British Navy was able to search ships for slaves. It led to the establishment of hospitals and missionary stations, where Negroes freed from the slave-herds and slave-ships were to be resocialized. Thus in 1787 the philanthropical Sierra-Leone Company established a station on the West African coast for blacks repatriated from the New World. In 1807, the year in which slave-trading was prohibited in Britain, the station was taken over by the British Crown. It became the first British Crown colony in West Africa and served as a reception area for the slave shipments captured by the British Navy.[17] In 1816 the Americans founded a colonial society for the rehabilitation of American Negroes in West Africa.[18] Four years later this society established a settlement on the West African coast; it became the nucleus of Liberia, which declared independence in 1847. When complete emancipation of the slaves was proclaimed for all the British colonies in 1833, many Boers of the Cape Country, thinking their very existence depended on the retention of slave labour, made their great trek into the interior of the country and founded the Orange Free State and Transvaal.

These are examples of the establishment of colonies or colonial settlements as a consequence of the humanitarian intervention of the British government and of philanthropic societies.[19] It would be biased to argue, as did some contemporaries, especially in France, that behind such establishments there was really some sordid economic motive, that the liberated slaves might be used as labourers on plantations to produce goods for European markets. In fact, the British government paid great sums to fight the illegal slave-trade. It made cash payments to Spain and Portugal for their consent to the abolition of the slave-trade; Sierra Leone was purposely accepted as a colonial settlement producing a deficit; the compensation paid to the settlers in the British colonies amounted to 20 million pounds sterling in 1833; patrol vessels on the African coasts,[20] numbering two dozen in 1850, cost the British taxpayer sums that have never been calculated, as did also the fifty or so treaties with native African chiefs, whose consent to abolition of the slave export had to be dearly paid for.

The Marxist view[21] is that Britain fought the slave-trade for economic gain, that the ostensible humanitarian impulse was thus only a cover-up for the economic motive or had only become important when pushed on by the economic factor. This interpretation does not hold water when the basic facts are examined. Marxists argue that the cultivation of sugar-cane in Britain's Caribbean colonies, combined with the sugar-cane production in Brazil and Cuba, led to an over-production of sugar. The British government, they contend,

was interested in curbing the production of sugar and consequently also of the slave-trade which was channelled to a large
extent to the West Indies. The Abolition Bills of 1807 and
1833 were therefore really meant to combat over-production.
In fact, however, Britain also fought the slave-trade with
Brazil[22] and thus jeopardized her good economic relations
with that country. Palmerston's policy against slavery and the
slave-trade must be seen as a blend of humanitarian and
economic motives. He sought rather to promote 'legitimate
trade' with West Africa[23] and to open up the West African
market for British goods, 'to encourage and extend British
commerce and thereby to displace the Slave Trade'.[24]

The bad conscience of Europe about the disgraceful and
abominable treatment of the black natives was stirred earlier
than the period of decolonization in the twentieth century. It
had already risen in Britain in the late eighteenth and early
nineteenth centuries. The humanitarian ideal, the sincere
wish to repair the wrong done to the blacks, became evident
in the report of a fact-finding committee presented to the
House of Commons in 1837 about the situation of the natives
in the Empire:

'He who has made Great Britain what she is, will inquire at our hands how
we have employed the influence he has lent to us in our dealings with the
untutored and defenceless savage; whether it has been engaged in seizing
their lands, warring upon their people . . . or whether we have, as far as
we have been able, informed their ignorance and invited and afforded
them the opportunity of becoming partakers of that civilization . . .
which it has pleased a gracious Providence to bless our own country.'[25]

These words evoke the concept of trusteeship, long before
similar ideas found expression in the twentieth century.

3.   RELIGIOUS MISSIONS AND THE ESTABLISHMENT OF COLONIES

It was usually Christian missionary societies which established
and maintained the stations for receiving and caring for the
former slaves. Their work and its results — not so much in the
religious but in the secular field — have become one of the
basic elements and preconditions of classical imperialism.
Missionary work and teaching natives European civilization
were regarded as one and the same thing. It was not enough
to teach the Scriptures to the blacks; they had to be taught
to earn a living. The cultivation of plantations and trading

their products was regarded as a secure and legitimate means of getting the blacks to settle down. As the French historian Henri Brunschwig put it, legitimate 'civilizing trade' should take the place of the abominable slave-trade. The demand for oil-products (machine oil, etc.) which suddenly increased due to Europe's industrialization provided a powerful impetus for the work of the missionaries in West Africa in the decades before 1860. Thus Samuel Crowther said in a report in 1857 on one of the Joruba tribes: 'Their head chiefs could not help confessing to me that they, aged persons, never remembered any time during the slave trade that so much wealth was brought to their country as has been since the commencement of the palm-oil trade for the last four years; that they were perfectly satisfied with legitimate trade and with proceedings of the British government [i.e. with cutting off the slave trade originating in Lagos] .'[26]

The great missionary and explorer David Livingstone was often heard to say that religious instruction and economic development – 'Christianity, Commerce and Civilization'[27] – must go hand in hand. The social reformer Thomas Fowell Buxton was convinced that only the Bible and the plough could lead Africa on to a higher level of existence. The plough, it was argued, would not only increase the yield of the soil, but would also free the native women from the heavy burden of hoeing the soil; moreover, the new methods of production would contribute to the abolition of the sinful practice of polygamy. The connection between missionary and commercial interests also becomes evident in Livingstone's endeavour to improve transportation in the areas of missionary activity by building roads, by introducing steamships on the major lakes, and finally by building railways. In this way, he argued, legal trade would be advanced and the plight of the carrier slaves would be alleviated.

The civilizing work of the missions and the establishment of factories in the early and middle Victorian ages were not intended to lead to the acquisition of colonies. If they did so, the result was accepted only with reluctance and reservations. In 1861 the delta region of the Niger, which had become the centre of the palm-oil export, had been placed under the protection of the British Crown because the commercial companies there were always quarrelling among themselves. Four years later, a House of Commons declaration on colonial policy considered inopportune the extension of the government's responsibility by new treaties of protection with the native tribes: 'The object of our policy should be to encourage in the natives the exercise of these qualities which may render it possible for us more and more to transfer to them the administration of all the Governments, with a view to our ultimate withdrawal from all, except, probably Sierra Leone.'[28]

This 'anti-colonial colonialism', as Henri Brunschwig called it, was at that time a characteristic of British policy. Disraeli in 1852 spoke graphically of the 'wretched colonies' which are 'a millstone round our necks'; he hoped they would become independent in a couple of years.[29]

The framers of British colonial policy during that period did not see any inherent contradiction between missionary aims and commercial interests. In the decades of classical imperialism the unity of these two factors came under considerable strain, but it never disappeared altogether. This new imperialism, which was now mainly pursued by the governments, was built on the peaceful work of the missions. The interrelation between *Pax* and *Imperium* is especially evident in the cases of Uganda and Barotseland. Here the famous phrase 'flag follows trade' could read 'flag follows the cross'.

Uganda was a land where European missionary work was especially successful. For one thing, it was a densely populated and a culturally developed country. Secondly, the advance of Islam, which had already established missions over large coastal tracts in East Africa, could be checked here. But the Christian missionary societies were incapable of pooling their efforts. Instead, there was strong rivalry among Catholic, Protestant, and Anglican societies,[30] a characteristic of imperialism. In the end, many missionaries were pure nationalists. There were even societies which wanted to work only in the colonies of their mother country. Thus the Berlin Evangelical Missionary Society for East Africa, among whose promoters was Carl Peters, was founded in 1886 exclusively to work in German East Africa. Despite tendencies to the contrary, the European missionary societies actually gravitated towards the colonies of their countries of origin. Missionaries from the United States, however, were active everywhere.

In the eighties British, French, and German missionaries

arrived in Uganda.[31] At the outset of the nineties the Imperial British East Africa Company, which originally administered Uganda, was on the verge of bankruptcy and was set to quit the country. Bishop Tucker of Uganda and the Church Missionary Society staged a money-raising campaign in Britain to postpone the departure of the Company by one year, during which time the British government might be induced to proclaim a protectorate over Uganda. The money which the IBEA Company thought necessary for the purpose was raised in a fortnight. This campaign and the accompanying clamour of public opinion were one of the major reasons why the government declared Uganda a protectorate on 18 June 1894.[32]

British protectorate status for Barotseland came about for other reasons. The French missionary François Coillard, at the request of King Lewanika, asked for British protection in order to eliminate tribal feuds in the interior and thus avert the danger of invasion by the Matabele, and to avoid the debasing contact with the gold-diggers.[33]

The nexus between 'Christianity and Commerce' was a risky one, because commercial activities could stifle the primary missionary goals and could in fact become degrading even in the hands of the missionaries themselves. There was very often a contradiction between idea and practice. The words of a popular saying of that time in South Africa about the missionary: 'When you came here we owned the land and you had the Bible; now we have the Bible and you own the land', were proverbial words which often corresponded to the truth.

On the other hand, it must be recognized that the work of the missions had a humanizing influence on imperialism.[34] The missionary societies were, so to speak, the conscience of European colonization. The stipulations of the General Act of the Berlin Congo Conference of 1885 advocating religious freedom, the struggle against the slave-trade, and the promise to preserve the tribal organization of the natives and to improve their moral and material welfare, were not empty phrases. They were the expression of the ideals of the humanitarian movement and of the missionary spirit of the nineteenth century, and they provided a yardstick by which the white man's rule could later be measured. The worst colonial scandals were discovered and exposed by humanitarian organizations and by missionaries as, for example, the abominable exploitation of the Congo region by King Leopold and his henchmen. A long-range effect of the civilizing work of the missionaries, above all of their introduction of the European educational system, was the creation of a large number of indigenous lower-ranking administrative officials without whom the 'imperial machinery' (as Charles P. Groves phrased it) would not have worked. They trained the first representatives of an intelligentsia who later became the critics and ultimately the heirs of European imperialism.

4. THE EXPLORATION OF AFRICA'S GEOGRAPHY

The activity of humanitarian organizations and missionary societies which provided the continuity and unity to European colonial policy before and after 1880, was but one of the fundamental and powerful impulses of classical imperialism. Along with the pioneering ranks of the missionary and merchant was the explorer of new lands, the discoverer of new frontiers.

Again, the connection between discovery and subsequent colonization and territorial acquisition can best be illustrated with African examples. But European interest was also focused to a certain extent on Asia, even though there had been contact with that continent for centuries. During the first half of the nineteenth century, Africa was indeed the 'dark continent'. Only the coastal regions were explored during the early voyages of discovery by the Portuguese. The hinterland and the interior were left blank on the maps. In the thirty years between 1850 and 1880 the blank spaces disappeared one by one.

The number of explorers venturing forth to Africa would comprise a whole book.[35] Among them were the most varied types, ranging from learned men to soldiers of fortune, from missionaries to officers. Most of them pursued more than one interest and thus embody the complex impulses and motives for imperialist or pre-imperialist activities. David Livingstone was a British missionary and an explorer, Gustav Nachtigal was a German diplomat and an explorer. Many of the discoverers were officers, such as the Russian Skobelev, the Frenchman Galliéni, the German Wissmann. They, as well as the pure adventurer, were anything but a blessing to the European governments, because they often acted on their own or against their instructions and surprised their governments with a *fait accompli*. They were the pro-consuls who acquired many a territory against the will of their governments. Because Michail Murav'ev in 1858–60 had concluded treaties on some territories on the Amur River on his own account, he was to be court-martialled. Carl Peters confounded Bismarck with his method of acquiring territories, that is, exchanging children's toys and liquor for deeds of cession from illiterate African chiefs. Archinard and Binger represent the type of the *officier soudanais* who acquired both Sahara desert strips and West African jungle tracts, one after the other, without the knowledge or against the wishes of the French Foreign Ministry, perhaps with the tacit approval of the Department of the Navy or the War Ministry. Some of these adventurers, explorers, and conquistadores actually became empire-builders. The most well known of them is Cecil Rhodes.[36] Another is Henry Stanley, who was sent into the interior of Africa in 1871 to search for Livingstone and who acquired during his expeditions the large Congo territory for the King of the Belgians; in this instance, the sovereign gave his whole-hearted support to the explorer.

5.   EUROPEAN NOTIONS OF AN ELDORADO

The geographical exploration of the African continent was a basic condition for the later colonization and acquisition of colonies, and in some cases even led to direct colonial occupation. Not unrelated is still another chain of motives for classical imperialism which may be termed the eldorado or bonanza myth.

The widely read dramatic accounts of explorers about their adventurous expeditions[37] aroused the expectation in their respective countries that unbelievable riches lay in the interior of the continent, especially within the hothouses of the tropics where trees seemed to reach to the sky. This image was magnified by the discovery of diamonds and gold in South Africa in the sixties and eighties which, of course, was reminiscent of the discoveries of the Spanish conquistadores of the sixteenth century. Legends, like the one of gold in the Sudan, were revived.

The effect of the treasure-trove myth on the acquisition of colonies can be studied in the case of the Congo region. French and Belgian historians (among them Henri Brunschwig and Jean Stengers) found out that the ratification of the Brazza–Makoko Treaty, which placed the area of the later French Congo under the protection of France, was forced upon the government under the pressure of a press campaign whipped up by de Brazza. The reports of the legendary riches of this region played an important part in this campaign. In its 2 October 1882 edition, the newspaper *La République fran-çaise* described the economic aspects in glowing terms.[38] It would be difficult, it said, to provide a complete list of the agricultural and mineral resources of the Congo region. In the valley of the Niari copper and lead were said to abound in fabulous quantities ('abondent en quantités fabuleuses'), numerous ore deposits were described as lying almost everywhere between Vivi and Stanley Pool (the rich copper-mines of Katanga several hundreds of miles away were not known of at that time). Gold, too, had been discovered in numerous cases. Ivory and caoutchouc were plentiful. The forests were real treasures: the natives were burning big logs of ebony and rosewood in their fireplaces. The extremely fertile soil would permit the growth of the most varied products.

These lyrical tones were echoed throughout the press during those days. According to the *Constitutionnel* of October 7, one could find in the Congo area 'a rich, vigorous and fertile virgin territory . . . It is as beautiful as India.'[39]

The comparison between Africa and India was a favourite topic in the propaganda of the colonial enthusiasts. It underlines again the inter-relationship of the first centuries of European colonial history and the age of imperialism. Many of the leading British imperialists and colonial officials regarded the development of India as a model for the opening-up of Africa, which would become the second India. Thus the British Colonial Secretary Joseph Chamberlain wrote to Salisbury on 2 June 1898 that the empire of Sokoto in the Western Sudan was in dissolution — a process which resembled the break up of the empire of the Great Moguls at the time of Robert Clives. He was therefore of the opinion that, 'in accordance with that precedent', a small European military force would be enough to install British rule there.[40] On 18 March 1901, Chamberlain declared in the House of Commons: 'From the moment we undertook responsibility for those spheres of influence [the

British colonies in Africa] . . . we made it our business to establish once and for all that great Pax Britannica which we established in India.'[41] Lord Lugard, the well-known British colonial official, established an administrative system in Northern Nigeria fashioned on the Indian model, in fact, 'a little India'. By that he meant the system of Lord Dalhousie in the Indian territories annexed after 1850, of which the main characteristic was, according to him, the retention of all powers, of the judicial as well as of the executive powers, in the hand of the Resident.[42]

The legendary riches of unexplored Africa tempted not only the colonial enthusiasts; even politicians and statesmen succumbed to the lure. King Leopold in his childlike fantasy was always dreaming of a great colonial empire: small wonder that he was captivated. The following passage of a letter which Leopold addressed to the Belgian diplomat Solvyns on 17 November 1877 is typical of his colonial aspirations *and* actions: 'We must at the same time be prudent and clever and act quickly [. . . in order to] secure for ourselves a part of that magnificent African cake.'[43] At the close of the seventies, Charles de Freycinet, who later became French Prime Minister, was one of the first to point to the supposed glittering commercial prospects in West Sudan. As Minister of Public Works, he embarked on an ambitious programme of transportation development in 1877. One year after that the building of a railway system in Algeria was added to the programme. After the Sudan was explored, the construction of railways was extended beyond Algeria through the Saharan Desert into the Sudan. In July 1879 a railway committee was formed to prepare a report on 'the railway connection of Algeria and the Senegal to the interior of the Sudan'.[44] In his report to the President of the Republic, Freycinet stated that the Sudan was accessible from three directions: from Algeria, from Senegal, and from the Niger. Railways would open up its interior, the last remnants of the abominable slave-trade could be eliminated, and its inhabitants could be given the blessings of European civilization; in short, France was to embark on peaceful conquests here. Freycinet apparently wished to convey the impression to the President that the population of these areas — 100 million according to his estimates[45] — were eagerly waiting to sell their products. They were very

industrious, and 'the elements of an international traffic seem
to exist there to a high degree'.

6.　THE TECHNOLOGICAL REVOLUTION

Freycinet's ideas and plans relate to still another basic preliminary condition as well as an important impulse for classical
imperialism, and that was the technical revolution. It is an
element peculiar to the age of imperialism and is not connected with the continuity of European colonial history.

On 30 July 1884 the *Pall Mall Gazette* wrote: 'Day by Day
the world perceptibly shrinks before our eyes. Steam and
electricity have brought all the world next door. We have yet
to re-adjust our political arrangements to the revolution that
has been wrought in time and space.'[46] With a more direct
reference to the colonies, Sir John Seeley, who was one of
those popularizing the imperial idea in Britain, had already
expressed this observation in his book, *The Expansion of
England*, published in 1883, in the following words: 'Science
has given to the political organism a new circulation, which is
steam, and a new nervous system, which is electricity. These
new conditions make it necessary to reconsider the whole
colonial problem,'[47]

The connection between the technological revolution and
imperialism can be more clearly understood by reviewing the
revolution in the system of transportation in so far as it induced the industrial powers to imperialist actions.

a) *Steam Navigation*

The development of steam navigation during the second
decade of the nineteenth century drew the continents closer
together. In 1825 a British ocean-going vessel used steam-
power to support its sails on its voyage to India. Speed, size,
and reliability of the steamships and thus the economy of
operation increased year after year. The first exclusively
steam-powered ship in 1825 required 113 days to travel from
Britain to India. The same distance was covered seventy-five
years later in one fifth of that time. Asia-bound ships from
Europe were henceforth independent of trade winds and were
no longer forced to take the detour via the South Atlantic.
Between 1852 and 1857 the first giant steamer, the *Great
Eastern*, was built on the Thames with a displacement of

27,400 tons. Steam navigation was responsible for revolution-
izing the structure of overseas trade. Sailing vessels were limited to transporting high-quality commodities, such as precious
metals, spices, and silk. But the steamship was now capable
of transporting bulk articles such as coal, grain, and peanuts
economically over a long distance. World trade expanded on
a gigantic scale.

b) *The Suez Canal and the Damming of the Nile*

When the isthmus of Suez was pierced through in 1869, the
commercial route between Europe and Asia shifted from the
Cape of Good Hope to the Mediterranean and the Red Sea
and to the old land routes in the Near and Middle East. The
construction of the Suez Canal,[48] a technical feat which was
admired and praised, is closely linked with imperialist actions
— for example, with the acquisition of bases by Britain,
France, and Italy on the east coast of Africa at the end of the
sixties[49] and with the occupation of Egypt by Britain in 1882.
Although the British government under Palmerston had opposed the construction of the Canal by the Frenchman
Ferdinand de Lesseps, the Canal route eventually became the
most important, but also the most vulnerable connection
between Britain and her Indian Empire. While in 1870 only
486 ships transited the Canal, it was used to capacity in 1882
with 3,000 ships. Almost four-fifths of them sailed under the
British flag.[50]

In 1875 Disraeli bought up seven-sixteenths of the Suez
Canal shares for the British government. The course taken by
Britain between this event and the occupation of Egypt seven
years later, however, was by no means consistent and straight-
forward. It is a widely held but wrong opinion going back to
Disraeli's opponents, and even supported by Disraeli himself,
that the *coup* of 1875 was but a first step in realizing a long-
cherished plan for the occupation of Egypt. In fact, Disraeli
did not entertain any such plan. For the time being he still
adhered without reservation to the traditional maxim of
British Eastern policy, that is, not to infringe the integrity of
the Ottoman Empire, of which the Khedive was a vassal. Even
after the purchase of the shares he continued to regard Constantinople as 'the Key of India, and not Egypt and the Suez
Canal.'[51] It was only from the end of the eighties onwards

that the British guardianship of the Bosporus was gradually replaced by guardianship on the Nile. As Disraeli's latest biographer, Robert Blake, has pointed out, the British Prime Minister, when purchasing the shares in 1875, pursued the aim of weakening French influence in Egypt and thereby forestalling a possible French occupation. At that time and even later on, the Canal was of more strategic than economic value. In 1875 the route via the Cape of Good Hope was still used by British ships more frequently than the route through the Suez Canal, with only one-tenth of Britain's overseas trade making transit through the latter. Strategically, it afforded speedy transportation of troops to and from India in such a contingency as an Anglo-Russian war, when reinforcements from India would no longer be forced to ply the much longer route around the Cape, as during the Crimean War. (During the war crisis of 1877-8 Indian troops had already been dispatched to the Mediterranean.) On the other hand, the Canal allowed speedier access of troops from Malta and Britain to India in case of a second Indian Mutiny. Stressing the priority of the strategic factor, Disraeli used the following general terms in a speech in the House of Commons on 21 February 1876: 'I have never recommended and I do not recommend now this purchase as a financial investment . . . I do not recommend it either as a commercial speculation . . . I have always and do now recommend it to the country as a political transaction, and one which I believe is calculated to strengthen the empire.'[52]

The opening of the Suez Canal worked in yet another respect as a motive force of imperialism. The man who built the Canal, Ferdinand de Lesseps, became the symbol of an optimistic belief in progress and in the achievement of science. His feat encouraged philanthropists, speculators, and technocrats in their belief that technology would help in opening up and exploiting the hitherto unexplored regions of the earth, especially Africa. De Lesseps was particularly admired and praised because he was neither an engineer nor a banker but originally came from the consular service. Especially impressive about him was that in his search for capital he did not rely on the financial magnates, but turned to the small subscribers. The Suez Canal, like the two other great European waterways, the Rhine and the Danube, was internationalized and thus contributed to increasing world trade. Because of this his contemporaries came to regard de Lesseps as a benefactor of mankind.

This self-made man encouraged many to emulate him. Practically all the African explorers of subsequent decades saw in him a source of inspiration. After traversing the Sahara desert, the French explorer of Africa, Paul Soleillet, wrote in 1879: 'The real conquests of the present epoch are industrial and commercial rather than military achievements. De Lesseps contributed as much to the glory of his country as Turenne and Bonaparte. All the nations praised him because they can all derive great benefit from his work.'[53]

In 1874 the French Captain Elie Roudaire developed a plan in the *Revue des deux mondes* to connect the salt lakes south of Tunisia and Algeria with the Mediterranean. He hoped that by extending the lakes into a large inland sea, the climate would change and fertilize the adjacent desert region.[54]

While this and other more or less fantastic canal-construction plans[55] were never carried out, another much discussed project created a political sensation. This was the attempt (or the threat) to dam the water of the upper course of the Nile and thus to cut the Egyptian lifeline. It is part and parcel of the factor of imperialist rivalry among the great powers, which suddenly intensified after 1882. It is also responsible for the reconquest of the Eastern Sudan by Britain and is therefore directly linked to an imperialist action.[56]

The idea of manipulating the headwaters of the Nile was none other than the revival of a legend which had originated centuries before in Egypt. In a thirteenth-century chronicle of the Saracen Empire there is mention of a diversion of the water of the Blue Nile. When the headwaters of the Nile were extensively explored in the second half of the nineteenth century, explorers and experts discussed the possibility of damming the waters of the Nile. One of the leading authorities on this subject, Sir Samuel Baker, suggested in a *London Times* article in 1888 that the biblical story about the seven arid years could probably be explained as having been a diversion of the Nile waters. He was of the opinion that a dam could easily be built on the Blue Nile or in the Atbara. So long as there was no European power wielding influence in the

Sudan, there was no prospect for these plans to be carried out. But, Baker went on, as soon as a European power, which in contrast to the Mahdi Dervishes had at its disposal the proper technical means, ruled in the centre of the Sudan, 'his first strategic operation would be to deprive Egypt of the water that is necessary for her existence'. Five years later the well-known French engineer Victor Prompt gave a remarkable lecture at the Institut Égyptien in Cairo about the problems of the White Nile and the Sobat. He argued that by building dams at these points, the course of the water could be regulated so as either to reduce the summer-time rate of flow to one half, or to inundate the whole Egyptian Nile valley all of a sudden. The construction of such a system would, he calculated, cost roughly half a million francs for each component dam.[57]

The influence of this lecture on great-power politics can be easily traced in the diplomatic documents.[58] The French government during the following six years were exploiting the threat of the regulation of the Nile waters in order to, as President Carnot put it, 'reopen the Egyptian question'.[59] In the debates of the French Chamber of Deputies and the British House of Commons the threat was brought up again and again. As early as 1893, by order of Carnot, a French mission headed by the African explorer Major Monteil was to advance from the West into the Upper Nile region to Fashoda, which is situated near the confluence of the White Nile and the Sobat. The plan was abandoned, however, because of the tense relations between France and Italy. In 1898 the famous Marchand mission finally reached Fashoda. For her part, Britain established a defensive position on the Upper Nile with mounting energy after 1893. Initially her efforts were at the diplomatic level; treaties were signed with the Continental powers which delimited spheres of influence on the Upper Nile. This later gave way to military campaigns which resulted in the reconquest of the Sudan and the Fashoda conflict.

c) *The Inter-continental Railways*

Above all, it was the construction of the railways that acted as a technological stimulus to classical imperialism. It is important to distinguish between railways as an instrument of imperialism, which was usually the case in the colonial-*exploitation* phase, and the railways as a motive force of imperialism, which they became in the colonial-*acquisition* phase.

As was the case with the construction of the Suez Canal, the completion of the first transcontinental railway over the United States from 1869 to 1872 represented a great technical feat which generated considerable enthusiasm. The Union Pacific Corporation undertook the task of linking both ends of the continent. The solid gold spikes and plates used to mark the joining of the railroads from east and west symbolized the importance attached to the venture.[60]

With the construction of the first inter-continental railway, the dream of a Napoleon to hold sway over a whole continent became reality. The Roman emperors had long before recognized that the expansion of their empire made rule more difficult and sought to correct the increasing disproportion by building an extensive network of roads. Napoleon was confronted with the same problem. At the peak of his power he said, 'I will never regret an expense which does away with the problem of distances. The vaster the Empire grows, the more one has to pay attention to the great means of communication.'[61] The railways, which the English historian Thomas Macaulay in his *History of England* described as the most important achievement of human civilization, along with the alphabet and printing, had created the fundamental condition as well as the most secure means of truly imperial domination.

After 1869 many railways were built which linked the world's oceans. In the United States the 'frontier' disappeared with the construction of new lines between the two coasts. Conditions were also created for increased trade with the Far East. Canada inaugurated her first transcontinental line in 1885. Between 1891 and 1903 the longest line of them all, the Trans-Siberian Railway, was constructed. In the European part of Russia and in Western Siberia its primary purpose was economic, but the more it was pushed toward the East, the more pronounced became its strategic and imperialistic character. It became Russia's most important instrument in dealing with Japan, her imperialist rival in the Far East. It served as the spearhead of Russia's political penetration of Manchuria and Northern China.[62]

In subsequent years China became the most important arena of the imperialist powers for railway construction.[63] It seemed to be much more attractive to private capital than Africa because the density of her population presaged higher profits. The Chinese government, however, were soon able to shake off foreign tutelage over their railway projects for several reasons: rivalry among the foreign powers, who, in contrast to the African situation, were joined by the United States and Japan; the sheer magnitude of the territory and of the population; and finally the capability of China to resist imperialism, as was shown during the Boxer Rebellion. The end of the Russo-Japanese war was a decisive turning-point in this process. After 1908 foreign financial control was systematically and successfully removed.

In the Near East the Baghdad Railway was the most effective motive force and the most important instrument of imperialism. Germany was the leading power in this area. The railway was started in 1869 between Sarajevo and Constantinople as a purely financial concern by the financier Baron Hirsch. Its continuation on Asian soil became the most visible expression of the German *Mitteleuropa* concept and of the idea of forming a large empire between Berlin and Baghdad. It was of strategic importance because of the real and imaginary threat to India. Withal, it served Turkish subimperialism by countering the centrifugal tendency of certain parts of the Ottoman empire, especially the Arab territories, and, as it were, by providing the body of the Empire with an iron spine.[64]

The schemes to span the African continent with railways largely remained on paper. Precisely because such plans did not materialize, however, the motive force they provided to such imperialist actions as political–territorial annexations can be traced all the more clearly. The blueprints for a trans-Saharan and trans-African railway and a Cape-to-Cairo connection are patent manifestations of the typically imperialist idea of amassing large territories. In the case of Cecil Rhodes, who was a passionate supporter of the Cape-to-Cairo line, they even bordered on megalomania as evidenced by that imperialist's well-known phrase: 'I would annex the planets if I could.'[65]

The plan for a trans-Saharan railway and the manner in which its very first sections were actually laid out are a good example of how the technological, the political, and the military factors in the imperialist movement influenced and strengthened one another.[66]

As early as 1875 there was talk of a railway linking Senegal and the Upper Niger regions. The French explorer Paul Soleillet was the first to carry out topographical work there, financially supported by the Governor of Senegal, Brière de l'Isle. Brière repeatedly urged his government to go ahead with such plans, and he was supported by Freycinet, the French minister and railway enthusiast. The engineer Adolphe Duponchel popularized the idea of constructing a trans-Saharan railway with the French public. His pamphlet 'Le chemin de fer trans-saharien', published in 1878, sold unexpectedly well. In May 1879 the parliament granted a first instalment of 200,000 francs for surveying the land. Six months later, both Chambers granted another sum three times that amount. In July Freycinet set up a study-commission acknowledging that the enthusiastic support of parliament had induced him to accelerate the plans. Merging and spurring one another on were the clamour of public opinion and the euphoria of a small group headed by Duponchel, Soleillet, and Freycinet[67] — men seized with 'railway fever'. Freycinet reported to the President of the Republic on 31 December 1879: 'It is in fact by the means of communication that civilization extends and establishes itself most securely. We must try to connect the vast territories located between the Niger and the Congo.'[68]

During the preparatory stage of the trans-Saharan project it soon became imperative militarily to secure the area to be traversed, which ran from the Figuig Oasis 2000 kilometres southward to Timbuktu. When Admiral Jean Jauréguiberry was appointed Minister of the Navy in February 1879, Freycinet found him completely on his side regarding his plans for railway construction and territorial expansion, and an authority who was certainly willing to put the necessary military means at his disposal. In the meantime Brière had succeeded in winning the government over on the idea of a railway from Senegal to the Niger, a line which would be incorporated in the trans-Saharan railway. This meant that military security would have to be ensured in West Africa from two directions.

Two historians, Colin W. Newbury and Alexander S. Kanya-Forstner, have analyzed the origins of the trans-Saharan plan on the basis of new documents and are of the opinion that the 'scramble for Africa' can be backdated to the year 1879 when the project of the trans-Saharan railway reached its first stage of realization. They regard Louis Freycinet, technocrat and politician, and Jean Jauréguiberry, the military leader, as the architects of France's new African policy rather than the geographical societies, the African explorers, or the business and banking world.[69]

In September 1879 Jauréguiberry appointed Major Gustave Borgnis-Desbordes commander-in-chief of operations in Upper Senegal, bringing the area to be crossed by the railway under military command. The primary reason for this action was to expand France's political influence in the Niger area; the question of economic profitability was of secondary importance. With this important decision 'Jauréguiberry had raised the curtain on the era of French imperialism in West Africa.'[70]

The greater trans-Saharan plan from Algeria was temporarily suspended after Tuaregs raided the reconnaissance party of Colonel Paul Flatters in February 1881. The massacre demonstrated what was already obvious from the American experience, that stringent security measures and political control were necessary before undertaking the construction of any railway. Although Jauréguiberry pressed ahead with the Senegal railway project, here, too, the prerequisite of military security was wrongly assessed. Half of the first instalment of 16 million francs which the Chambers had granted for constructing the railway went instead into the building of forts and the sending of diplomatic missions. As a result, the parliament became less willing to grant further credits. The railway project became an appendage of the military task.

Several decades passed before the section from Dakar via Bafoulabe to Bamako was completed. These railway projects, however, had sparked off France's military expansion in West Africa. That they generated a dynamism which spread beyond the sphere of transportation is an extraordinarily important element of the phenomenon of imperialism. The Sahara and the Sudan were to become the domain of the French military and would set the pattern for French imperialism in West Africa regardless of the uncoordinated objections of the politicians and economic viability.[71] This is the gist of the important work recently published by Kanya-Forstner.[72]

The trans-Saharan project, practically buried after the massacre of the Flatters expedition, eventually was revived again and again in various forms. In parliament too, it was discussed several times, for the last time in 1941. Quite a number of pamphlets were written on the project.

In the nineties the idea of a trans-African line was propagated as an outgrowth of the trans-Saharan project. In 1893 the French engineer Amédée Sébillot proposed the construction of the following rail network:[73] from Algiers to Ahaggar in the Sahara; from there a branch-line would run to Obok on the Gulf of Aden; the main line would continue to Lake Chad; from there another branch-line would bifurcate to Ouidah on the coast of Dahomey; after having crossed the Congo, the main line would finally end at Johannesburg where it would join the line to the Cape. The gauge of this trans-African line was to amount to 200 centimetres. Fast trains would reach an average speed of 100 kilometres per hour and the duration of journeys between Europe and the other continents would be cut considerably. The journey from Bombay via Obok to London, for example, would be reduced from 24 to 11 days; from Cape Town to London from 35 to 20 days; from Rio de Janeiro via Ouidah to London from 18 to 14 days — a calculation which was typical of the belief in technical progress. The security of the line would be guaranteed by 'mobile forts', i.e. by armoured trains; its profitability would be safeguarded by potential African travellers numbering 200 million. Furthermore, one could count on a quarter of a million emigrants per year who would want to settle in the newly opened regions.

Projects similar to that of Sébillot were also propagated by the well-known French political economist Leroy-Beaulieu. In 1914 Major Roumens published a pamphlet, 'L'impérialisme français et les chemins de fer transafricains', in which he proposed a railway from Algeria to the Upper Niger, and a second line to Lake Chad.

The French railway projects in Africa did not progress beyond the initial stages. Although the similarly grandiose Cape-to-Cairo project was more successful, it never reached completion. The idea seems to have been born at the same time as its French counterpart, i.e. several years after the completion of the first American transcontinental railway. The most ardent promoter of the trans-African railway was

Cecil Rhodes with his British South Africa Company. The rail plan was closely linked to the acquisition of colonial territories;[74] This became most obvious in the leasing to Britain in 1894 of a 25-kilometre-wide corridor by Leopold II, situated between the Albert Edward and the Tanganyika Lakes, which was to link up British East and British Central Africa. In 1910 one-third of the over-all length of 9,300 kilometres was completed in South Africa between Cape Town and Broken Hill via Buluwajo, and in Egypt several sections were also completed. To date, a satisfactory study of the Cape-to-Cairo railway and its connection with imperialist expansion has not been written.[75]

The concept of transcontinental railways is an important ingredient of the ideology of imperialism. The various branch-lines were built from the African coast into the interior for the purpose of economic penetration and military security after the colonies had been effectively occupied. By contrast, the trans-Saharan, trans-African, and Cape-to-Cairo railway projects were conceived for reasons that went beyond economic profitability; they were to be a grand manifestation of the imperial will. They were therefore called by contemporaries 'imperialist' railway projects. They were vivid examples of the extra-economic motivation of economic projects as described by John Maynard Keynes: 'If human nature felt no temptation to take a chance, no satisfaction (profit apart) in constructing a factory, a railway, a mine or a farm, there might not be much investment merely as a result of cold calculation.'[76] Indeed, a quick calculation will make the unprofitable nature of the above-mentioned railway projects quite obvious. For most of its 2,500 kilometre length the trans-Saharan railway (as far as Lake Chad) was to cross desert country. It was therefore impossible that any passenger or freight traffic worth mentioning would develop. Only the Niger and Senegal rivers could be regarded as natural inlets and outlets. When the promoters of the projects put forward economic reasons, or when they proposed to offer a pilgrimage at a certain point of the trans-Saharan railway where people would travel in long trains, their enticements actually concealed a will to power and the strategic importance of the railway. In the decades of Anglo-French colonial rivalry troops could have been quickly moved from Southern France

and Algeria across the Sahara to West Africa. Neither the
trans-Saharan nor the Cape-to-Cairo railways would ever have
developed any economic importance. The lines from the coast
did serve to open up the hinterland. For transit traffic, however, the Cape-to-Cairo railway could never have competed
with the much cheaper sea route. Moreover, the three different
guages of the existing sections in the Cape Country, Uganda,
and Egypt, and the use of the lakes of Central Africa in
between, would have necessitated costly and frequent re-
loading of freight.

7.   THE PRINCIPLE OF CONVENIENCE IN DIPLOMACY

When examining the factor of continuity in the political and
historical explanation of imperialism and in doing so looking
at the political calculations of the government of each of the
imperialist powers, it becomes obvious that great-power
politics before and after 1880 are closely linked.

a) *The European and the Colonial Balance of Power*

Imperialism on this level is the direct sequel of the cabinet
policy of the European powers during the eighteenth and the
first half of the nineteenth centuries. Their policy of maintaining a balancing of potential was based on the principle of
convenience and compensation, that is, on the principle of
the balance of power.

The idea of the balance of power is intrinsically a mechan-
istic principle. In the age of imperialism the increasingly
important economic–industrial and demographic elements
were associated with this concept. Contemporaries used the
products of the mining and heavy industries as a yardstick to
measure economic strength — more specifically the output of
coal, iron, and steel. Comparing statistics in these fields was a
common game among the great powers and served in an
almost magical way to define their sense of security based on
political-power potential or as a warning of the increasing
strength of a neighbour. The burgeoning German economy,
for example, aggravated the already deep-rooted sense of
inferiority and decreasing power status among the French.
The widening disparity in the demographic growth of the two
countries was viewed, according to the largely irrational theory
of social Darwinism, as positively traumatic. After the turn of

the century, Britain and Germany used the criterion of naval power as another method of assessing each nation's power resources. Among the powers as a whole the statistical game was based on the strength of armies. In Germany, where the numerical inferiority of the army was obvious, military authorities took comfort in pointing out the army's superior quality.

To the economic, demographic, and military ingredients of power was next added the colonial criterion. The concept of a European balance was extended to include colonial balance and in the process was redefined to mean a world balance.

The principle of the balance of power means that none of the great powers is allowed to increase its power to such a degree that it creates an imbalance intolerable to the other powers and thereby provokes resistance by means of alliances, threats to resort to force, or by actually using force. An alteration of the great-power structure can be avoided if the intended or real increase of power is neutralized by offering adequate compensations to the others. In European politics compensations were agreed upon at the cost of small or medium-sized nations, in colonial policy at the cost of the colonized peoples or the weak colonial powers (Holland, Spain, Portugal).

In the eighteenth century balance-of-power politics was restricted to the European Continent with the exception of south-eastern Europe and the Ottoman Empire, and the overseas colonies. The exclusion of these areas was practicable since in each case only two of the four or five powers were affected — Russia and Austria in south-eastern Europe and Britain and France in the colonial areas.

In the nineteenth century these excluded areas were gradually opened up to all the powers. The 'Eastern Question' became a part of the balance-of-power principle when both Britain and then France claimed to have an interest in the Ottoman Empire. The Eastern Question was, as it were, internationalized with balancing established in south-eastern Europe as a subsidiary principle of the idea of the European balance.[77] This process was started with the Greek war of independence. Britain acted as a guardian of the balance of power whenever the power-scales were tilted by Russian or French pressure — in 1833 on the occasion of Russia's protectorate treaty of Unkiar-Skelessi with Turkey, in 1839–41 regarding the Straits question, in 1854–6 in the Crimean War, and in 1878 in the Russo-Turkish war.

In a similar way colonial balance was being advocated and integrated into the general system of the balance of power when, at the beginning of the eighties, Anglo-French colonial rivalry was revived and when other powers, namely Belgium and Germany, presented their colonial claims. In the nineties the idea of the European balance became global in scope when Germany clamoured for a share in overseas 'power' and when the United States and Japan joined in the imperialist expansion.

The relationship between the traditional idea of the balance of power and new overseas expansionism was much more obvious to the traditionally and historically minded people in the nineteenth century than it is to many a scholar of the present day. Diplomats were so deeply rooted in or even captivated by the balance-of-power idea that they tended to be reluctant to accept new factors such as vigorous economic expansion[78] which would upset the traditional system.

The above-mentioned relationship was also present in the minds of contemporary intellectuals as well as professional diplomats. It is vividly expressed in the colonial novel of the Frenchman Eugène-Melchior de Vogüé. The hero of the novel, a colonel in the colonial service named Louis Tournoël, talks to a higher-ranking officer about this point in the following terms:

Diplomacy used to be concerned with the Mediterranean and the Bosporus; now it has to do with China, the Niger and the Congo . . . The great states of Europe are dividing up the other continents of Africa and Asia, in the same manner they would divide such countries as Italy or Poland . . . What used to be a European balance of power is now a world balance of power, but it is subject to the same laws, and any country which does not wish to become less important must obtain as much new territory relatively as our rivals are doing.[79]

b) *The Congress of Berlin*

The close connection between the traditional Eastern Question and the emerging colonial question became most tangible in the case of the Berlin Congress of 1878. Delegates to the Congress negotiated not only the Eastern Question (i.e. the integrity of the Ottoman Empire, which was construed differently by the British and the Russians), but also, less officially, the colonial question in terms of the vassal states of the Ottoman Empire in North Africa. During the Eastern Crisis of 1875–8 Bismarck repeatedly recommended as a sweeping settlement that, in return for Russia's dominant influence in the Balkans, Britain should receive Egypt, France should acquire Tunisia, Austria should get Bosnia, and Italy should receive Albania. This barter deal was in fact partially realized in the Congress of Berlin negotiations at the expense of the 'sick man of the Bosporus'. Britain reserved to herself the isle of Cyprus from the Sultan as a *place d'armes* to counter the preponderance which was granted to Russia in the Caucasus. Austria received the right to occupy Bosnia and Hercegovina as a counterweight against Russia's increased influence in Bulgaria and eastern Rumelia. France received from Britain and Germany the promise of a free hand in Tunisia as compensation for her consent to the British foothold in Cyprus.

That Tunisia was exclusively regarded as an indemnity becomes evident in the commentary of Waddington, the French foreign minister and delegate to the Congress: 'What we will do in Tunis, we do not yet know.'[80] Italy, which was not yet a full-fledged great power, had an eye on Tripoli because of Austria's strengthened position in south-eastern Europe. The Austrian foreign minister who was disposed not to leave the Italian scale empty, dropped the following hint: 'We are most willing to examine benevolently Italy's wish for compensation — either for an island, a harbour, for Tunisia or Tripoli — and even to support her in concert with the cabinets.'[81]

The occupation of Tunisia three years later could not have been carried out by France without her being able to fall back upon the promise given her in 1878 and above all without the toleration and even encouragement of Bismarck: 'Tunisia', he said, 'is as ripe as a pear in the August sun.' The occupation of Egypt by Britain in 1882 was an action intimately linked to the Eastern Question as well as one that helped to set off the 'scramble for Africa'. It must not be forgotten when examining the age of imperialism that the Eastern Question remained the most important problem in international relations before the First World War, just as it had been in the decades before 1870–80 when, though for a short time only, it was equalled in importance by the problems of Italian and German unification. Because of its intricate nature, it was a favourite theme in the training of diplomats; only by successfully mastering the labyrinth of the Eastern Question could one be regarded as a genuine diplomat.[82]

c) *Great-Power Treaties on the Distribution of Colonies*

The principle of convenience regulating the Eastern Question, that is, making compensations to check a marked rise in influence of one of the powers, was automatically transferred by diplomats and politicians to imperialism in its colonial applications. This became evident in the numerous treaties of the colonial powers for the delimitation of newly opened areas and spheres of influence. The British lawyer Edward Hertslet has compiled these agreements in *The Map of Africa by Treaty*. According to his collection, thirty-one frontier agreements were concluded between Britain and Portugal, twenty-six between Britain and Germany, and thirty-six between Britain and France from 13 January 1869 to 25 February 1908.[83] This number and the contents of the colonial treaties show that the powers tried to settle colonial conflicts, as far as possible, by the traditional means of adjusting their interests and by barter agreements. A colonial stock exchange was set up where colonies were quoted[84] and where the powers pursued a sort of cartographic imperialism. It was Bismarck who took the lead by applying to the colonial sphere the considerable crisis-management skills he acquired while dealing with the Eastern Question. Undoubtedly this spirit of compensation greatly softened the aggressiveness and brutality inherent in imperialism. It was the underpinning of all the colonial treaties of the powers from the end of the seventies until World War I, the finale being the Anglo-German treaty concerning Portugal and the Baghdad Railway. A few examples from the period after the Congress of Berlin may serve to illustrate this point.

When Britain annexed the Transvaal on 12 April 1877, the delimitation of the hinterland of Mozambique became urgent. At that time Portugal controlled only the narrow coastal strips of her African colonies except for Mozambique, where she was also claiming the hinterland *vis-a-vis* the British. When Portugal granted concessions to Britain in this area, she demanded and obtained as compensation the recognition of her claims to the Congo delta region. France, supported by Bismarck, protested against this settlement because it would bar access from the Atlantic to the Congo basin, which had been explored by de Brazza and Stanley and which was coveted both by France and by Leopold II. This, in turn, led in 1884 to the Berlin Congo Conference at which the controversial points were settled — at least for the time being.[85]

The great colonial partition treaties of 1890 (Britain–Germany, Britain–France); of 1898-9 (Britain–France, Britain–Germany); and 1904 (Britain–France), as well as the two conferences dealing with Morocco in 1905 and 1911, are excellent examples of the political principle that the renunciation of claims in one region must be compensated for by concessions in some other region. In the earlier treaties there was always the phrase that the *lignes idéales* drawn at the green table had to be replaced by lines which would be determined by frontier commissions on the spot and that in doing so care had to be taken 'not to favour one of the two parties without granting fair compensation to the other'.[86]

In later treaties claims and concessions were bartered in spheres of interest situated in very different geographical regions. Thus in 1899 the settlement of the Samoan question was linked to the shifting of borders in West Africa. In the treaty of 1904 Britain not only granted financial compensation to the French Newfoundland fishermen who stood to lose their fishing grounds; she also acknowledged that 'some territorial compensation is due to France in return for the surrender of her privilege in that part of the Island of Newfoundland referred to in Art. II'.[87] France received this compensation in Senegambia. The protracted negotiations leading up to the settlement are an excellent example of the traditional diplomatic horse-trading. There was the ritual of petty bargaining and haggling regarding fishing baits, for example, which kept negotiations on the more important questions stalled for weeks on end. The French made their intention known from the start that they would 'not relinquish any of their titles without obtaining adequate compensation elsewhere'.[88] When Declassé demanded the Los Islands off Conakry for France during one stage of the negotiations, Lansdowne countered: 'We are not disposed to throw these islands into the bargain, unless the French Government, for its part, adds something else to the scales. We suggest that to make the transaction equal France should accept the British protectorate over the New Hebrides.'[89]

During the Moroccan crises, however, the traditional methods of give-and-take were abandoned because there were several parties to the negotiations who confronted each other in two main opposing camps. The two sides not only negotiated according to the rules of chess but also exerted pressure and uttered threats that were not to the point. One of the contracting parties, Germany, worked herself into such a state of mind that she felt encircled; her efforts to suppress her reactions were partly irrational and uncontrollable.

Nevertheless, settling disputes in a calculable manner, especially when only two parties were involved, was still possible right up to the First World War, as was the case with the Anglo–German negotiations on the Baghdad Railway and on Portugal. On the whole, it can be argued that imperialism in the shape of colonialism was hardly a motive underlying the origin of World War I.[90] The First World War broke out, not because of colonial problems, but because of the Eastern Question. The two major early waves of European colonization had proceeded in a disorderly and dangerous fashion. The freebooter, the merchant adventurer, the conquistador — they all respected only the right of the strongest. The mercantilist notions of the seventeenth and eighteenth centuries made it possible to hunt for colonies without restraint; rivalry was fought out with brute force. There were numerous colonial wars. One of the most devastating, the Seven Years' War, was of world-wide dimensions and involved the European Continent. Colonial imperialism after 1880, however, was for the most part managed by the great powers without seriously disturbing world peace.

The transfer of the rules of the European balance-of-power policy and of the European Concert relates rather to the form of colonial conflicts and their settlement than to their origin. In order to elucidate the latter, we must again revert to comparing the Eastern and the colonial questions. The Eastern Question existed in the eighteenth century and its very origins go even further back. But in the eighteenth century it was the domain of only two great powers, Russia and Austria.

In the wake of the French Revolution and owing to the results of the Congress of Vienna, which drew Austria's attention to Central Europe, Russia was even in the position to monopolize the Eastern Question. Only when Britain and France each claimed a share in handling the Eastern Question did it take on a pluralistic character. From then on it was Europeanized; the antagonism became universal and more intense among the great powers.

The colonial question developed in an analogous way. After the War of the Spanish Succession it was mainly Britain and France which carried on a colonial quarrel. In 1763 Britain emerged victorious from the colonial struggle. Her position of monopoly, together with the revolt of the North American colonies and the spreading of the free-trade doctrine, fostered within Britain an anti-colonial attitude. As Lord Shelburne characterized the mood in 1783, 'We prefer commerce to dominion.'[91] Underneath the surface, however, Anglo-French colonial antagonism lingered on. Although scarcely noticed by the public, there was a virulent Anglophobia in the French navy, whose sense of honour was offended by the cession of the strategically important Mauritius Islands in 1815. This was regarded as contradictory to the principle of the colonial status quo.[92]

8. THE RIVALRY OF THE COLONIAL POWERS

By the end of the 1870s, Anglo–French colonial rivalry again came to the surface. The French Minister of the Navy told the Senate on 17 February 1881: 'We have . . . implacable rivals who constantly seek to counter the influence we exercise in the Senegal.'[93] And the head of the African department in the British Foreign Office, H. Percy Anderson, wrote in a memorandum in June 1883: 'If there is one thing clearer than another, it seems to be that the French have a settled policy in Africa, both on the East and West coast, and that policy is antagonistic to us.'[94] At first, only those directly affected were conscious of rivalry in West Africa: soldiers, seamen, explorers, merchants, missionaries, and government officials. The various conflicts in North Africa, however, such as the 'War of the Consuls' in Tunisia and especially developments in Egypt, were watched by an attentive and interested public. This was because the scene was geographically nearer to Europe and because it revolved around the well-known Eastern Question.

The decisive separation of the old and the new colonialism came when Anglo–French colonial dualism was transformed into a pluralistic, multi-national, colonial rivalry. The sudden burst of dynamism in the imperialist movement, with expansion in Africa and in the Pacific assuming sometimes hectic proportions, is best explained by this factor of universal rivalry.[95] Contemporaries appropriately characterized this accelerated pace with terms taken from the sporting and hunting language when they spoke of a race, a steeplechase, a *course au clocher*. Once started, the scramble gained momentum, as it were, according to the law of acceleration. It had a snowballing or stampeding effect. It was like a gold-rush, a run on the stock exchange, a mass panic, an inflation with its various effects. The imperialist movement developed, as have revolutions, wars, and all great historical processes; it had a self-propelled momentum which spread further and further from its origin as it developed.

Contemporaries, above all politicians, regarded this pressure to move and to act with greater importance than did scholarly analysts later on. Anderson explained the British reaction to France's activities in West Africa in his memorandum of 11 June 1883: 'Action seems to be forced on us . . . Only one course seems possible; that is to take on ourselves the Protectorate of the native States at the mouth of the Oil Rivers, and on the adjoining coast.'[96] Protectorates, he went on, are unwelcome burdens, but in this case it is 'a question between British Protectorates, which would be unwelcome, and French Protectorates, which would be fatal'. Jules Ferry, in a very informative foreword to a book which he edited in 1890, *Le Tonkin et la mère-patrie*, wrote: 'An irresistible movement drives the great European nations to conquer new territories. It is like a steeplechase moving headlong towards an unknown destination.'[97] He then observed that the steeplechase, under way for barely five years, was accelerating annually 'as if propelled by its own speed'. Answering the reproach that his colonial policy was diverting attention from the more important national task of concentrating the country's energies on Germany, he rhetorically asked, 'Should we steer French policy into a blind alley with our eyes transfixed on the Vosges

Mountains, leaving everything to be done, managed, and decided on without us and around us?' A policy of clean hands would quite obviously mean, 'Italy in Tunis, where we are being cheated; Germany in Cochinchina and Britain in the Tonkin; both of the latter countries in Madagascar as well as New Guinea — in a word, the bankruptcy of our rights and hopes, a new Treaty of 1763 but one that lacks the excuse of Roßbach and Madame Pompadour.' Ferry characterized colonial policy as the 'international manifestation of the eternal laws of competition'.

Rivalry breeds fear in all those concerned; it spurs counter-actions and leads to a chain reaction of even greater anxieties and defensive actions. On 18 September Leopold II wrote to de Lesseps about de Brazza's activities in the Congo: 'I fear he will drive his country down the road of annexations and conquests, which will inevitably lead other countries to seize other parts of the Congo.'[98] France, on the other hand, suspected Leopold to be Britain's proxy for the Congo. De Brazza accordingly wrote in a letter sent to Paris on 27 December 1883: 'It is to be feared that Belgium is being duped in this affair and that Britain is trying to start again here what she did in Egypt.'

As previously mentioned, the scramble for Africa was set in motion by the treatment of the Congo problem. In the seventies Britain had negotiated with Portugal regarding the latter's claims to the area around the mouth of the Congo. As the price for recognizing these claims, Britain demanded that free trade and other concessions be granted in this area. The negotiations dragged on. The Foreign Office pursued them with vigour only when Brazza brought his treaty with Chief Makoko to France. In 1884 the negotiations were concluded, and Britain accepted the Portuguese claim to the Lower Congo. However, Bismarck and France refused to recognize the Anglo-Portuguese treaty. The ensuing diplomatic entanglement led to the Berlin Congo Conference. The way in which the numerous claims, demands, and counter-demands clashed, can be illustrated as shown in the diagram below.

A similarly tense situation was developing in East Africa, on the Upper Nile where British, French, Italian, and even Russian[99] interests crossed in many ways and mingled explosively. Britain, however, managed to reduce the tension

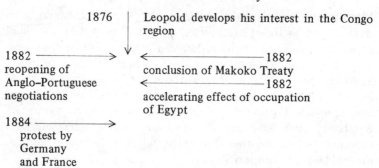

1876 | Leopold develops his interest in the Congo region

1882 ———————> V <——————— 1882
reopening of   conclusion of Makoko Treaty
Anglo–Portuguese   <——————— 1882
negotiations   accelerating effect of occupation
                       of Egypt

1884 ———————>
   protest by
   Germany
   and France

through several bilateral treaties in 1890, 1892, and 1894 and finally to remove it in 1898 by threats of war during the Fashoda conflict. In the Pacific the Samoan islands developed into an area of tension involving Germany, Britain, and the United States.[100]

The latter two cases suggest that the imperialism of individual nations may spawn a local, autochthonous, or sub-imperialism which joins the main stream of imperialism. In East Africa, Abyssinia under Menelek II took part in the imperialist scramble and even managed, thanks to the use of modern arms, to defeat her Italian rival in a pitched battle at Adowa in 1896.[101] In the Pacific, when Australia's imperialism came into the existence she demanded, for security reasons, the complete annexation of the Samoan islands — thereby embarrassing her British tutor.[102]

Morocco and China were also colonial danger areas where more than two rivals were in competition and where imperialistic penetration was being accelerated. In the case of China, however, the involvement of several competitors actually saved the Empire from partitioning and therefore from the most intensive stage of imperialism.

Rivalry among the powers led to a very peculiar variety of imperialism which may be called prophylactic or preventive imperialism. Sometimes the terms 'anticipatory' or 'pre-emptive annexations' or 'preclusive imperialism' have been used. Lord Rosebery alluded to preventive imperialism in a speech in 1893 couched in the language of mining: 'We are engaged . . . "in pegging out claims for the future". We have to consider not what we want now, but what we shall want in the future.'[103]

9. COLONIAL IMPULSES

Another aspect of the phenomenon of imperialism which must be seen in conjunction with the continuity of the history of colonial expansion is the pull of local impulses which, after having passed through several preliminary stages, may end up with territorial annexation. In this context, mention must also be made of the quasi-'natural' drive to expand and round off territory. This drive, which originates from a local (but also from a central) initiative, comes into play whenever a powerful entity is presented with a power vacuum or with an area of much reduced power at its borders. A case in point is the retreat of the Ottoman Empire from Europe and Russia's urge to fill the evacuated areas. Applied to the colonial regions, the phenomenon can be illustrated in the case of the expansion of the United States, where the 'frontier' was pushed westward against the unsuccessful resistance of the Indians; or when, after 1850, the colonial government in Batavia annexed those parts of the Indonesian archipelago which were not yet under Dutch domination; or when, in the second half of the nineteenth century, Russia expanded in Asia in a southeasterly direction. This drive is often set off by impulses on the spot when energetic generals or adventurers create situations which usually leave the central government no other choice than annexation.[104]

The dilemma of a government with locally staged *faits accomplis* is vividly expressed in an 1867 letter from Petr N. Stremoukhov, the head of the Asian Department in the Russian Foreign Ministry, to a high-ranking officer:

Various points in Central Asia have continually been indicated to us as necessary acquisitions to strengthen our position and serve as a base and a bulwark for our possessions . . . It has constantly been said that for the glory of Russia, for the raising of her prestige, it is necessary to take some stronghold or other to smash the Asiatic hordes in the field: strongholds have been taken one after another, the hordes have been utterly defeated, good borders have been attained, and then it has invariably turned out that one more stronghold is lacking, that one more final victory is necessary, that the really perfect frontier lies somewhat farther off, that our prestige is still insufficiently raised by our former successes. Your Grace will rightly agree that such a form of action ought finally to be ended, because it is compatible with neither the dignity nor the true interests of the government.[105]

Many instances could be cited of local initiatives carried out in Africa. In contrast to the Eurocentric *driving* force emanating from Europe, one should speak of the Afrocentric *tugging* effects; the latter mingled with the former and pressed for intervention. This pattern varied. The Egyptian situation ended up in 1882 with an intervention that Britain neither planned nor wished. It was the result of a xenophobic movement led by Arabi Pasha. Especially conspicuous in the army, this agitation fatally weakened the power of the Khedive Ismail and brought about domestic chaos.[106] The helplessness of the Egyptian government rendered vulnerable not only the financial interests of the numerous British and still more numerous French creditors *vis-à-vis* the state, but also, more importantly, the security of the Suez Canal, the British lifeline to India. (The creditors could not by themselves have accounted for the intervention; indeed, French, rather than British, action would have redounded more to their advantage.) The occupation was an improvised action. Although Britain repeatedly announced the intention of 'restoring and retiring', the occupation was not withdrawn because of continuing domestic instability and also because of France's stiffening opposition.[107]

In South Africa the expansion took place in confrontations amongst the Boers, the British settlers, and the Bantus. The land hunger of the settlers and the cattle thefts of the natives produced constant friction. In the 1820s the British colonial administration tried to protect the eastern parts of the Cape Country by setting up homesteads (just as the Austrian 'military frontier' was established against the Turks in Eastern Europe). The conflicts between the settlers and the native tribes, however, continued. The administration tried its luck by further expanding the frontier areas. But this cramped the living-space of the natives and automatically heightened the tensions. During this process the Cape Colony expanded into Basutoland, Griqualand, and Natal. This urge to secure the frontiers, which can be explained in psychological terms and which strongly contributed to imperialism later on, may be called the borderland mentality or the '*limes* complex'. Another case in point from the period after 1880 may serve to illustrate it.

In Abyssinia the commander-in-chief of the Italian troops

in Keren was pressing to occupy the important stronghold of Kassala in the Sudan in order to gain better protection against the much-dreaded attacks by the Mahdis. In 1888, criticism of the expansionist policy in East Africa was expressed by Ruggiero Bonghi, a member of the Italian Parliament: 'If we leave the security questions to the generals, they will demand all of Africa.'[108]

In the Western Sudan the expansion also resulted from the initiative of the generals, who developed great skill in defying the orders of the metropolis just as did the military leaders during the colonization of Algeria after 1830.[109] Beyond this urge to secure the hinterland,[110] to pursue pacification as a prerequisite for the construction of railways, and to satisfy the soldiers' thirst for action, there was the geopolitical idea of creating a direct link between the North African territories and the possessions on the West African coast and the Congo region. This strategy was also pursued by the metropolis when Eugène Étienne, an ambitious and convinced expansionist, occupied a key position in the central government.[111] Étienne and the Comité de l'Afrique française pursued a systematic and far-reaching plan, the aim of which was to weld together all the African possessions north of the equator into a cohesive bloc of territories from Bizerta to Brazzaville and from Dakar to Djibouti. The French take-over of Morocco, one of the last unoccupied territories in Africa, can be viewed in this context. Of this, Delcassé wrote as early as May 1900: 'If France must search for a complement to her Algerian–Tunisian empire, this complement lies in the west.'[112]

Such far-reaching territorial plans are to be found in Cecil Rhodes's idea of the all-red line, that is to say, the creation of an uninterrupted link between the Cape and Cairo. (At that time maps traditionally depicted British colonies in red.) They also are reflected in the plan of the German government (under Bethmann Hollweg) which provided for a compact bloc of central African territories from the Cameroons to German East Africa at the expense of the Belgian Congo.[113]

Finally, the strategic factor must be cited in the attempt to explain imperialism historically in terms of power politics. Strategy was of fundamental importance in Britain's seizure of East Africa. As Robinson and Gallagher have demonstrably shown, the official policy-makers in London established clear priorities in their West Africa and East Africa policies. Although the West African territories offered better prospects for marketing goods and supplying raw materials than East Africa and the valley of the Upper Nile, the reflections of the British government centred around these economically poorer regions. 'These regions of Africa which interested the British investor and merchant least, concerned ministers the most.'[114] The territorial claims to Uganda, the east coast, and the Nile delta, they argued, were not caused by a drive for markets and trade. Nor was any belief in the value of an African empire in itself responsible for it, in contrast to Rhodes, for example. It was, rather, a search for greater security for the lines of communication to the Indian Empire.

III. The National- and Social-Psychological Attempt at a Definition

The overriding factor of rivalry leads to the second comprehensive interpretation of the phenomenon of imperialism —to the explanation in terms of national and social psychology.

Rivalry on the international level arises when two or more nations of roughly the same strength take the measure of each other's power status and then identify some real or imaginary differences which they try to level down. The power structure of the predominant nations dealt with here was subject to constant changes resulting mainly from interior and exterior crises, from social tensions and revolutions, and from wars. Defeat in war affects the way in which the vanquished nation assesses its strength. It reacts by streamlining its internal resources. Defects in the internal fabric are discarded — in the social structure, in the instruments of power, above all in the armed forces. Reforms become a major concern of the government. Thus when Prussia had lost her wars against Napoleon, administrative and military reforms were introduced. Russia inaugurated a comprehensive programme of reforms in seeking to overcome the backwardness in her social structure (serfdom) and in her industrial development which was exposed by the Crimean War. The slogan was *recueillement* in domestic policy and *abstention* in foreign policy. Sadowa resulted in the *Ausgleich* between Austria and Hungary. The internal regeneration of the Hapsburg Empire was designed to raise her prestige abroad and to free her from her isolation among the powers. France's catastrophic defeat in 1870–1 resulted first in the collapse of the Second Empire, then in the uprising of the Commune, and finally in the prolonged birth pangs of the Third Republic. Her foreign policy could be reactivated only when her domestic situation had considerably improved.[115]

Well-known contemporaries at the turn of the century and the scholars of a later period regarded imperialism as an exaggerated form of nationalism. The turning-point of 1870–1 is undoubtedly of special importance in this respect because it deeply affected nationalism and sentiments of prestige in Western and Central Europe. The connection between nationalism and imperialism as well as the social–psychological elements of imperialism in general point to its irrational aspects. Although this irrationalism is elusive on the theoretical level and its impact on imperialism difficult to assess, it is rather more easily susceptible to empirical explanation and analysis.

1.   PRIDE OF EMPIRE AND JINGOISM IN BRITAIN

The idea of the nation state had finally become reality in Central Europe in the decade between 1861 and 1871, first in Italy, then in Germany. With the unification of Germany by Prussia, a completely new power factor on the chess-board of international relations had come into existence in the centre of Europe. The traditional power structure had been totally recast.

In Britain, Disraeli, the leader of the Conservatives, felt deep concern about this upheaval of the international situation. On 9 February 1871 he stated in the House of Commons: 'This war represents the German Revolution, a greater political event than the French Revolution of the last century . . . The balance of power has been entirely destroyed, the country which suffers most, and feels the effects of this great change most, is England.'[116] The power status of Britain seemed to be somewhat depreciated by this revolutionary change on the Continent. As seen by Disraeli, the way to restore it was through increased activity in foreign policy, especially in re-activating imperial policy. In a speech delivered on 24 June 1872, his programmatic exposition went as follows:[117] Liberalism had been responsible for the loosening of the bonds between the mother country and the colonies. Colonial policy had always been regarded exclusively from the financial point of view — which view he himself had espoused.[118] For this reason the colonies had been granted self-government, and it had been expected that they would sever their bonds with the mother country as the North American colonies had done. Contrasting with this attitude, which had led to the 'disintegration of the Empire', was Disraeli's 'great policy of Imperial consolidation'. It would not exclude the principle of self-government, it would include an imperial tariff system, an agreement on mutual military obligations and rights, and the right of representation of the colonies in the government of the mother country.

Disraeli's foreign policy in his second cabinet from 1874–80 may be seen as a reaction to the changes of the power structure on the Continent. Derby, his pacifist Foreign Secretary, regarded it as a policy of 'occupy, fortify, grab and brag'[119] and therefore opposed it. Derby resigned when Disraeli embarked on a warlike course in the spring of 1878. Those were the days when 'jingoism' sprang up, a passionate outburst of Russophobia of the same kind as at the beginning of the Crimean War.[120] The refrain of a popular song which was introduced in a London music-hall and then spread throughout the country went as follows: 'We don't want to fight, but, by Jingo, if we do, we've got the men, we've got the ships, we've got the money, too.'

Disraeli's active foreign policy and especially his desire to strengthen the Empire was called 'Disraelian imperialism' by his contemporaries. This version of imperialism did not yet mean territorial expansion; it simply called for consolidation of the existing colonial empire. It did not exclude, however, gaining a foothold on foreign territory as happened with Cyprus. But it was completely subordinated to the consolidation and protection of the Empire. Disraeli's regeneration of the Empire was thus a 'consolidationist imperialism', not an 'expansionist imperialism' as it developed a few years later, it was not an end in itself, but was meant to serve as a counterweight against increased power potential on the Continent.

Disraeli's Empire policy reflected a strong trend of public opinion which was rediscovering the value of the colonies. Its major spokesmen were three Empire protagonists: Charles Dilke, who wrote his *Greater Britain* in 1868;[121] John Robert Seeley, who in 1883 published lectures he had given in 1879 under the title *The Expansion of England*; and James Anthony Froude, whose book *Oceana, or England and her Colonies* came out in 1886.[122]

All three books, classics of British Empire ideology, have in common the view of imperialism as an outgrowth of nationalism, with economic, politico-strategic, and other such elements receding into the background. Moreover, they are concerned only with the white-settled colonies and not the dependent territories (with the exception of India).

The success of Dilke's book played no small part in his being elected Member of Parliament in 1868; twelve years later he became Under-Secretary of State in the Foreign Office. In Dilke's view, the strength of the British Empire was based on the common cultural bonds of its individual parts and on the superiority of the 'British race'. The US were also part of this Pan-Anglism: their declaration of independence had not severed the bond of blood. 'Greater Britain' signified the unity of the mother country and of all those regions of the world where people of British stock were found. Although originally this did not mean the extension of Britain to include peoples of different races, the term was eventually liberalized to take on such a meaning and was used as a catch-phrase to characterize British imperialist expansion. Following suit, the French coined the equivalent phrase, *la plus grande France*. In Germany Paul Rohrbach took the lead in attempting to popularize the notion of a *Größeres Deutschland*, by which he meant political–economic rather than territorial expansionism beyond Germany's frontiers, which would be purified by the export of *Kultur*.[123] Bülow used the term 'Greater Britain' to justify Wilhelmine imperialism. On 11 December 1899 he told the Reichstag: 'When the French speak of a *Nouvelle France*, when the Russians are opening up Asia, then we likewise can claim a '*Größeres Deutschland*.'[124]

Amongst the contemporary literature of imperialism, it was historian John Seeley's book which exerted the strongest influence in Britain. It became a best seller and was reprinted almost every year. Seeley, like Charles Dilke, did not recommend a programme for further extending the British Empire. He rather sought to interpret the significance of past expansion, to exploit the Empire for beneficial gain in his own time by esteeming its value as an 'extension of the British race into other lands' and by enhancing national pride in this great cultural achievement. In the past, he explained in a phrase that has become famous, 'we seem, as it were, to have conquered and peopled half the world in a fit of absence of mind'.[125] The Empire came into existence not according to a careful plan, but by chance. The sheer size of its area represented a compelling stimulus to assume a paramount moral and spiritual position in the world.

The historian James Froude did not stress the superiority

of the British race as did Dilke, but he, too, advocated the maintenance of the Empire, which he regarded as a historically mature entity.

It is important to stress that the most conspicuous elements of British imperialism at its onset were a sense of belonging together, born of nationalism, and a pride in the Empire. Later on, however, it formed the soil which bore the less pleasant fruits of nationalist imperialism. The initial surge of jingoism of 1878 was an isolated phenomenon which had sprung up in the moment of acute danger. It was only in the nineties, by which time imperialism had grown into a hectic expansionist movement, that it escalated into a xenophobia which was first directed towards France and Russia, then towards the Boers, and after the turn of the century towards Germany. Again it must be borne in mind that this perverse nationalism was latent in nature; it needed to be ignited by a crisis in foreign policy. (One cannot, after all, hate another nation for ever.) The difference was that it now erupted with greater and more mercurial frequency. Rosebery described this as 'wild-cat imperialism', not to be confused with 'sane imperialism', by which he meant, as did Dilke and Seeley, a 'greater pride in Empire'. 'Sane imperialism' was nothing but 'a larger patriotism'.[126] The ambiguity of the concept of nationalist imperialism was well evoked by Gooch, who spoke of a patriotism 'which ought to mean the love of country, [but] has with many come to denote the love of more country'.[127]

Hobson was one of the shrewdest contemporary critics of imperialism and is generally regarded by scholars as the chief authority on the theory of economic imperialism. But he assigned special prominence to the nexus of jingoism and imperialism, for he saw its effects in the Boer War — an experience which caused him to reflect on the nature of imperialism. 'It is quite evident', he wrote in his 1902 book *Imperialism*, 'that the spectatorial lust of Jingoism is a most serious factor in imperialism.'[128] Hobson made a distinction between the jingoism of his time which took hold of the masses and the 'nationalist warlike spirit' of former times; modern jingoism, he felt, was related to the living conditions of the industrial age.

2. IMPERIALISM IN THE BRITISH PRESS AND LITERATURE

Without getting lost in details, attention must be drawn in this connection to the demographic explosion of the nineteenth century which was an accompanying circumstance as well as an effect (and in certain respects also a cause) of industrialization. The urbanization of a population gives rise to a neurotic urge for gratification. The modern media of communication are themselves products of industrialization and serve to appease this appetite in a quick and widespread way. The cheap, sensationalist, mass-circulation press, which sprang up in the last third of the nineteenth century, both profited from and promoted the upsurge of imperialism. Alfred C. Harmsworth, later Lord Northcliffe, recognized the inter-relationship between the popular sensationalism of journalism and imperial questions and commercialized it. One of his staff wrote: 'We realized that one of the greatest forces, almost untapped, at the disposal of the Press was the depth and volume of public interest in Imperial questions.'[129]

Inspired by the 'yellow press' in America, Harmsworth launched the halfpenny *Daily Mail* morning paper in 1896 which, because of its efficient news service, reached a million-strong readership just five years later. The *Daily Mail* regarded itself as the megaphone of the imperialist movement. When it was founded, it stated that it stood 'for the power, the supremacy and the greatness of the British Empire . . . The *Daily Mail* is the embodiment and mouthpiece of the imperial idea. Those who launched this journal had one definite aim in view . . . to be the articulate voice of British progress and domination. We believe in England. We know that the advance of the Union Jack means protection for weaker races, justice for the oppressed, liberty for the down-trodden. Our Empire has not exhausted itself.' The historical and cultural arguments of Dilke and Seeley for a dominant British position were now modified to appeal to the masses. In 1900 Arthur Pearson founded the rival paper the *Daily Express*. Its first leading article of 24 April proclaimed, 'Our policy is patriotic; our policy is the British Empire.'[130]

The popular mass-circulation press accelerated the imperialist movement. Even in its early stages it was among the promoters of imperialism. The London *Daily Telegraph* and *New*

York Herald newspapers jointly financed Stanley's second journey to Africa. At least as early as the turn of the century the press was massively influencing imperialist policy, as evidenced by contemporary observations. The British journalist William T. Stead, who became a pacifist following his meeting with the Russian Tsar and agitated against the Boer War, described how much influence the press exerted on international relations in 1898: 'The fact is that the intervention of the Press in international disputes tends daily to become more and more hostile to peace and civilisation.'[131] In a similar vein, Lord Salisbury stated in 1901: 'The diplomacy of nations is now conducted quite as much in the letters of special correspondents, as in the dispatches of the Foreign Office.' He regretted that the antagonistic hatred fomented by the press in Britain and Germany made more difficult an agreement which the governments of the two countries were negotiating at the time. In 1902 the British press actually prevented German–British co-operation in the Venezuela conflict.

The governments, of course, recognized that the press could also serve as a propaganda weapon. Utilized as such, however, it quite often became a double-edged sword. According to recent detailed research by Klaus Wernecke,[132] a student of Fritz Fischer, the German Foreign Secretary Kiderlen-Waechter indeed harnessed the press for his policy, but then found he could not coax the genie back into the bottle so to say. Certain elements of the German press made unbridled colonial demands of France that went far beyond what the government had set as their policy; so much so, in fact, that relations between the government and press cooled considerably and that the crisis in Morocco was blown totally out of proportion.

In Britain, the mass-circulation press and, therefore, nationalist imperialism are likely to have profited decisively from the two electoral reforms of 1867 and 1884 as well as from the introduction of compulsory school attendance by the laws of 1870 and 1880 — in short, from important advances in democratization. It was only in the great reservoir of the emancipated masses that the yellow press could find its readers. In a sociological sense, therefore, it was not only the middle class but also the workers who were susceptible to and could be captivated by imperialism.[133]

Hobson and many other contemporary liberal critics of imperialism deeply deplored and pilloried imperialism's appeal to the more brutal and aggressive instincts of the masses. Jingoism, he said, did not mean the quickening of an individual's aggressive urges into actual personal involvement in a fight. Rather, it was the vented emotions of a spectator participating, with hosts of others, in violence, but from a distance. 'Jingoism is merely the lust of the spectator, unpurged by any personal effort, risk, or sacrifice, gloating over the perils, pains, and slaughter of fellow-men whom he does not know, but whose destruction he desires in a blind and artifically stimulated passion of hatred and revenge.'[134]

The military aspects of imperialism were glorified in literature[135] as well as the yellow press. This phenomenon can best be illustrated in the case of Britain, where the literature on imperialism is more extensive and of higher quality than in Germany or France, for example. As in the case of most other aspects of imperialism, here, too, the question whether this type of literature was the root of imperialism or its fruit cannot be answered unilaterally. It was as much one as it was the other. At the most one could argue about how intense was the interplay between the two.

A typical characteristic of the literature of imperialism was that it tended to oppose the materialism of the time and to strive for lofty ideals. The subjects treated were conscientiousness, forbearance, glorification of the *pax Britannica*, and the admonition to maintain and extend the Empire. Psychologically speaking, the literature suggested a need to compensate for the unromantic hardships of life in the industrial society, the yearning for adventures in an exotic world untouched by civilization.

Carlyle may be regarded as a forerunner of imperialist ideas in literature.[136] In his work he challenged the prevailing rationalistic–utilitarian outlook of his day and instead glorified heroism and hard work. Robert Louis Stevenson, whose *Treasure Island* appeared in 1883, popularized adventures and travels in foreign continents. Stevenson, like Dilke and Froude, the latter a disciple of Carlyle, drew on his own adventures in the colonies; he had made a two-year voyage into the South Seas and in 1890 settled on the Samoan island of Upolu. Reports on military events in the colonies were read with great eagerness. Father Ohrwalder's *Ten Years Captivity in the Mahdi's Camp* (1892) was re-edited ten times in one year; George W. Steeven's *With Kitchener to Khartum* reached thirteen editions in 1898 within a few months. The Boer War produced an extensive literature, including books by Hobson and Winston Churchill.

Britain's foremost literary spokesman for imperialism was probably Rudyard Kipling. From 1882 until 1892 he worked as a journalist in India. His work embodied the idea of the British Empire and glorified Britain's colonization as a religious mission. Greater Britain was the real home of the English; the native colonial peoples were to be subjugated, not educated and developed. The refrain in one of his poems of the *White Man's Burden* — which became the slogan of British imperialism — must be understood in this context. In his *Barrack-Room Ballads* and in his soldier stories Kipling idealized the colonial work of the Englishman and at the same time stirred the warlike instincts of the white race, prototypically the British, portrayed by him as superior to the natives. As the literary hero of the day, Kipling inspired both the general public and the torch-bearers of imperialism themselves, such as Cecil Rhodes and Carl Peters.

3. NATIONALISM IN FRANCE

As in Britain, nationalism prepared and promoted the imperialist movement in France. However, its advent and its effects were quite different in a number of ways.

Until 1870 nationalism in France was not a mass phenomenon as it was in Germany, Italy, and Poland. In connection with colonialism it was restricted to the French navy. This circumstance gives a clear indication of its origin: the humiliating feeling of defeat and a longing for compensation.

The French navy's nationalism after 1815 was essentially an 'anti-British reflex'.[137] which undoubtedly originated in eighteenth-century Anglo-French rivalry and which grew especially strong after the naval defeats of the Napoleonic wars and the loss of colonial bases. As the French saw it, the relations between the two navies were characterized by morbid distrust and the desire for self-assertion. The struggle of the British navy against the slave-trade was suspected of having an imperialist bent. The British navy's obligation to honour French ships with a salute was zealously monitored.

The defeat of 1870-1 was a catastrophe not only for the French navy, but for France as a whole. More than the loss of the Indian Ocean base of the Isle de France, it meant the renunciation of Alsace and Lorraine which, worse still, had been gained by force with no consideration for self-determination. There were two additional instances in the nineteenth century of humiliation which affected French imperialism. These were the ousting of France from Egypt in 1882 and the confrontation at Fashoda in 1898. In both cases France suffered a feeling of inferiority which in turn triggered an imperialistic reflex. In comparison with these reverses, however, the 1870-1 defeat was positively traumatic. Imperialist expansion was now seen as a way of supplanting the trauma and proving to the world that France had not yet forfeited the stamina to be a great nation.

Documentary evidence of this sentiment is so numerous that any selection would be arbitrary.[138] It is, above all, important to keep in mind the special origin of French nationalism: the national catastrophe. French imperialism was fed from this specific nationalism, not from any pan-movement as the British one was from pan-Anglism, the Russian one from pan-Slavism, the German one from pan-Germanism. (Although there was a sort of Latinism or pan-Romanism, it was restricted to small intellectual groups.)[139]

The interrelation between French nationalism and imperialism makes it especially evident that nationalism does not necessarily have to lead to imperialism: on the contrary, radical nationalism in France in the shape of anti-Ferryism and of Boulangism was hostile to imperialism. Striving for overseas expansion, they felt, diverted from France's foremost national duty: the struggle against the 'German danger'.[140]

None the less, the desire for self-assertion and for assertion to the world remained powerful enough to impart strong impulses to imperialism. The further one goes beyond the year 1880 in studying French imperialism, the more difficult it becomes to attribute to this assertiveness a motive force of imperialism or merely a justification for it. In most cases, however, both elements cannot be separated.

The manifestation of the desire for rehabilitation, of the yearning to regain the former great-power status, became almost a ritual in public gatherings, in political meetings, during scholarly banquets and the like. Bébin, the General Secretary of the Geographic Society of Valenciennes, stated in 1881 that, although France must still exercise great restraint in Europe, she must draw her attention overseas: 'It is there that the nation's vital forces, which are beginning to feel constricted by the narrow limits of the treaty of Frankfort, will be able to expand unhindered, and when once the events which we hope to see occur have come about, it is impossible to say where our flag will not one day fly . . . If a nation wishes to remain or become great, it must undertake colonisation.'[141]

Colonization and imperialism were regarded as a means of moral and national regeneration. Georges Leygues told the Paris Colonial Congress in 1906: 'Just after 1870 it was colonial policy which gave us a fresh energy, renewed our courage and once more brought to our spirits a taste for action and life. It enabled us to prove that our trials had not deprived us of sufficient confidence in ourselves for us to embark on the greatest undertakings and to carry them to fruition.'[142] In the same year, Jules Charles-Roux stated at the opening of the colonial exhibition at Marseilles that defeat had long compelled France to renounce colonial ambitions. 'We were yearning to recover from both the moral and the material blows we had suffered, both in our own eyes and in the world's.'[143]

Looking back at the colonial activities of the Third Republic in Indo-China, Joseph Chailley-Bert declared at the North Africa Congress of 1908: 'We had been beaten in 1870. We had been demoted . . . from our position as the dominant power in Europe and almost master of the world to the status of a second-class power. We were dreaming of some event or effort through which we should later seek to recover our position as a first-class power.'[144] Such an event took place in the advance on the Red River and the colonial operations of Gambetta, Ferry, and Étienne after the Congress of Berlin.

In 1912 Chailley-Bert expressed before a banquet of the *Union Coloniale*[145] his fascination for the sheer magnitude of the colonial empire and even exhibited a touch of megalomania typical of the colonial enthusiasm of that time. Had it not been for the men who had devoted themselves to colonization after the terrible year of 1870, he said, France would not be where she was now in Europe; she would have remained a small nation of 35 to 38 million inhabitants, confined within 500,000 or 600,000 square kilometres, which would be of no great significance in modern times. But now France was 'a great nation, exercising authority over an area of between six and eight million square kilometres and with 50 million subjects, in addition to our 39 million citizens'. With this mass of territory and with this number of people, declared Chailley-Bert, France was very much in a position to meet those who challenged her and to maintain her position amidst the world powers.[146]

Such enthusiasts seemed not to want to realize that the masses of colonial territory consisted to a great extent of deserts, steppes, and virgin forests. The magnitude alone was sufficient to convince them; the quality and the economic value counted much less, if at all. Commenting on how megalomania gripped German colonial enthusiasts, the Imperial Chancellor Caprivi told the Reichstag on 12 May 1890 that 'it was commonly believed that once we came in possession of colonies, then purchased an atlas and coloured the continent of Africa blue, we would become a great people'.[147]

The desire to lift France from her deep humiliation of 1870 was in no way limited to the propagandists of the colonial movement. Politicians also harboured it, and it was they who acted upon it. In a report of 26 January 1881 the French Ambassador in Berlin encouraged his government to take action in Tunisia: 'An act of firmness . . . and we shall recover our position in the esteem of nations.'[148] A few months later, after the conclusion of the Treaty of Bardo, Gambetta expressed his satisfaction to Ferry at this event: 'France is recovering her position as a great power.'[149] To Gabriel Hanotaux, foreign minister between 1894 and 1898, the desire for rehabilitation was the core of his doctrine of imperialism: 'Having seen the war of 1870, I suffered from the humiliation of the Fatherland and I instinctively searched for the laws undergirding its grandeur.'[150] His successor Delcassé capped his speech before the Senate on 3 April 1900 with the following proud conclusion: 'France is, above all, a great European power

. . . which, has become, or rather has recovered its position as, a great colonial power.'[151] People once thought that France was beaten. But she had demonstrated again that she possessed an exuberant vitality by having created an empire beyond the seas which was more magnificent than the one she had lost a hundred years before.

Bismarck's support of the French colonial policy was due to the consideration that the defeated opponent should be allowed to regain his position among the powers even if only in his self-assessment. This conciliatory attitude, regarded today by some scholars of imperialism as immaterial, was viewed by contemporaries in a different light. The London *Daily Chronicle* wrote on 4 June 1884: 'France, largely out of consideration for her reverses fourteen years ago and her decline as a European Power, has been allowed a free hand — a too free hand indeed — in divers quarters of the globe.'[152]

As a matter of fact, the practice of allowing an adversary to overcome the sting of defeat can be observed again and again in the nineteenth century after great wars and peace treaties. After 1815 France was soon able to reoccupy her position in the European Concert. After 1856 Russia received several offers to revise the Paris Peace Treaty. Bismarck tried to show greatest consideration to Austria in the Peace Treaty of Nikolsburg of 1866. Britain's policy of appeasement after the Treaty of Versailles towards the Weimar Republic and towards Hitler is to be seen in the same light.

Apart from the defeat of 1870-1, French imperialism, as already mentioned, was psychologically affected and promoted by the serious set-backs in the colonial sphere *vis-à-vis* Britain. Although not powerful, the effects became evident more quickly because the imperialist movement was already under way.

4. THE BRAZZA-MAKOKO TREATY Of 1882 AND 'COLONIAL FEVER' IN FRANCE

Analysis of the attendant circumstances clearly indicates that public opinion in the form of a sudden and extensive press campaign literally forced ratification of the Brazza–Makoko Treaty on the French government in the autumn of 1882. Indeed, this is one of the rare examples of nineteenth-century history in which one can reconstruct the gradual evolution of factors — crowned by 'public opinion' — towards a politically far-reaching decision. Another good illustration is the decision taken by the British Cabinet during the summer and autumn of 1853 to drive home to the Russian government that Britain was prepared for war. According to the results of research undertaken by Kingsley Martin, that decision was forced by the pressure of public opinion.[153] As to the Brazza–Makoko Treaty, Jean Stengers has come to a similar conclusion after having analyzed the stages leading up to the final decision in a critical and methodically convincing way. During the first stage the French government took no interest in the treaty. Subsequent stages are characterized by a massive intervention of the chauvinistic press. In the final stage the government's decision in favour of ratification came about in quite unusual forms and was another indication of the power of public opinion.[154]

In the summer of 1882 de Brazza returned from a two-year trip to Africa with two documents which he himself called his treaty with Makoko. In reality they were pieces of paper which were of doubtful validity in terms of international law and which displayed an ignorance of basic facts of law as it related both to the African and to the European partners. In the first document de Brazza declared that he had obtained from King Makoko, ruler of the territories north of Stanley Pool (Brazzaville), 'the cession of his territory to France'. As proof of his consent, Makoko had put an 'x' underneath the declaration. In the second document de Brazza declared that, in the name of France, he occupied that part of the territory bordering on the Congo at Stanley Pool.

The fate of this 'treaty' seemed certain. As in many a precedent when an enterprising explorer or officer had come to an agreement with an African chief without the knowledge of the home government, the responsible official, Navy Minister Jauréguiberry, did not bother to have a look at the documents. On 19 July 1882 he informed Freycinet that he was not inclined to 'come to any direct decision relating to the negotiations which M. de Brazza seems to have set in motion'.[155]

At that point de Brazza was pessimistic and in September told the Foreign Minister in Brussels that 'he was convinced that neither the government nor the Chambers would do anything'.[156] After his return to Paris in the second half of September, however, he had several reports published in the press about his exploring expeditions, the advantages of his treaty with Makoko, and the great economic prospects in the Congo Basin. The reports were reprinted and were repeatedly the subject of comment. The press unanimously demanded ratification of the treaty. 'The whole French press,' wrote the *Temps* on 4 October 1882, 'with a vehemence it has never displayed before in colonial matters, is pressing the government to ratify the treaty which M. de Brazza concluded with the chiefs of the Congo territories.'[157] The Navy Minister, who refused to have anything to do with the matter, passed it on to the Foreign Minister on 26 September, stating that since the treaty might lead to diplomatic complications, he declared it to be not in his department.

King Leopold II threw out hints in Paris about his displeasure at the French claims on the Congo. He called upon Stanley, his agent, who had also returned to Europe in 1882 from his African expedition, to minimize the value of the treaty with Makoko in public. Stanley spread the news that Makoko had never intended to cede his territory and was quite ignorant of the consequences of the 'x' put underneath de Brazza's declaration. Hoisting the French flag in Stanley Pool did not mean anything to the Africans, he said; they would regard the flag as a piece of cloth, having a commercial value but no symbolic meaning at all.

Such public statements were bound to add more fuel to the fire. The French press, seeing the tricolour compared to a rag, did not fail to react at once. But it was not Leopold's opposition with its unexpected consequences that had really kindled the enthusiasm of the press. Rather it was caused by Britain's behaviour in Egypt since July of that year. By establishing a foothold at Stanley Pool, France sought revenge against Britain for her occupation of Alexandria: she wanted to compensate for the advantage Britain had gained. This psychological factor was regarded by contemporaries as the main cause of the passionate attacks by the press against the government. De Brazza exploited it in his public lectures. Both the French and the international press treated it again and again. The *Journal de Bruxelles* wrote on 7 October 1882: 'It is obvious that in the Congo affair France seeks revenge for the Egyptian affair.'[158] The *Koelnische Zeitung* commented upon the events on 22 November 1882 in the following words: 'It was regarded as an enterprise of great patriotism. France wants to recoup her eviction from the Nile by the English by evicting the Belgians and the Portuguese from the northern parts of the Congo territory.'

Politicians and diplomats, too, explained the motives behind the French reaction in psychological terms. Thus King Leopold remarked in a letter to Queen Victoria on 12 October 1882: 'In Paris they are raging; they seek a twofold revenge, against the Germans and for the success of the British in Egypt. They want to expand in every direction. Tunis is not enough; they want the Niger and the Congo in Africa.'[159] The Dutch envoy to Paris summed up the situation as it had developed since the summer: 'Initially, the French government was not very inclined to take the treaty seriously, but public opinion, roused by newspapers of every bent, forced, so to speak, its attention on the matter more than was its original intention.'

Duclerc succeeded Freycinet, who had resigned for domestic reasons shortly before the *coup* in the Egyptian affair and and had thus paralysed the government in foreign policy. The new foreign minister allowed himself to be swept along by the chauvinism and broke with the traditional procedure of ratification. Instead of ratifying it by decree, as was usual with treaties with native chiefs, the treaty was submitted to the Chambers. The committee, appointed by the Chamber of Deputies to report on the treaty, originally intended to make a statement on the opposition of the Navy Minister to the treaty. But it omitted the censure. On 22 November the treaty was unanimously approved by the Chambers.

The stages leading up to the final decision can be clearly retraced from the documents. They show the intrusion of irrational elements into the careful calculations of the politicians. Without examining the material value of the treaty and without assessing its financial and international implications, a step was taken into the unknown, a step into the shadows of the dark continent. The French government did what a government normally should not do: they embarked on an adventure in foreign policy under the pressure of public opinion and without much reflection.

5. THE FASHODA CRISIS OF 1898

The date of November 1882 is especially important in the
history of classical imperialism. That was the first time that the
'colonial fever' typical of the subsequent years and decades,
mixed with a strong amount of xenophobia and nationalism,
seized upon public opinion in one of the industrial nations and
forced on the government an action that would not have been
undertaken in a calm atmosphere free of external pressure.

The Fashoda crisis of 1898 is another outstanding example
of the way in which the 'imperialist fever' worked. There are
also instances when a government itself promoted colonial
frenzy and profited therefrom for its own political purposes.
Thus Bismarck in 1884 exploited the agitation of the German
colonial movement — a subject not yet fully studied — for
the domestic aim of influencing the Reichstag elections to the
advantage of the government. However, the 'colonial fraud', as
Holstein and Bismarck called it,[160] seemed to have been a
disappointment, for Bismarck never utilized it again in subsequent years. On the contrary, he sought to minimize its
troublesome results, particularly its financial consequences.

Before dealing with the Fashoda crisis from the point of
view of national psychology, yet another observation must be
made relating to the factor of public opinion in the imperialist
movement. Neither public opinion nor 'great politics' was
constantly occupied with imperialist affairs from 1880 to
1914. One should speak not of a continual pressure of public
opinion to influence policy-makers in matters of imperialist
expansion, but rather of outbursts of public opinion which,
at irregular intervals, transformed colonial squabbles among
the powers into full-fledged crises. Between these eruptions
there were long periods of indifference which defied professional agitators of the colonial movement. In order to illustrate
the interaction between public opinion and official policy,
one should not speak of an undulation, but of a temperature
curve so as to better describe the nearly incalculable ups and
downs of the influence of public opinion on matters of
imperialism.

The gravity of the Fashoda crisis of 1898 was caused by
the coincidence of a number of special factors, among them
an extraordinary outburst of public opinion on both sides of

the English Channel. According to recent research,[161] the documents relating to the conduct of both governments concerned do not admit of speaking, at any moment of the crisis, of a readiness to let matters come to a clash. The outburst of public opinion in France in the autumn of 1898 resulted from the coincidence of two crises — the Dreyfus affair and Anglo-French colonial rivalry — which arose independently of each other and developed in parallel for awhile until they merged and intensified each other.[162]

The famous mission of Captain Marchand to the Upper Nile, the origins of which go back to the year 1893, was caused by the desire to compensate for the defeat of 1882 in the Egyptian affair. It was not supported by a widespread public enthusiasm. It was not even supported by the official policy-makers of the French government. It was the work of the *Comité de l'Afrique française*, a small colonial pressure group founded in 1890 by the Under-Secretary of State for the Colonies, Étienne, and a few bureaucrats in the Colonial Office (Roume, Benoît, Archinard). The latter knew how to profit by a structural weakness of the French governmental system, that is, such chronic governmental instability and such frequent changes of ministers that policy continuity was mainly bound to be maintained by them — the everlasting bureaucrats. The methods employed to obtain Cabinet consent for Marchand's mission are tinctured with conspiracy.

Marchand's intention, fully shared by the promoters of the mission, was to reopen the Egyptian question and then to 'resolve' it at an international conference in a way satisfactory to France. A foothold was to be established on the Upper Nile in order to have a bargaining chip. 'The question of the evacuation of Egypt naturally springs from that of the Egyptian Sudan', wrote Marchand in a memorandum on 10 November 1895.[163] The organ of the *Comité de l'Afrique française* defined the aim of French policy in East Africa in the following terms: 'Our task is to bring about military evacuation of Eygpt.'[164] As late as July 1898 the Quai d'Orsay was still hopeful: 'Having an excellent pawn, we can wait and see when negotiations begin.'[165] The territories in the Sudan would be evacuated if, in return, British troops evacuated Egypt.

The main incentive of French policy in the Sudan was to

restore French prestige. Demands were raised in public and in diplomatic conversations for a *debouché sur le Nil* for France. This clamour, however, was camouflage for the underlying psychological motive. The territory on the Upper Nile was not in itself of value to France. It could not become a market or a transit area for French goods because trade on the Upper Ubanghi did not exist. However, it could acquire a certain strategic value in the grandiose plan for a future continuous strip of territory from West to East Africa. Whatever the secondary motives, it is a singularly outstanding example of the 'imperialism of prestige'.[166]

After the encounter between Marchand's mission and Kitchener's troops at Fashoda on 19 September 1898, it was pretty certain that the British demands and the French counter-demands would be treated and settled according to the normal rules of compensatory cabinet policy and diplomacy. During September of that year, however, incidents occurred on the domestic scene in France and in Britain which made a smoothly negotiated settlement appear uncertain. The long-standing differences between the French Foreign Ministry and the Ministry for the Colonies relating to the question of jurisdiction in colonial matters — another surviving structural defect of the French system of government impacting on French imperialism — burst into the open at the end of September when the Minister for the Colonies, Trouillot, complained in the press about difficulties in communicating with Delcassé. Much more important was the suddenly increasing tension about the Dreyfus affair, which had entered a new phase when it was submitted to a court of appeal after the publication of Emile Zola's article *J'accuse* and which threatened to split the public into two camps, the Dreyfusards and the anti-Dreyfusards. In the second half of September the usual demonstrations in the streets of Paris entered a dangerous stage because of mounting strikes. The army headquarters prepared for a *coup*.

In view of such an aggravation of the domestic situation, the French government was not disposed to settle the Fashoda affair in accord with the British demand that Marchand be recalled from Fashoda in exchange for territorial compensation in the Bahr el Ghazal. Dissent within the French nation should not be exposed to the world by backing down in a matter of colonial prestige.

The British ambassador to Paris, Sir Edmund Monson, tried to elucidate to his government this relationship between the crisis in foreign policy and the highly critical situation in domestic policy in his report of 1 October:

Delcassé has judged quite correctly as to the utter impossibility of the French Government conceding the recall of M. Marchand. Such a step would involve, I am convinced, the immediate fall of the Cabinet, and would be disavowed by their successors. The irritation of the Army and of a large portion of the public over the Dreyfus 'affair' renders the situation of the Government more than usually delicate; and any symptom of weakness on the Fashoda question would be the signal for their downfall within twenty-four hours of the meeting of the Chamber.[167]

According to the opinion of the British government, which was strongly influenced by Monson, France seemed to be on the verge of a civil war; despite her internal weakness, however, she seemed to be willing to act uncompromisingly and aggressively.

On the British side, too, although not to the same degree, the government's willingness to compromise, which they usually displayed in colonial conflicts, was impaired by special factors. The overriding importance of the strategic element to Britain's presence in Egypt and for the subsequent advance into the Sudan is as evident as ever. As Robinson and Gallagher have shown, the primacy of the strategic factor cannot be doubted in view of the large documentary evidence in this respect. But the more elusive factor of prestige, too, played a part. As far back as 1887 Salisbury referred to the encroachment of this element upon the calculations of the politicians. 'I heartily wish we had never gone into Egypt', he wrote to Sir Henry Drummond Wolff in Cairo.[168] 'Had we not done so, we could snap our fingers at all the world [especially Bismarck]. But the national, or acquisitional feeling has been roused; it has tasted the fleshpots and it will not let them go.' On 15 October 1889 *The Times* observed that, regardless of the commercial and economic value of Africa, there were still other reasons why Britain should take the lead in the movement of the partition. People on the black continent must not be made to believe that Britain's 'imperial prestige' was on the wane. Queen Victoria, who knew how to express seemingly complex psychological phenomena in plain words, wrote once to Salisbury with regard to Egypt, 'Giving up what one has is always a bad thing.'[169]

It was almost inevitable that a French advance to the Upper Nile would meet with a strong British resistance that stemmed not only from strategic motives but also from considerations of prestige. In December 1894, d'Estournelles de Constant warned his government from London: 'No one doubts that this Sudanese question attracts general attention. The ultimate solution will be important in itself, and will be the touchstone of British power. Possibly it is Britain's greatness that is at stake. It is, therefore, a question of life and death.'[170]

It is only from this perspective that the Fashoda crisis is thrown into its proper dimension. In the last resort the heart of the matter was neither the Turkish fortress nor the African village of Fashoda, nor the Sudan or the security of the Nile waters. It was, rather, the concern of Britain and France for status as a great power.[171] Viewing it in this light was, of course, not limited to the age of imperialism. Frederick the Great picked a quarrel with Austria in 1740 about Silesia solely for the purpose of raising his prestige before the world. France in 1840 played with the fire of war because she thought her honour was hurt by the threatening attitude of the other great powers in the Egyptian question; Russia launched the Crimean War and the war with Turkey in 1877 because she believed her national honour suffered due to the stubbornness of the hated Turks.

In the age of imperialism, however, politicians played more intensively and more frequently with points of honour which were then interpreted as vital questions. German naval policy is evidence of this dangerous exaggeration: the egregious backwardness of German naval power *vis-à-vis* both Britain and the other great powers was to be compensated for by a precipitate naval armament. Italian imperialism just before the First World War stemmed basically from the psychological desire to repair the national catastrophe sustained at Adowa. Russia's stiffening attitude after the Bosnian crisis was due, among other things, to the defeat suffered at the hands of Japan. French, Italian, and Russian imperialism was intended, to a large extent, to restore national prestige; Britain's imperialism was defensive, intended to maintain and possibly raise the prestige gained in the past, in view of the loss of the colonial monopoly; German imperialism was aggressive, aimed at reaching the power level of the other world powers as quickly as possible despite unfavourable historical conditions.

The firm British reaction to Fashoda was also determined by a factor of personal prestige. George Sanderson and Zara Steiner have pointed out that Salisbury's position as Prime Minister was at stake during the crisis.[172] The British government's reaction to Russia's acquisition of Port Arthur in March 1898 was generally regarded as weak by the public, and this increasingly spawned the opinion in the press that Salisbury was no longer in control of the situation. The Cabinet ministers, too, became alarmed 'lest some untoward event should occur'.

During the crucial meeting of 28 October 1898, the British Cabinet decided to mobilize the navy. This step marked the turning-point of the crisis. France could now no longer evade Britain's demand, published in a blue book on 10 and 23 October, for an unconditional recall of the Marchand mission. The Brisson government resigned. The new government had to surrender in view of Britain's overwhelming naval supremacy. The defeat of Fashoda was precipitated by the domestic crisis of the Dreyfus affair and was sealed by the mobilization of the Royal Navy.

There is controversy over just *when* Delcassé, who was not an Anglophile when entering the Colonial Ministry, had made up his mind to work towards an entente with Britain — whether as far back as 1898 or only from 1902. Recent research favours the earlier date.[173] The discovery of private letters written by Delcassé during the Fashoda crisis makes it quite plain that Delcassé regarded this entente as pivotal in his *idée politique générale* which he developed after entering the Foreign Ministry in 1898. The reasons for this change of mind towards an Anglophile attitude are not quite clear. The result, however, is plain. Delcassé realized that Britain would not permit having her preponderance in Egypt reduced to the status of the English–French condominium of 1882 and that French claims to Egypt ought to be compensated by Paris's claims elsewhere in the world. An obvious equivalent were those parts of North West Africa not yet occupied by Europe. By establishing herself in Morocco, France would erase the feeling of humiliation of 1898 and at the same time succeed in turning it into a political asset. Fashoda was directly linked up with the *Entente cordiale* of 1904 with Delcassé as the main architect.

6.   THE DOCTRINE OF WORLD EMPIRES

The Fashoda crisis illustrated the struggle of France and Britain for status as great powers, or rather as world powers. This was also a general characteristic of international relations in the age of imperialism. Imperial policy is essentially empire policy. The predominant feature of the age of imperialism was the idea that the ascendant powers, as they had developed in the eighteenth and nineteenth centuries, would maintain their great-power status only by increasing their might and demonstrating this by expanding beyond their frontiers,[174] especially by expanding overseas. This was obvious everywhere — in the press of that time, in scholarly debates, and in the self-esteem of government policy-makers, the governments. Borrowing a term used in contemporary debates, it may be called the theory of world empires.

In Britain the number of foreseeable world empires was seen as being limited to three: the British Empire, the United States, and Russia. In Germany, on the other hand, the doctrine of four world empires was established with Germany extending her power base to include the economic resources of the *Mitteleuropa* area and, of course, a colonial empire. A special feature of the latter doctrine is that policy-making and the definition of over-all resources were based on the notion of 'large areas': Not only should an extensive geographical base be regarded as an imperial prerequisite; a world empire ought to be a dynamic one, with an ingrained tendency to grow and expand. Since Germany's geographic base was disproportionately small, an attempt was made to correct the imbalance by rapid economic expansion: with the economic concept of *Mitteleuropa*: in some quarters also with the economic and geographical concept of the Berlin–Baghdad axis; and later on with the *Mittelafrika* idea. Obviously, this doctrine of world empires and Nazi Germany's geopolitics, with its demand to combine geographic and political concepts, had much in common.

The origins of the doctrine of world empires seem to go back to the very beginnings of the imperialist movement.[175] In his book *Études sur les colonies et la colonisation au regard de la France*, published in 1877, the French publicist Pierre Raboisson stated that there has never been a great power without colonies.[176] 'The grandeur of empires always reaches its apogee when colonial expansion has reached its maximum, and their decadence always coincides with the loss of their colonies.' That a great power is in decline because it does not possess colonies or is losing them was typical of French colonial doctrine. Underlying this idea was the concern to guard against recurring symptoms of the 'decadence' that had been apparent in the history of France's overseas territories.

In Britain, the advocates of Empire Seeley and Dilke were particularly enthusiastic about the geographic factor when defining the qualities of a world empire. They drew conclusions from the geographic development of the great powers of their time and applied them to the future so as to portray a hierarchy of world powers and of second- and third-rate powers. According to Seeley, history provides many examples of 'nations cramped for want of room' that had irresistibly pushed beyond their frontiers and swamped thier neighbours.[177] 'If the United States and Russia hold together for another half century, they will at the end of that time completely dwarf such old European states as France and Germany and depress them into a second class. They will do the same to England, if at the end of that time England still thinks of herself as simply a European state, as the old United Kingdom of Great Britain and Ireland such as Pitt left her.' This was clearly a warning of decadence unless geographic boundaries were extended. So confident was Seeley of the homogeneous racial character of Greater Britain (apart from India), as contrasted with the racial and religious diversity of the Russian Empire, that he expected Britain to move to no less than the second rank among the world powers, behind the United States.

Dilke described the broad material basis of the British Empire in his 1890 book *Problems of Greater Britain*, and finally set up the same hierarchy as Seeley: '. . . So far more rapid is the increase in the strength and the riches of the British Empire and of the United States that, before the next century is ended, the French and the Germans seem likely to be pigmies when standing by the side of the British, the Americans, or the Russians of the future.'[178]

The German reaction to this doctrine, which in subsequent years was frequently put forward in numerous varieties, was to propagate a German *Weltpolitik* comprising colonial, naval, and *Mitteleuropa* policies. The intellectual framework was provided by historians, above all by the followers of Leopold von Ranke, with their doctrine of the organic development of the European balance-of-power system into a global balance-of-power system; by political economists such as Gustav Schmoller, Max Sering, Paul Voigt, and Karl Rathgen with their *Mitteleuropa* ideology; and finally by 'liberal imperialists' such as Friedrich Naumann and Paul Rohrbach with their notion that an energetically pursued *Weltpolitik* would cure domestic evils and would in turn be invigorated by an internally unified nation.[179]

Since a world empire was regarded as a quasi-economically self-sufficient unit, there were warnings and representations against it, but they could not detract from the popularity of the idea. The German educator and pacifist Friedrich Wilhelm Foerster, following the arguments put forward by the political economist Heinrich Dietzel, viewed the establishment of large self-sufficient world empires as impossible for 'very basic economic reasons, because international division of labour in trade, in the output of raw materials and in agriculture, is growing at such a pace that in the long run the isolation of individual groups is no longer possible'.[180]

That the doctrine of world empires is a dominant feature of the age of imperialism becomes especially evident from the fact that politicians, above all such exponents of imperialism as Ferry or Joseph Chamberlain, but also Salisbury, were both attracted to it and espoused it.

In his great speech which he delivered on 28 July 1885, immediately after his fall from power, and in which he developed his *système de la politique coloniale*, Ferry entered into this aspect of the expansionist movement of his time. As a Frenchman, he was so concerned about the demographic growth in neighbouring Germany that he reviewed the international position in France with alarm. In view of the increase of the German population and of the ever-growing number of colonial competitors, 'a policy of containment or abstention' would mean abdication as a great power; it would simply mean taking 'the broad road leading to decadence! In the present period, the greatness of nations is due exclusively to the activities they develop.'[181] The appeal of French culture, 'the peaceful radiance of institutions' which, in the past had held great sway over other nations, would not be sufficient unless supported by political expansion. 'To radiate without acting, without taking part in the affairs of the world . . . would result in abdication . . . It would mean that we should . . . become a third- or fourth-rate power.'

To Chamberlain the doctrine of world empires was a centre-piece of his political ideology. In a speech he delivered at the Royal Colonial Institute on 31 March 1897 he said: 'It seems to me that the tendency of the time is to throw all power into the hands of the greater empires, and the minor kingdoms — those which are non-progressive — seem to be destined to fall into a secondary and subordinate place.'[182] To this he added the cliché that the British Empire should draw closer together. A united Greater Britain could not be surpassed by any other empire in terms of square miles, size of population, abundance and variety of resources. This idea was constantly repeated by Chamberlain in his public statements, as, for example, in a speech in 1902: 'The future is with the great Empires, and there is no greater Empire than the British Empire.'

In a speech printed in *The Times* on 5 May 1898, Salisbury divided the nations of the world into living and dying ones: 'The weak states are becoming weaker, and the strong states are becoming stronger . . . The living nations will gradually encroach on the territory of the dying, and the seeds and causes of conflict amongst civilized nations will speedily disappear.'[183] Here *imperium* and *pax* were seen as a unit; imperialism was regarded as the means by which domination will guarantee peace.

Another rationalization for the doctrine of world empires was the stereotyped reference to the fate of the Spanish colonial empire. The example of Spain seemed to leave the champions of this doctrine with only the alternative of expanding in order to maintain or arrive at the status of a world empire, lest there be shrinkage, decadence, and desolation. When the French ambassador to Berlin on 26 January 1881 urged his government to take action in Tunisia, he warned: another sign of weakness, 'and we end up by finding ourselves on a par with Spain'.[184] In Ferry's above-mentioned speech of 28 July 1885, he did not fail to draw a comparison between the France of his days and the former Spanish empire. Unless France took a part in the movement of colonial expansion which had seized all the European powers, 'we shall meet the fate . . . which has overtaken other nations which played a great role on the world's stage three centuries ago but which today . . . are now third- or fourth-rate powers'.[185] Chamberlain's 'non-progressive' kingdoms which were doomed to relapse into an inferior position express the same idea.

The decline of the Spanish colonial empire eventually became visible to everybody at that time. As a result of the war with the United States in 1898, Spain lost Cuba as well as her possessions in the Pacific area. More than ever, the doctrine of world empires was to appear as an inexorable law of evolution in the life of nations. In Spain, which was plunged into a national crisis similar to the one in France in 1871, a literary movement called 'the generation of 1898' was created and demanded reform of Spanish society as the prerequisite for increasing Spain's international reputation.[186]

7. NAVALISM

Along with the doctrine of the three or four world empires, the theory of the importance of naval power must be regarded as an ingredient of classical imperialism. It was delayed and popularized by the American naval officer and historian Alfred Thayer Mahan. In 1890 he published *The Influence of Sea Power on History*. In subsequent years two more studies on naval history came out. The first book ran to more than thirty editions, each amounting to a large number of copies. (The first edition, for example, sold 23,000 copies in the United States alone.) Contemporary naval experts described it as epoch-making. There are some defects in the historical line of argument and the main ideas were, after all, not so original as Mahan pretended them to be. Nevertheless, there has hardly been another historical work in the last one hundred years which exerted such a great impact on political developments.[187] It took Britain by storm; its influence on the naval concepts of Alfred Tirpitz is evident;[188] and its impact on Japanese naval imperialism was decisive.

The ideas Mahan put forward in his first major work centre around the following points: modern history between 1660 and 1783 (in subsequent books historical reflections are carried on to Britain's naval victory of Trafalgar) furnished unequivocal evidence that Britain was raised to the status of a world power only through a powerful navy. The struggle between Holland and Britain as well as between France and Britain shows irrefutably that in naval warfare battleships and not cruisers are the decisive instrument. In the War of the Spanish Succession, Louis XIV withdrew his naval force from the high seas for financial reasons and instead waged a war of privateering with cruisers from the Channel coast in order to harass and paralyze British commerce. To be sure, France had scored a temporary success by crippling Britain's merchant shipping. In the long run, however, this damage could be repaired; more importantly, Britain with her battleship fleet was now undisputed master of the high seas. The Seven Years' War, in which France applied the same strategy, only confirmed this result.

Mahan, the military writer, drew the lesson from the events of the past for his own time. This is why his ideas came to exert a deep influence. The introduction of steam navigation in the nineteenth century appeared to have revolutionized not only world trade, but also naval warfare. Naval strategy as it had evolved in the age of sailing was no longer regarded in many quarters as valid, but a new strategy had not yet been developed. France had resurrected the idea of cruiser warfare propogated by the *Jeune École*.[189] The Royal Navy was placing primary emphasis on numerical superiority over the second and third strongest powers (two-power standard after 1889), rather than on a superior strategic concept. In Germany, the navy was merely living from hand to mouth. In the midst of this stagnation appeared Mahan's sweeping study, which tried to demonstrate that it was the strength of navies at sea, and not the strength of armies on land, which was decisive for securing the existence of a great power, and that the old basic rules of naval warfare still applied to his time, all the more so since sea power would of necessity grow in importance in the new overseas expansion.

Mahan's ideas, called Mahanism or navalism, indisputably had great impact in the years after 1890. In Britain this can be seen in the wide circulation of Mahan's books and especially in the annual rise of the navy estimates. In 1894, the Navy League was founded for the purpose of making propaganda for a strong navy. The Royal Navy seemed to recover its self-confidence which had been lost after preference had been given to the army following the Crimean War. In Germany Mahan's 'philosophy of naval warfare' and his naval strategy based on the battleship became effective through Tirpitz. At the instigation of Tirpitz and Admiral Knorr, Mahan's first book was translated into German and 3000 copies of the first edition were distributed for propaganda purposes to support the Navy Bill of 1898.[190] It was only now that the navy gained a higher degree of independence after having been over-shadowed by the glorious army.

8.   IMPERIALIST ASSOCIATIONS

Mention of the Navy League introduces the factor of imperialist associations as yet another aspect of the over-all phenomenon of imperialism. These societies were the pillars of the imperialist and, above all, of the colonial movement. The rise and existence of imperialist associations bring two points into special focus. For one thing, there was an indissoluble link between nationalism and imperialism. On the other hand, imperialist opinions were advocated only by a minority, and the task of the associations was to propagate them and to remove all obstacles in the way of their dissemination.

Nationalist associations such as the German National Association (*Deutscher Nationalverein*) of 1859 or the *Società Nazionale* in Italy can be regarded as forerunners. In Russia the propaganda of the Russian imperialist movement flowed directly from Panslavism with its numerous Slavic committees. Elsewhere there were scholarly associations, especially geographic societies that served as connecting links. Their political influence was greatest in the French colonial movement.[191] The *Société de Géographie de France*, founded in 1821, had just 300 members in 1860, but in 1873 there were 780 and in 1881 as many as 3000 members. Eleven new societies were established between 1871 and 1881 in the provinces. After 1871 they coupled the geographical exploration of overseas territories, especially of Africa, with the political demand for the acquisition of colonies. In support of this they put forward the subjects already mentioned: the necessity of France's rehabilitation, of fulfilling her central mission, and of expanding her trade.

In the eighties the imperialist movement started directly organizing itself everywhere. Soon imperialist associations cropped up like mushrooms. The rapid proliferation of such societies, their increasingly distinguishable character as mass organizations (apart from some notable exceptions), their propaganda methods, their management, which was increasingly assumed by functionaries, and finally their attempts to influence and exert pressure on governments — all were typical of the age of imperialism. The history of these associations is often quite inadequately explored.

Suffice it to characterize the most important groups briefly. The direct reason for founding an imperialist association was often a colonial-policy action which had provoked public criticism. The German Colonial Society (*Deutscher Kolonialverein*) came into being in 1882 after the failure of the Samoa Bill in the Reichstag in 1880. The Pan-German League (*Alldeutscher Verband*) was founded in 1891 by Carl Peters and Alfred Hugenberg as a reaction to the Heligoland–Zanzibar treaty. It was a challenge to a government which regarded colonies as pawns on the chess-board of diplomacy and did not see in them any intrinsic merits. The *Comité de l'Afrique française* was established in 1890 at least partly as a protest against the Anglo-French colonial treaty of 4 August 1890, which Salisbury, in a sarcastic statement before Parliament, had called a triumph for Britain.

The imperialist associations in general regarded themselves as non-profit organizations, not affiliated with political parties, and desiring to raise sympathy for the idea of expansion and colonization and to promote the great work of colonization in such areas as emigration. Individually, the differing objectives of the associations corresponded with the imperialism characteristic of each of the powers.

a) *In Britain*

In 1884 the Primrose League and the Imperial Federation League were founded in Britain. The Primrose League was established in honour of Disraeli by Sir Henry Drummond Wolff, a diplomat, and Lord Randolph Churchill, MP. Its purpose was to propagate imperialist and conservative principles in foreign and domestic policy. They are neatly summed up in its motto *imperium et libertas*, which was taken from a speech Disraeli had made in 1879: 'When one of the greatest Romans was once asked what his politics consisted of he replied — imperium et libertas.' This was a quotation probably bowdlerized from Tacitus's original combination of *'principatus et libertas'*. In any event, it expressed Disraeli's desire to pursue a resolute, energetic foreign policy as well as his faith in the liberal traditions of English history.[192] Although Disraeli himself did not recognize a direct intrinsic link between foreign and domestic policy, but regarded both as independent entities, with foreign policy the more important, the dialectical connection between imperialism and social reform became an essential feature of British imperialism later on as it was pursued by the so-called liberal imperialists. The Primrose League grew into a mass organization numbering some 1.7 million members in 1906.

The Imperial Federation League[193] aimed not at the extension of the existing Empire, but rather, in consonance with the imperial themes of Dilke and Seeley, at its consolidation. A closer union between Great Britain and the self-governing colonies was to be promoted by trade measures (establishment of a tariff and commercial union), by increased participation of these colonies in the defence contribution of the mother country, and by establishment of an Imperial Council in which Great Britain was to be represented by Cabinet members and the self-governing colonies by members of their governments. The League was soon dissolved, but its various functions were taken over by new associations which grew up in the nineties. Among them were the United Empire Trade League and the Imperial Defence Committee. Their original purpose was partly fulfilled through conferences of the leading ministers of the colonies with the Colonial Office, through contributions of the colonies to the defence expenditures of the mother country, and through the dispatch of colonial troops to the theatre of war in South Africa. But a preferential tariff system for the Empire which would have implied abandoning the principles of free trade was never established. The driving force behind the League and its successor organizations was Joseph Chamberlain, who was appointed Colonial Secretary in 1895. Among the leading members were politicians of both parties.

b) *In France*

The formation of imperialist associations in France went along somewhat different lines. In the seventies and eighties imperialist ideas were mainly propagated by the geographic societies. Independent pressure groups — a 'colonial party' as they were briefly called by contemporaries — were established only in the nineties. The most important were the *Comité de l'Afrique française*, founded in 1890, the *Union coloniale française*, established in 1893, and the *Groupe colonial.*[194] All three groups shared, to a large extent, the same members — a general feature of pressure groups of the imperialist age, including those influencing domestic policy. The record for accumulated membership was held by Eugène Étienne, who was Under-Secretary of State for the Colonies for a time and the master-mind of the *Group colonial.*

The *Comité de l'Afrique française* was founded in the autumn of 1890 by a group of persons 'animées d'un zèle patriotique', as its first declaration put it, under the leadership of the writer Hyppolite Percher (Harry Alis). Its aim, according to a statement in the society's magazine, was to take part in 'something that has never before been seen in history: the veritable partition of an unknown continent'.[195] France, it was said in conformity with the prevailing mentality of rehabilitation and compensation, had a claim to the greater part of Africa in view of the renunciation of her rights in Egypt and in view of her cultural achievements in Algeria and Tunisia, in Senegal, and in the Congo Basin. In other words, this was a claim to those territories between the north and west African coast that were not yet French. In the Anglo-French colonial agreement of 1890, France seemed to have renounced the formation of a continuous block of territories in this part of the continent. It was against this renunciation that the Committee wanted to make a stand. The Committee was secretly supported by Étienne who was dissatisfied with the policy of the Quai d'Orsay.

The sociological composition of the committee members is shown in a statement published by the committee itself. Of the twenty-nine original members ten were members of parliament, nine deputies, one senator, seven were military officers, five were teachers; the remainder were made up of writers and scholars. Economic groups were represented by some of the members of parliament. At no time, however, did they have any decisive influence on the committee's activities. The Rothschilds, for example, were not members of the committee. In the following ten years membership increased by only sixteen.[196] A 'Bulletin', which never had more than 4,000 copies printed, served for public relations. From the funds which had accumulated from subscriptions, a sum of one million francs was spent in the period between 1891 and 1914, two-thirds of it for exploring expeditions in Africa, the remainder for propaganda purposes.[197]

The *Union coloniale française* was an association of trading firms that entertained commercial contacts with the existing French colonies. In contrast to the *Comité*, it was thus a pure pressure group pursuing its own interests, and its capital assets were accordingly higher. Membership increased from 234 in 1894 to 1,219 in 1900. Besides representing economic interests in the exploitation of the colonies, the Union regarded as its task the promotion of emigration.

The *Groupe colonial* came into existence through the initiative of Étienne, deputy for Oran and former Under-Secretary of State for the Colonies. It was like the managing group of the Imperial Federation League or even more so like that of the Pan-German League, an interparty union of those Deputies who advocated the idea of colonial expansion. As Henri Brunschwig has shown, it reflected, sociologically speaking, the composition of the Chamber of Deputies; the main body (two-thirds) came from the broad centre of parliament, the Republicans of every colour; the representation of the numerous peripheral groups decreased in relation to their political radicalism. As to the numbers, the ninety-two original members consisted of twenty-five lawyers, thirteen merchants, industrialists, and shipowners, eleven journalists, nine land-owners, six diplomats, five civil servants, four officers, four engineers, three doctors, three teachers, three notaries, two former prefects, one forester, one pharmacist, one artist, and one banker.[198] Thus members of the liberal professions predominated; after them came civil servants and representatives of trade and industry.

As to specialized imperialist associations, the navy associations everywhere became the most popular. Their relatively large membership may be explained by the fact that in the age of imperialism with its stormy technical progress, the navy appeared to be the most striking fulfilment of the belief in such progress, the most visible expression of the abilities and efficiency of the whole people, and the best guarantor of the nation's self-assertion in the imperialist competition. By means of a strong and modern navy the flag could be shown everywhere on the high seas, i.e. national power could be demonstrated and a nation could regard itself as globally omnipresent. Moreover, the hasty buildup of navies, from the latter nineties on, was the exact equivalent of the hectic scramble for colonies after the beginning of the eighties. Just as there had been a scramble for colonies, a scramble for ships was now setting in. Although both enterprises were costly and meant a drain on the nation's wealth, nationalism did not find a more satisfactory expression.

c) *Governments and Associations*

It is very difficult to assess the influence exerted by imperialist associations on the policy-making process of the government concerned. Looking for a common denominator is bound to blur differences. General statements, therefore, can only be made with reservations. It must also be kept in mind that research on the relations between associations and governments has not yet been carried very far.

Generally speaking, it can be said that the imperialist associations, just as did all other pressure groups, opposed governments much more frequently than they collaborated with them. This is, after all, a matter of course. Pressure groups advocate group interests, whereas a government represents the collective interests, or at least is supposed to do so. From the outset there is an unbridgeable gap between the usually extreme programmes and objectives of pressure groups and their practicability. It is therefore to be taken for granted that pressure groups cannot dictate a political course, but can at best influence it. Finally, pressure groups are also essentially antagonistic to each other; their means of influence are limited for this very reason. Imperialist associations after all, came into existence not only to arouse and maintain an interest in expansion, but also to combat resistance to expansion.

It may therefore be said that governments were never taken

in tow by imperialist associations. Normally, the relationship was just the other way round, as in many cases it was certainly meant to be so right from the start. In such cases the associations were only serving a useful function: they were harnessed to the government's cart only as long as this seemed opportune. While Bismarck was acquiring colonies, the German Colonial Association and the Society for German Colonization were beating the drum for him. In the same manner Tirpitz used the Navy League as a noise screen in order to improve the prospects of his naval demands before parliament and before his colleagues in the government. Kiderlen-Waechter collaborated with the Pan-German League during the second Morocco crisis in order to extract concessions from France.

Those examples suggest how dangerous the use of pressure groups could be for the governments. The agitation could get out of control and disturb or even frustrate political calculations by the intrusion of irrational elements. When Tirpitz after 1900 realized the failure of his extravagant navy plans, he denounced the agitation of the Navy League; and Kiderlen-Waechter, after the second Morocco crisis, was on the worst possible terms with the pan-Germans whom he had tried to use for his colonial plans. There is no important instance where the German imperialist associations effectively influenced the government's policy, let alone dictated it.

At first sight it might appear that the importance of the Imperial Federation League and its successor organizations was especially strong in the policy-making process of the British government because it had several politicians among its members. However, the basic differences between German and British imperialism must be kept in mind. The League's foremost task was the conservation and strengthening of the existing Empire, less so its expansion. In view of the totally different starting-position of Germany, however, expansion was the sole and necessarily aggressive aim of the German imperialist associations. The consolidation of the Empire, primarily seen as a defensive measure, could very well be a common platform of both the associations and the government. Not even a 'Little Englander' such as Gladstone could evade the dialectical demand of strengthening the defensive by offensive means, as was shown in the occupation of Egypt. Although originally the French 'Colonial Party' in 1892 consisted of 92, and later on of almost 200 deputies (from among 600), its main disadvantage was its relative aloofness from the nation. Because of the low membership of the French imperialist associations and the poor appeal of their propaganda, it may be safely said that they remained a sectarian group.[199] Pretty much as the Pan-German League, the Colonial Party opposed the most important decisions of the government's colonial policy. Thus it condemned the bills of 1892 and 1910 on protective tariffs because the *mise en valeur* would thereby be sacrificed to the interests of a few branches of the economy in the mother country (export industry, agriculture). It regretted that capital took no interest in the colonial business which was bound to have adverse effects on the exploitation of the colonies. It opposed the army bills of 1905 and above all of 1913 because they drained the defence potential of the nation to such a degree that nothing was left for emigration to the colonies.

9.   SOCIAL DARWINISM

The last important element in the social- and national-psychological attempt at interpreting imperialism is social Darwinism. Like most of the factors already discussed, social Darwinism functioned both as an impulse to imperialism and as its justification.

Social Darwinism is the transfer of Herbert Spencer's evolutionary theory and of the biological laws in animal and plant life discovered by Charles Darwin to the interpretation of the development of human society. Whereas evolutionary theory wants to explain the *past* evolution in the organic world, social Darwinism projects the evolutionary idea on to the *future* development of mankind. This distinction should be applied in scholarly debates more often than it is for the sake of greater clarity.

Although social Darwinism was an intellectual trend perhaps even more powerful than Socialism and Marxism and although in many points there exists close kinship between both models of explaining the world (turning away from all kinds of metaphysics, materialism, belief in progress, belief in the possibility of changing man), the former does not reach the latter's consistency in the structure of ideas. Social Darwinism did not have such an outstanding intellectual father as Marxism had in Karl Marx, who, in 1859 described Darwinism as the natural-history basis of his doctrine.

The varying interpretations of social Darwinism, above all of its applicability, are as numerous as its adherents. Social Darwinists were found above all in the natural sciences, not only in biology, but also in sociology, in ethnography, and anthropology, and also in the humanities, from philosophy to the history of law and music. Like Marxism, social Darwinism appealed to the intellectuals as well as to the workers, but also to many people in the middle classes, above all to those groups which had been uprooted by the transformations of industrialization and had run into difficulties adjusting to new circumstances. To the intellectuals as well as to the half-educated it offered a plausible explanation, a 'terrible simplification' of the enormous and brutal changes working within industrial society, of the varying speed with which the imperialist expansion cracked down on the resistance put up by the natives, of economic competition, of the arms race, and of war. There were few who were not spellbound by the teachings of social Darwinism.[200]

The centre-piece of Darwinism is the theory of natural selection, according to which only the fittest species in organic nature survive (the slogan 'survival of the fittest' was first used by Spencer), whereas the unfit become extinct. The doctrine of natural selection appeared to be one of the most important causes of evolution in the organic world.

During the first half of the nineteenth century people in Britain were already using the theory of evolution[201] in order to explain and justify the unrivalled position that Britain had occupied in the world by then; it was accordingly used to vindicate cosmopolitanism, pacifism, and the *laissez-faire* principle. When, however, Britain's monopoly in world trade and colonial policy was challenged by new competitors, it was the other way around: reinforced by Darwinism, the theory appeared to be a moving force and a weapon for British imperialism.

Contrary to Darwin's intentions, his theory of evolution and selection was soon, without much reflection, applied to human society. The German zoologist Ernst Haeckel completed the logic of Darwinism in 1863 by claiming that man was descended from the animal world and by calling progress a law of nature 'which can never be permanently suppressed by human power, be it by the force of tyrants or by the curse of priests'.[202]   In Britain the political economist and writer Walter Bagehot applied the doctrine of natural selection to politics, albeit during the early stages of human civilization. His book *Physics and Politics*, first published in 1872, contained such phrases as, 'In every particular state of the world, those nations which are the strongest tend to prevail over the others; and in certain marked peculiarities the strongest tend to be the best.' and: 'The strongest nation has always been conquering the weaker; sometimes even subduing it, but always prevailing over it.'[203]

In his books *The Struggle for Existence in Human Society* (1888) and *Evolution and Ethics* (1894), Thomas Huxley, an ardent preacher of Darwinism, pleaded that the evolution of man and mankind cannot be explained by biology alone, but that the spiritual and psychological world are subject to independent laws. Acting in accordance with ethical standards, he wrote in the second book, for example, that practising virtues such as charity, self-denial, and self-control means a way of life that is exactly the reverse of the struggle for existence in which merciless and unfeeling selfishness towards competitors predominates. It is less aimed at the survival of the fittest than at making as many as possible fit for survival.[204] At the same time Huxley believed that the application of ethical standards favours the reproduction of the biologically less suitable stock and that therefore the social organism will end up destroying itself. In order to avoid self-destruction or at least to remove it to a remote future, Huxley suggests war with neighbours and rivals as one alternative, but also the possibility of strengthening and concentrating the nation's resources in order to be able to resist the rival, thanks to a higher degree of social homogeneity.

Huxley set forth the distinction between two forms of social Darwinism which was elaborated by later advocates and adherents of the doctrine: the distinction between an internal social Darwinism, which is active among the individual members of a social organism, and an external social Darwinism, which works among the larger social organisms – the nations. Huxley advocated, as did the English sociologist and philosopher Benjamin Kidd, a lessening of tensions of the class struggle, one of the main forms of internal social Darwinism, so that energies could be better concentrated on the struggle of external social Darwinism, the struggle among the races.

In his 1894 book, *Social Evolution*, Kidd called for more 'social efficiency' in the English nation.[205] By this he meant virtues that promote group discipline — resoluteness, readiness for sacrifices, devotion, conscientiousness, public spirit. In his book *National Life from the Standpoint of Science* (1901), the eugenicist Karl Pearson wrote that the 'true statesman' was obligated to 'treat class needs and group cries from the standpoint of the efficiency of the herd at large', and 'to lessen, if not to suspend, the internal struggle, that the nation may be strong externally'.[206] He believed that the elimination of class and property distinctions in this way would result in Socialism in the true sense of the word, that is, in a highly developed 'sense of common interest'. The similarities to social imperialism become evident at this point.

Others, however, welcomed the working of internal social Darwinism. They opposed all measures taken by the state or by church and charitable organizations for the protection of the socially weak. The English social Darwinist John B. Haycraft in 1895 called the tubercle bacillus 'a friend of our race' because it removed sickly people in accordance with the process of selection. The German anthropologist Otto Ammon regarded infant mortality as the 'operation of natural selection which is the basis of the health and strength of country people'.[207] The unemployed were regarded by him as 'the lowest section of the lower class in which defeat in the struggle for life is already certain'. The German industrialist Alexander Tille, who called such ideas social aristocratism, welcomed alcoholism and social misery as the safest means 'of weeding out' the unfit and found his bizarre views confirmed in the slums of East London with their high mortality rates.

Basically such views can be interpreted as the desire to escape the inhuman effects of the industrial revolution and the egalitarian tendencies of democracy, as well as the striving for a 'whole' world, in which society is stratified according to traditional values and where civilization has grown in an 'organic' way. Cultural pessimism, anti-industrialism, anti-modernism, *fin-de-siècle* mood, 'local art' movement are typical forms of expressing these ideas.

External social Darwinism, in contrast with the internal variety, is directly linked to imperialism. It served to explain the rise and decline of nations in history and justified and enlivened competition among the nations of the present time.

The Austrian sociologist Ludwig Gumplowicz set up the theory of superstratification, according to which the 'race struggle' (as he titled a book published in 1883) leads to the formation of ever larger social groups and to correspondingly bigger clashes among them. The struggle for mastery is the eternal law of universal history. In a book that appeared in 1886, the Russian sociologist Jakov A. Novikov defined the foreign policy of the states as 'the art of pursuing the struggle for existence among social organisms'.[208] A few years later he described social Darwinism as the 'doctrine which regards collective homicide as the cause of progress of mankind'.[209]

The English zoologist P. Charles Mitchell anonymously published an essay entitled 'A Biological View of Our Foreign Policy' in the *Saturday Review* of 1 February 1896. The foreign policy of nations, he wrote, serves the struggle for existence. Weak races will be swept away from earth and a few major races will prepare to aim their weapons at each other. With the whole world having been conquered and the expansionist movement continuing, Britain, as the largest race, will have to wage a life and death struggle against one rival after another. The hardest struggle will be against the German rival, whose race is the most akin to the British.

Against the background of the Boer War, the English eugenicist Karl Pearson gave a reinterpretation of the whole history of mankind.[210] There is no progress without wars, he wrote. In South Africa the situation must not develop in such a way that the whites co-operate with the blacks. The blacks, although belonging to an inferior race, would crush the whites owing to their greater fecundity. The Kaffirs should therefore be thrown back across the equator. 'The path of progress', Pearson concluded in his survey of history, 'is strewn with the wreck of nations; traces are everywhere to be seen of the hecatombs of inferior races, and of victims who found not the narrow way to the greater perfection. Yet these dead peoples are in very truth, the stepping-stones on which mankind has arisen to the higher intellectual and deeper emotional life today.'[211]

As for France, research on social Darwinism is still very fragmentary, but it indicates that the debate concerning Darwinism's hold on the sciences was not so intense as in Germany or in the Anglo-Saxon countries. The reasons for this difference are that the rationalism of the age of Enlightenment still exercised a powerful intellectual influence; on the other hand, France's political-power status had weakened since 1871 with the result that there was a corresponding sense of inferiority.[212] Notwithstanding, one of the most persistent social Darwinists was the Frenchman Georges Vacher de Lapouge.[213] His ideas were based on the doctrine of the inequality of the human races. This led him to glorify the Aryan race. But he did not meet with much interest in France in such views. In the war of 1870-1 he saw the law of the survival of the fittest in operation. He developed far-reaching eugenics programmes and recommended that they be used not by such nations as France (or Germany, for that matter), but by the great nations, such as the Anglo-Saxons, the Russians, and the Chinese. For the remote future he prophesied that, following a period of smaller wars, there would be a great racial war. 'Then we will see the yellow race, the white race, the black race at one another's throats.'

Probably the most virulent and historically the most far-reaching consequence of such ideas was the growing glorification of war and the spreading notion of its inevitability. War was regarded as a mechanism of evolution. It is sometimes pointed out in this context that the harshly Germanophobic articles which appeared in the *Saturday Review* following 1896 were by no means characteristic of British public feeling towards Germany. Although (British and European) public notions regarding war in the two decades before 1914 have not yet been systematically examined, it may be said that the opinion expressed in the *Saturday Review* was no exception. Newspapers and magazines such as *The Times, Nineteenth Century, London Quarterly Review*, and *Fortnightly Review* were treating the subjects of 'war' and of the 'German peril' year after year. In 1899 the publicist Harold F. Wyatt described war as the only means, which history had confirmed many times, by which the strong nations had replaced the weaker ones. In 1911 he called war the 'test . . . which God has given for the trial of peoples — the test of war'. 'Victory in war is the method by which, in the economy of God's providence, the sound nation supersedes the unsound, because in our time such victory is the direct offspring of a higher efficiency, and the higher efficiency is the logical outcome of the higher morale.'[214]

Similarly, the arms race among the imperialist powers was defended and welcomed with arguments deriving from social Darwinism. Again, it is difficult to establish whether social Darwinism in this context was used as a means to an end or whether it worked as an impulse. The former may usually have prevailed. But the latter was never missing. The doctrine of the importance of sea power as developed by Mahan shows that both elements are indissolubly linked together.

The following phrase used by Nathaniel Barnaby, an advocate of navalism, in his 1904 book *Naval Development of the Century* may be regarded as typical of the social-Darwinist mentality with regard to the arms race. 'While injustice and unrighteousness exist in the world, the sword, the rifled breechloader and the torpedo boat become part of the world's evolutionary machinery.'[215] In the German navy arguments along similar lines were being used. The effects of Mahanism on Tirpitz have already been mentioned. One of Tirpitz's departmental chiefs, Hunold von Ahlefeld, wrote in a letter of 12 February 1898: 'The struggle for life exists among individuals, provinces, parties and states. The latter wage it either by the use of arms or in the economic field – we cannot help this – ergo we wage it; those who don't want to, will perish.'[216]

The most important question when dealing with the effects of social Darwinism on imperialism is the extent to which leading politicians of that time absorbed social-Darwinist ideas, and the extent to which such ideas influenced their political actions. The second part of the question can be more easily answered than the first. It would be hardly possible to interpret any of the major imperialist actions as having been predominantly caused by social Darwinism. The answer to the first part of the question requires more details.

Cecil Rhodes and Theodore Roosevelt are those statesmen who were most strongly affected by social-Darwinist ideas. The influence which the writer and African explorer William Winwood Reade exerted on Rhodes with his book *The Martydom of Man* (London, 1872; seventeenth edition, 1902) is quite evident.[217] The idea of racial war deeply affected both his imperialist dreams and his actions. As for Roosevelt, social-Darwinist arguments were exploited extensively. Most other leading politicians used them and were affected by them in varying degrees. The policy-makers' arguments were often linked to a belief in a civilizing mission based on nationalism. The previously mentioned notion that the great powers would finally be reduced to three or four world empires borders between nationalism and social Darwinism.

The early 'classical' imperialists had already evinced a feeling of superiority of their own race or of the white race. Disraeli once said, 'all is race: there is no other truth'.[218] Ferry stated in his great speech of 28 July 1885, in which he white-washed his colonial policy: 'It must be openly said that the superior races have rights over the inferior races.'[219]

The racial element played an important role in the books of Dilke, Seeley, and Froude. Froude linked the old English ideals of liberty to imperialist Britain's claim to world domi-nation. 'Freedom', he wrote in 1888, '. . . is only obtainable by weak nations when they are subject to the rule of others who are at once powerful and just.'[220] Dilke, who was Under-Secretary of State in the Foreign Office from 1880 to 1882, considered the Anglo-Saxons as the 'only extirpating race on earth' and regarded the extermination of inferior races such as the Red Indians as a law of nature.[221] Seeley, equating the formation of the British Empire with the 'diffusion of the English race' across the earth, exerted a deep influence on Rosebery and on Chamberlain. After entering office as Prime Minister, Rosebery evolved a philosophy of 'efficiency', the core of which was the implicit claim to the 'rule of the fittest'. Chamberlain was proud of being called the 'apostle of the Anglo-Saxon race'. In his speech of 11 November 1895 he described 'the British race' as 'the greatest of governing races that the world has ever seen'.[222]

The emphasis laid on the supposed superiority of the Anglo-Saxon race in the nineties was also due to misgivings that the old British Empire had crossed the zenith of its power and was now in decline, giving way to newer and more dynamic powers. This view was widely held in Britain herself and in Germany, especially around the turn of the century. This was at a time when Britain was waging war on the small Boer people which looked like a contest between David and Goliath. The British imperialists exalted the greatness and nobility of the British Empire in order to work against feelings of decadence.

As to Rhodes and Chamberlain, this line of argumentation based on social Darwinism must at least partly be regarded as an impulse for imperialist actions. In 1891 Rhodes wrote to his friend, William T. Stead, 'Your people do not know their greatness; they possess a fifth of the world and do not know that it is slipping from them.'[223] In an 1895 speech, Chamberlain said he saw no reason to doubt that the old British spirit was still alive. Indeed, the speeches and writings of British politicians during those years drew upon the social-Darwinist vocabulary again and again. In the previously mentioned speech of 4 May 1898 by Salisbury, for example, the world was divided into living and dying nations. Living nations, he contended, would gradually encroach upon the territory of those countries approaching their demise.[224]

From the nineties on, thinking and arguing in terms of social Darwinism was common amongst practically all the leading politicians and military figures of the imperialist powers.[225] Greatly facilitating the penetration by social Darwinism of nearly all the sciences, of politics, of state philosophy, and of the *Zeitgeist* in general was the fact that its central idea — that man is subject to evolution just as is the rest of nature — bore innumerable similarities to conventional notions on human life, and that it seemed to set up a goal to human evolution as did Socialism (although from a differing perspective): that of progress and continued development. For imperialism this provided both an impulse and a vindication.

IV. The Economic Theory of Imperialism

Explaining imperialism in primarily economic terms has become a doctrine in the Marxist interpretation of imperialism.[226] But this is also done, although with various modifications, by scholars who do not classify themselves as Marxists.

The economic theory of imperialism is fascinating at first glance, because it seems to provide a cogent formula for completely explaining this chameleon-like phenomenon. Those who popularized this theory usually overlooked the fact that such critics of imperialism as Hobson and Lenin had cautioned against using their catchy or aphoristic interpretation as a passe-partout for examining the phenomenon in all its individual aspects. They also overlooked the fact that the great books of Hobson and Lenin on imperialism were meant not as scholarly treatises comprehensively addressing all the elements of the phenomenon, but rather as political pamphlets which featured one important element as the centre-piece of their arguments — for Hobson, criticism of the wayward course imperialism had taken; and for Lenin, demonstration of the supposed accuracy of a law of the social-economic development of mankind.

The economic motives behind imperialism are of such complexity that a thorough analysis is surely justified. There are such aspects as marketing, supply of raw materials, the formation and investment of capital, the economic policy of a country (foreign-trade policy, tariff policy, protectionism, free trade), the role of economic pressure groups and the interplay between them and the government. As in the case of most of these motives, the economic factors in themselves do not constitute imperialism. Such a statement would be a monstrous over-simplification. In fact, for all their evident importance, they do not even represent the decisive aspect of imperialism. An economic motive does not necessarily underlie an imperialist action, whereas a power–political motive will, as a rule, be present.[227] Actually, it is not even a question of whether the power–political or the economic factor is of greater importance. An ideal definition comprises all elements previously mentioned as well as those yet to be discussed. However, there is always a combination of only some of these motives in each new, concrete, and different historical case.

Would it be correct to say that classical imperialism differed from the imperialism of other periods because of economic factors?

Trade has always played a significant role in European colonial history, and so it is no special feature of post-1880 imperialism. However, the massive export of investment capital which led to economic and political expansion is a peculiar feature of classical imperialism. Still, in the decades before 1880, capital had been exported by Britain and France with no consequent imperialist actions. The economic policy of the state reverted in various respects to mercantilist practices, called neo-mercantilism. However, use of the term mercantilism to describe the economic conditions of the imperialist powers as a whole is more misleading than elucidating. The large-scale growth of pressure groups was associated with the reshuffling and regrouping of industrial society. Pressure groups such as trading companies and shipping firms, which attempted to influence government colonial policy, already existed before that era. But in the age of imperialism they were joined by a large number of new groups — economic associations, nationalist societies, and, in a broader sense, also by the modern political parties — so that their means of influencing the imperialist policy of governments became much more effective.

1.   JOHN A. HOBSON'S THEORY OF IMPERIALISM

Of the numerous economic theories of imperialism, those developed by Hobson and Lenin will be dealt with more closely, since they had the strongest impact on contemporary debates and on scholarly discussions of later times.

In 1902 the liberal English publicist and political economist John Atkinson Hobson published a book with the short title *Imperialism. A Study*.[228] Up to now it has remained the most influential non-Marxist economic interpretation of imperialism.

The economic analysis of imperialism which Hobson developed in this book was not original. He adopted numerous ideas and results of debates conducted for more than a century by political economists. As far back as 1776, Adam Smith had pointed out the importance of the colonial market for the 'surplus produce' of the European nations, especially of Britain, herself then embarking on industrialization. In the 1830s and the 1840s the 'Philosophical Radicals' anticipated many elements of the later critique of imperialism. Thus Edward Gibbon Wakefield called into question — as did Hobson after him — Say's law, according to which production stimulates a corresponding demand so that over-production does not occur. A book published anonymously in Edinburgh in 1845, which Karl Marx later used for the third volume of his *Capital*, points out the phenomenon of the accumulation of surplus capital. A few years later, John Stuart Mill was advocating the export of capital to the colonies and abroad as an effective means of checking the decline of the profit-rate of investments.[229]

During the 1890s Hobson himself already was discussing questions of the capitalist economy in various journals and had touched on or developed major ideas which he later incorporated in his book of 1902. On the whole, Socialist critics on the continent during the 1890s saw an essential link between over-production and accumulation of capital on the one hand and imperialism on the other.[230] In a series of articles on *Old and New Colonial Policy* published in 1898, Karl Kautsky distinguished between capital accumulated by industry, which is used for expanding and marketing production, and the capital of 'high finance', that is, the big banks. The latter, he wrote, realizes such a high surplus value that it can no longer be invested in the home markets at anticipated profits and therefore expands abroad. The state protects capital export of high finance; in fact, it is forced to do so, being completely in the hands of the financiers.

Similar ideas were developed by the German–Russian Socialist Alexander Helphand in his book, *Marineforderungen, Kolonialpolitik und Arbeiterinteressen* (*Navy Demands, Colonial Policy and Workers' Interests*), also published in 1898. The exploited working classes of the industrial countries are capable of consuming only a fraction of what they produce, he argued. The surplus capital of the financiers is profitably invested in railway construction and in the mining industry, as well as in the plantations of the backward territories of the world, particularly in China. Helphand demanded that purchasing power in the home market be raised by repealing the corn duties and excise taxes and by introducing a progressive income tax in the Reich affecting the wealthy classes. He called for the reduction of armament expenditures, especially for the navy programme, and an Anglo-German entente. Capitalism, by introducing social reforms, would be able substantially to weaken the impact of its eventual, inescapable downfall. If it were to embark on a colonial policy, however, the impact of its collapse would increase out of all proportion. His alternative was: 'Either social reform and social revolution or a world crisis and social revolution.'[231]

The resolution of the German Social Democratic Party rally of 1900 reads in reference to 'World Politics': 'World and colonial policy is pursued for the purpose of capitalist exploitation and for displaying military force . . .; it corresponds first and foremost to the greedy desire of the bourgeoisie for new opportunities to invest its ever-increasing capital which is no longer content with exploiting the home market, and to the desire for new markets which each country tries to usurp to itself.'[232]

Thus Hobson's ideas as expressed in 1902 had antecedents. It is additionally helpful to consider the political climate of the time he wrote his book. Like many of his contemporaries in Britain, Hobson took a deep interest in the Boer War which broke out in 1899. In that year he visited the war theatre and sent back reports to British newspapers which he then published in book form in 1900. With his 1902 book on imperialism he wanted to join the political debate of the day, especially to address himself to the causes and consequences of the war. His was an indictment as well as a reform pamphlet. Hobson tried to expose the causes of the war and at the same time to show an alternative for their elimination. He shared the view of many of his contemporaries that the capital interests behind the South African mining industry were responsible for the outbreak of the conflict, and he used the deep public interest in the war to popularize the social-reform proposals he developed in the nineties. He was not really concerned about imperialism, but about the social question of England.

The years of the Boer War were also a period of considerable social unrest. There was a major strike movement which at times adopted syndicalist forms, and there was also vociferous suffragette agitation. At the same time the Irish question again took a turn for the worse. The British perceived that there was growing economic competition from Germany, behind which loomed an increasingly visible German naval programme, and this was regarded as an increasing threat. The deep concern over Britain's foreign and domestic policy led to a widespread effort to trace the causes and the culprits of the conflicts that had arisen. Coming as it did at the height of the ensuing debate, Hobson's book, set forth in easily understandable and vigorously formulated ideas, was a veritable battle-cry that met with resounding success.

One final perspective may help toward a better understanding of Hobson's book. It has already been pointed out that, contrary to the widely held view, Hobson admitted that there were a number of extra-economic factors which fuelled imperialism. He dealt with such irrational elements as the spirit of adventure and discovery, the atavistic traces in industrial mass society ('the savage survivals of combativeness'[233]) and its passion for satisfying its psychic desires, the idealization of Britain's imperial past, and nationalism and its jingoistic perversion. As for the political aspects of imperialism, Hobson believed that international relations had regressed from a cosmopolitan internationalism, which had respected the power interests of the nations, to a Machiavellian *Realpolitik* and to a brutalized diplomacy in which the 'national interest' was regarded as an absolute value. Finally, he also considered the social-Darwinist elements of imperialism as important.

In piecing all these elements together to define a total phenomenon, Hobson showed a peculiar inconsistency. When discussing the economic aspects he did not attribute any independence to the non-economic motives, whereas in other passages he regarded them as decisive. On the one hand, he tried to refute the racist motivation of imperialism; on the other hand, he displayed a strong affinity to Pearson's social-Darwinist ideas.[234] He even indulged in anti-Semitism.

In summing up Hobson's economic critique of imperialism, mention must first be made of the two basic theses of underconsumption and oversaving. Hobson regarded both phenomena as typical features of a certain stage of development of capitalist economy and of imperialism. He believed that there was a clear distinction between the post-1870–80 imperialism and the colonial expansion which went before it, and he saw imperialism as a specific corollary of the modern industrial economy.

The theory of underconsumption, which Hobson had already formulated before 1902 in a number of articles and essays, was an explanation of the economic crises of the industrial states after the 1870s: of over-production, of the decline of the rate of profit in capital investments in the home market, of pauperism, and of unemployment. Capitalism produced more than it was able to consume. Although the wealthy classes had the means to buy more goods, they felt no urge to do so because their material desires had been satisfied; the lower classes indeed had such an urge but did not possess the means to appease it.

It was the rigid, unjust distribution of the gross national production which Hobson believed was responsible for over-production in the home market. He combined this observation with the perception that competition under the *laissez-faire* principle was gradually being replaced by a process of concentration. Trusts and monopolies were being formed which led to a reduction in the over-production of goods at the same time that they brought about an even greater accumulation of capital. Since this capital could no longer be profitably employed in the home market where it would only increase the tendency towards over-production, it was channelled abroad.[235] 'Large savings', said Hobson, 'are made which cannot find any profitable investment in this country; they must find employment elsewhere.' Such pressure was the fundamental cause, 'the taproot', of imperialism.

Hobson distinguished between the effect on imperialist government policy which resulted from the over-production of goods and from surplus capital. Industry and commerce were as a rule interested only in intensifying foreign trade; the capitalist, however, demanded not only government protection, but also the extension of political control over those areas where he invested his capital, so that they would be as secure for his profits as the home market. However, certain sectoral interests, even in industry and commerce, were pursuing an aggressive, annexationist imperialism. Hobson identified firms engaged in building warships and transports; the armament industry, including subsidiary trades; and major firms satisfying newly arisen economic needs in annexed territories — in other words, textile and hardware industries engaged in colonial trade. These commercial interests were primarily concentrated in the economic centres of Manchester, Sheffield, and Birmingham. They were able to bring pressure to bear upon the government through parliamentary representatives, chambers of commerce, and such groups as the British South Africa Company or the China League. They were joined by the political and military services in the colonies, that is, the colonial bureaucracy, particularly the Indian Civil Service, and by the army and navy. Colonial policy, according to James Mill, offered the members of these services 'a vast system of outdoor relief'.[236]

More important than these sectoral interests, which represented only a fraction of the total economy and of society, was the investor to Hobson. His observation derived from a fundamental structural feature of the British economy well known at the time: the share of profits derived from foreign capital investments in national income was larger than the corresponding share of profits from foreign trade, and Britain was abandoning her position as the 'workshop of the world' in favour of becoming banker of the world. It is no exaggeration to say, Hobson concluded, that the foreign policy of Britain was primarily a struggle for profitable markets for investments. This also provided an answer to the question as to who derived most of the profit from imperialism: the investor, of course.

In the figure of the investor Hobson had found, as it were, the *deux ex machina* for the explanation of imperialism. He sought to avoid over-simplification, however, and rejected indirectly the possible charge that he had interpreted history in overly narrow economic terms. The motive forces of imperialism were not chiefly economic; rather, they were made up of 'patriotic forces which politicians, soldiers, philanthropists, and traders generate',[237] and of the enthusiasm for irregular and blind expansion. The investor would feed off these forces and manipulate them. An ambitious statesman, a frontier soldier, an over-zealous missionary, an aggressive trader — each would possibly initiate an imperial action or suggest to patriotic public opinion the necessity for more expansion. But the final decision rested with the small clique of financial magnates.

'Does anyone seriously suppose that a great war could be undertaken by any European State, or a great State loan subscribed, if the house of Rothschild and its connexions set their face against it?'[238] This rhetorical question was perhaps the clearest indication of the politicizing, combative, and pseudo-scientific character of Hobson's treatise on imperialism. Proof of that assessment was not necessary. Who would contest it, after all? The sordid war in South Africa and the influence of the major banks over the press should have made it obvious to anyone who was pulling the strings of policy.

Hobson was not content with exposing the causes of imperialism and pillorying its parasites. He supplemented his analysis by demonstrating that the colonies annexed since the end of the seventies were a burden to the national economy. He was convinced that the 'condition of England question' could be solved, that is to say, that aggressive, parasitic imperialism was not a terminal disease.

In an effort to demonstrate that the more recently acquired colonies were burdensome, Hobson prepared a table showing British acquisition over the thirty preceding years. He included only those territories which were under definite political control and concluded that the newly annexed lands amounted to one-third of the Empire as it existed in 1900.[239] Hobson noted that practically all the territories lay outside the temperate zone and were hardly suitable for European settlers. On the basis of import and export statistics, he stated that Britain's trade with her newly acquired possessions was infinitesimal compared to over-all trade and embraced goods of the lowest quality. Furthermore, the proportion of trade with the Empire was generally decreasing in relation to trade with foreign countries. Hobson thus ridiculed the notions of those imperialists who demanded colonies as an outlet for settling surplus population, selling goods, and procuring raw materials. None the less, he believed that the territories had been annexed because — quite apart from the above-mentioned marginal economic and social groups — the almighty investor needed them as areas for capital investments. To buttress the point, Hobson adduced another table listing income from

British overseas investments between 1884 and 1900.[240] He did not distinguish between foreign investments and Empire investments, let alone a specification of the Empire investments in settlement colonies, crown colonies, and, above all, the newly annexed tropical colonies.

As to the second question — whether imperialism was a policy which sprang by necessity from a certain stage of development of the capitalist economy — Hobson's answer was in the negative. At this stage he introduced his ideas of social reform which he had advocated in earlier years. The pressure to export capital could be avoided, he believed, by redistributing the national income through taxation and social-policy measures. Excess capital would be taken from the wealthy through increased taxation, and the workers' consuming power would correspondingly be elevated. The home market should be capable of absorbing goods to the extent that foreign trade need be employed not to absorb over-production, but only to purchase those goods from foreign countries that cannot be produced at home.[241]

By employing savings, through higher taxation of the wealthy classes and higher wages for the workers — which would stimulate the masses to spend more — the most important condition for dismantling aggressive imperialism would be fulfilled. To Hobson the latter was only the reverse of the domestic and social aspect of imperialism which he was really concerned about. By draining the financial power of the small capitalist clique, their political power would automatically be cut and the road would be opened to a true liberal democracy. Throughout Hobson's interpretation of imperialism was the notion that the 'new imperialism' leading to militarism and the brutalization of international relations also required an autocratic regime at home in which the government and bureaucracy triumphed over popular parliamentary representation. The imperialists demanded 'national efficiency' and homogeneity of the nation, so Hobson reasoned, only in order to divert attention from the necessity of social reforms at home and thus to preserve the existing social structure.

The economic side of imperialism had its necessary counterpart in this social aspect. In this way Hobson arrived at an interpretation of imperialism which later authors called social imperialism.[242]

According to Hobson, these social–political demands had to be accompanied by the establishment of 'genuine' and 'organic democracy', in which political affairs would be managed by the people and for the people through representative organs. Rather than simply be 'organized', genuine democracy could only grow organically. The legislature, in other words, would have to possess the confidence of the people. In order to develop this institutional bond, a long process of education would be necessary. Only when the nation produced a group of specialized, competent politicians as its leaders, whom it could control and call to account, could the danger of rule by bureaucratic tyranny be erased.

Establishing genuine democracy was also for Hobson the precondition for overcoming imperialism (or what was left of it) in foreign policy, by realizing the idea of a federation of nations. 'Secure popular government, in substance and in form', he wrote, 'and you secure internationalism: retain class government and you retain military imperialism and international conflicts.'[243] Hobson regarded a federation of the Anglo-Saxon, Germanic, Slavic, and Latin nations as a preliminary step towards realizing the principle of a worldwide federation in international politics. In this way Hobson's critique of imperialism ended with the vision of stability and harmony in the interior of the industrial states as well as in their relations among each other.

2.   LENIN'S THEORY OF IMPERIALISM

Before examining the contents of Hobson's thesis of imperialism in the light of present-day knowledge, it would seem appropriate to outline briefly Lenin's theory of imperialism. Lenin deliberately followed Hobson's ideas, but differed on a number of points and proceeded to a totally different practical application.[244]

Like Hobson, Lenin is wrongly regarded as a representative of a theory of imperialism defined in narrow economic terms. This assessment is mainly due to the fact that his theory of imperialism, as well as Hobson's, is not regarded as what it is and what it seeks to be: a theory pursuing a specific political design rather than a purely scholarly exposition. Lenin would have called an impartial scholarly analysis 'naive', 'mawkish', and 'bourgeois'. He believed that historical investigation should be pursued not for its own sake but rather for a political purpose. His theory of imperialism served as a weapon on behalf of his most important political goal, the proletarian revolution; it was intended as 'guidance for action'. It was part and parcel of his activist theory of revolution. His treatise on imperialism of 1917 (to which earlier and later remarks by Lenin on imperialism must be added) is, therefore, to be taken as a pamphlet with a distinct tendency.

The reason why Lenin occupied himself so intensively with imperialism is mainly a psychological one. Like many other Socialist theorists after the turn of the century[245] — Rudolf Hilferding, Rosa Luxemburg, Karl Kautsky, and others — Lenin felt embarrassment over having to provide reasons why, contrary to Marx's predictions, capitalism had not collapsed. Although perhaps feeling himself cornered in view of the gap between the theories of Marx and the way capitalism actually developed, he was not one to accept the dilemma in resignation. On the contrary, he preferred to take the offensive against the sceptics among his followers and, of course, against capitalism. Thus his pamphlet on imperialism of 1917 was also a weapon in the struggle against revisionism. Under the leadership of Eduard Bernstein, revisionists had particularly questioned Marx's theory of concentration (absorption and monopolization of small- and medium-sized enterprises by large firms); his theory of catastrophe (collapse and replacement of the capitalist system by Socialism); and his theory of the pauperization of the workers. Revisionists pointed out that small- and medium-sized enterprises continued to exist, that capitalism was capable of stabilizing itself despite the economic crises, and that the material position of the workers was constantly improving.

Even as Lenin interpreted the outbreak of the First World War to be the confirmation that capitalism, with its inherent contradictions, would culminate in an explosion, his 1917 pamphlet on imperialism served the additional function of boosting his demand, repeatedly raised during the war, for the right of self-determination of peoples. The struggle for independence of the oppressed peoples — the minorities in Europe and the backward peoples in the colonies — was to him a struggle against their oppressors and exploiters, that is, a struggle against imperialism.

Attention must finally be drawn to another misunderstanding in the historical and historiographical assessment of Lenin's theory of imperialism. Lenin was not primarily concerned with establishing a connection between the colonial expansion of the industrial powers during the last quarter of the nineteenth century and the development of the capitalist economy of that time, as some critics (such as David Kenneth Fieldhouse) have assumed.[246] Lenin acknowledged, with some inconsistency, that the hunt for the world's undeveloped territories was finished by 1900. His idea of imperialism was rather applied to the one decade and a half *after* the turn of the century.[247] A redistribution of the earth could be observed during this time, he believed, and a redistribution in more than just the territorial sense.

In his 1917 publication dealing with imperialism Lenin repeatedly defined these chronological limits. In the preface to the French and German editions of 1921 it was unequivocally stated that the main purpose of this book was 'to present . . . a *general picture* of the world capitalist system in its international relationships at the beginning of the twentieth century and on the eve of the first world imperialist war'. It would prove 'that the war of 1914–18 was imperialistic (that is, an annexationist, predatory, plunderous war) on the part of both sides; it was a war for the division of the world, for the partition and repartition of colonies, the 'spheres of influence' of finance capital, etc.'[248]

It was the struggle after 1900 for the division and redivision of the world which Lenin called capitalist imperialism. He fully acknowledged, as already stated, that there were transitional forms and other varieties of imperialism, but he did not elaborate on them. He emphasized that 'we shall not be able to deal with non-economic aspects of the question, however much they deserve to be dealt with.'[249] He spoke of the 'vast diversity of economic and political conditions' of imperialism, acknowledged 'numerous "old" motives of colonial policy'[250] (without describing them), and applied the term imperialism to history in general — Ancient Rome had pursued imperialism, for example. The foundation of the British Empire, wrote Lenin, was British colonial imperialism; its expansion in the nineteenth century was capitalist colonial policy, which he distinguished from the export of French loan capital in the nineteenth century and at the beginning of the twentieth century. The latter he called usury imperialism.[251] In another passage Lenin cautioned that, although his brief definition of imperialism as 'the monopolistic stage of capitalism' conveniently summed up the main points, it was 'nevertheless inadequate'.[252]

What were the specific characteristics of capitalist imperialism as Lenin saw them? *In nuce*, they were expressed in his book title, which he borrowed (with characteristic modification) from a work by Rudolf Hilferding published in 1910 under the title *Das Finanzkapital. Das höchste Stadium des Kapitalismus*. Lenin changed it to: *Imperialism, the Highest Stage of Capitalism*, and added the significant subtitle: *A Popular Outline*. His term capitalist imperialism could be replaced by market imperialism, market defined first as the financial market and second as the commodity market.

Lenin summed up the essence of capitalist imperialism in the following five basic definitions:

1. The enormous growth of industry was accompanied by a process of concentration of production. A few large-scale enterprises in the most important branches of production accumulated a larger and larger share of the over-all production. The importance of small enterprises decreased. Production associations called cartels, syndicates, and trusts came into existence and impeded or eliminated competition, which was the hallmark of the 'old capitalism'; in other words, they occupied a monopoly. As examples of monopoly organizations, Lenin cited the Rhine–Westphalian Coal Syndicate in Germany and the Standard Oil Company and the Steel Corporation in the United States. The process of cartelization was fully under way at the turn of the century. In Germany and the United States it was protected by tariff walls; in Britain it came about within the free-trade system. Lenin did not mention any important data of relevance for Britain.

2. At the same time, the process of concentration occurred in the banking system. Big banks crushed the small ones by absorbing more and more money deposits. They merged with one another until two or so major banks came into existence in each of the industrial countries. In the United States there were Rockefeller and Morgan, who disposed of capital amounting to several thousand million dollars. In Germany the

Deutsche Bank and the Berlin-based Disconto-Gesellschaft became dominant; in France it was the Crédit Lyonnais, the Banque de Paris et des Pays-Bas, and the Société Générale. During the process of monopolization the banks, with their expanding credit potential, outgrew their original role purely as financing agencies and adopted such new functions as amalgamating their share holdings with those of the large industrial and commercial enterprises and occupying seats on their boards of directors and executive committees. With this amalgamation of personnel and by this fusion of bank capital and industrial capital, the process of monopolization and concentration of capital was accelerated. A small financial oligarchy disposed of thousands upon thousands of millions and in this way dominated the banking, commercial, and industrial operations of the whole capitalist society.

3. The capital, including industrial capital, which was at the disposal of the banks, and which they offered to industry on certain conditions, was called by Lenin finance capital, a term he borrowed from Hilferding. This finance capital accumulated in the few rich industrial countries at the turn of the twentieth century to such an extent that it could no longer be invested in the domestic market at the traditional rates of profit. The unprofitable surplus capital was exported abroad, preferably to the backward countries, where usually there was maximum profit in store due to the scarcity of capital, because competition could easily be eliminated, and because prices for real estate, raw materials, and wages were low. This export of capital, together with the domination by the monopolies, characterized the 'new capitalism', whereas the 'old capitalism' featured the export of goods on competitive conditions. Since the beginning of the twentieth century the export of capital had acquired gigantic dimensions. Three industrial countries which exported their finance capital were Britain, France, and Germany. The United States, which Lenin mentioned in his listing of monopoly formations, were passed over in silence.

4. At the instigation of finance capital, the struggle for the redivision of the earth would continue and intensify.

In drawing his conclusions from statistics used by 'bourgeois' authors such as Hobson and from their connection with monopoly capitalism, however, Lenin became involved in contradictions. He identified imperialism with monopoly capitalism as the highest stage of capitalism and repeatedly cited the turn of the century as the beginning of extensive and speedy formation of monopolies. He did not, however, label the two decades preceding 1900 as the pre-monopolistic stages, but rather the years before 1876, so as to establish a connection between the acquisition of colonies and monopoly capitalism.

The period between 1876 and 1900 was described as the transition of (pre-monopolistic) capitalism to monopoly capitalism. As to the acquisition of colonies by the great powers, Lenin did not draw up statistics for the period between 1876 and 1900,[253] but rather for the years between 1876 and 1914. He arrived at the conclusion that Britain's colonial expansion was most important in the years 1860–80 and that the colonial possessions of all the six great powers taken together had expanded enormously between 1876 and 1914 — from 40 to 65 million square kilometres. In order to substantiate his statement that the transition of capitalism to the stage of monopoly capitalism was linked with an intensification of the struggle for partitioning the world, he stated that it was such semi-colonies as China, Persia, and Turkey that were increasingly becoming objects of the struggle for redistribution and that the search for sources of raw materials was intensifying.

The acquisition of colonies and the competition for semi-colonies were to Lenin but one aspect of imperialism. Another was the struggle for the redivision of territories among the great European powers (Germany's appetite for Belgium and France's appetite for Alsace–Lorraine, for example). And still another was the struggle to partition and repartition the world's markets.

5. The intensified antagonism among the imperialist great powers was to Lenin the surest indication that capital in its highest stages was dying and decaying. Lenin admitted that finance capitalism succeeded in drawing a considerable part of the work-force over to its side, that it stripped the workers of their revolutionary conscience by channelling part of its 'extra profits' into the improvement of the material situation of the workers, which really meant bribing them. This 'opportunism' on the part of the workers, however, was only a

transitional phenomenon. As a parasitic phenomenon, capitalism was destined to rot away[254] and would ultimately perish, for the time would arrive when finance capital in each nation was bound to expend all its profits for the struggle that would take place among the powers.

Treaties of alliance of the imperialist countries and their agreements on delimiting spheres of interest which Kautsky had described as symptoms of a permanent nature were only respites before the outbreak of new struggles. What expedient could there possibly be, Lenin exultantly asked as he pointed to the World War, for capitalism to solve its intrinsic contradictions? The latter he saw arising from irregular and erratic economic growth, that is, in the development of individual enterprises, of individual branches of industry, and of individual states; and from the constant shifting of forces which coalesced to form monopolies. Other inherent contradictions he identified as the antagonism between monopolies and free competition (which still survived); between the gigantic transactions' of finance capital and 'honest' business in the free market; and between cartelized and non-cartelized industry.[255]

Lenin's activist approach, which was really the mainspring of his analysis of imperialism, was most evident in his polemic against Kautsky's notion that the inter-imperialist alliances would point to a peaceful elimination of imperialist policy.[256] Kautsky's 'theory' was described as a 'most reactionary method of consoling the masses with hopes of permanent peace being possible under capitalism, distracting their attention from the sharp antagonisms and acute problems of the present era, and directing it towards illusory prospects of an imaginary "ultra-imperialism" of the future'. The contents of Kautsky's 'Marxian' theory was 'deception of the masses — there is nothing but this' in it.[257]

Lenin did more in his analysis than criticize imperialism. He actually welcomed it as a necessary stage of transition on the road to Socialism: monopolies were 'an immense progress in the socialisation of production'.[258] Under the old capitalism, free competition had been anarchical. Manufacturers had produced their goods out of touch with one another and without knowing the needs of the market. The movement towards concentration would bring calculation into the chaos and, using the term coined by Bukharin and Hilferding, 'organized' capitalism would be formed.[259] 'Capitalism in its imperialist stage arrives at the threshold of the most complete socialisation of production. In spite of themselves, the capitalists are dragged, as it were, into a new social order, a transitional social order from complete free competition to complete socialism.'

In this way the most opportune moment would arrive for the revolutionary action to be launched. Since the socialization of production had been accomplished to a large extent, it would only be necessary to transfer the social means of production from the private ownership of a small number of persons — the monopolists and the financial oligarchy — into the hands of the proletariat. This was the major aim of Lenin's critique of imperialism until the October Revolution of 1917: to drive home to the proletariat and to the suppressed nations the necessity of a revolutionary uprising against the domination of the monopolies.

After the Revolution had obtained its partial success in Russia, Lenin employed his theory of imperialism for new objectives: for safeguarding the Bolshevist regime against the danger from outside (Allied intervention), in view of the hostility of the imperialist powers, and at home against the counter-revolution (civil war); for justifying the continued existence and strengthening of the power of the Bolshevik party; and finally, for stimulating the liberation movements in the colonies, particularly in India and China.

Although there were minor differences, Hobson and Lenin agreed in their discovery of the fundamental causes of imperialism — paramount among which was the drive of capitalism to acquire new fields of investment — they differed, however, completely when they assessed and accounted for the causes. Hobson believed that imperialism would become superfluous if underconsumption were overcome, that is, when social reforms were introduced. Lenin believed that this was a necessary, final stage on the road to the Socialist revolution. Hobson was the physician prescribing a remedy to an ailing capitalism; Lenin was the prophet forecasting its collapse.[260]

3.   A CRITIQUE OF THE ECONOMIC THEORY OF IMPERIALISM

When critically analysing the theory of capitalist imperialism, this important difference should be kept in mind. Generally speaking, it is difficult to question Lenin's view of imperialism, not because it includes the unsubstantial notion of informal (market) domination, and is therefore not linked to territorial domination, but because it is a dogma. Arguments that appeal to reason cannot convince a person who proclaims and advocates an article of faith. If, however, one is studiously impartial and objective — the only possible position for a non-Marxist scholar — which is to say that one considers the theory of capitalist imperialism as a hypothesis, then its weaknesses are readily identifiable.

Attention must again be drawn to the fact that Hobson's and Lenin's ideas were not original. Hobson's views leaned heavily on the results of the debate waged for a century by classical political economists over colonial policy. Lenin, who proceeded from the premiss that capitalism developed according to certain laws, based his statistical data on Hobson, Hilferding, and a number of 'bourgeois' scholars and even adopted their views to some extent, but then proceeded to hammer out a dogmatic theory. Having chosen capital export from a large number of elements working together in various ways and having proclaimed it the decisive motive force of imperialism, while regarding the other elements as merely existent but not necessary symptoms, Hobson and Lenin reduced a complex phenomenon to a catchy but unduly simplistic formula. Being rational men, they believed they could retrace the behaviour of the imperialists of the pre-war period according to a rational pattern.

The historian is bound to do precisely what Lenin derided as treacherous, backward, and deceitful when he attacked Kautsky's explanation of imperialism. That is, he must analyse the main motives of each major imperialist action of the industrial powers. In the end, the sum of these individual inquiries is the utmost that the historian can gain. General statements must not be proclaimed as universally binding and applicable, but must always be made with reservations.

In order to point to the weakness of the purely economic critique of imperialism, Kautsky had contrasted the figures of Britain's trade with Egypt for the years 1872 to 1912 with those of her total foreign trade, and in doing so had found that Britain's trade with Egypt was lagging behind the development of her over-all trade.[264] He had then drawn the conclusion that there was no reason to assume that Britain's trade with

Egypt would have grown less without the military occupation
of Egypt by the sheer weight of the economic factors; in
other words, that the expansionist drive of capitalism was not
necessarily promoted by the brutal methods of imperialism
(which in Lenin's view were a constituent part also of informal, non-territorial imperialism), but much more so by 'peaceful democracy'.

a) *Hobson and Britain's Capital Export*

When Hobson wrote about the importance of the colonies as
markets for selling goods and as sources of raw materials for
the industrial powers, he started on the basis of available
foreign-trade statistics that the new colonies were of very
small value; in fact, that from the point of view of the national
economy, they actually were a burden.

When Hobson, however, analysed the importance of overseas investment, he discovered from the data of the Statistical
Department of the Board of Trade (Sir Robert Giffen, Direc-
tor) that the profits accrued from these investments and
assessed for income tax had nearly doubled in the period
between 1884 and 1900 (from £33.8 to £60.3 million).[262]
Hobson, however, did not bother to specify these overseas
investments, to examine their geographical distribution, and,
above all, to distinguish between colonial and foreign investments as he had done in his foreign-trade statistics. He then
went on to place a table of colonial acquisitions of the same
period alongside the table of investments made up indiscriminately of 'foreign and colonial investments'. Having
spotted a notable increase here as well, and having depreciated
the connection between the annexation of colonies and the
export of goods, Hobson came to the conclusion that the
acquisition of colonies could only have been brought about
under the pressure of the above-mentioned financial cliques.

This conclusion, however, was wrong. A close investigation
of overseas investments — which can be done more precisely
today than in Hobson's time — shows that British overseas
investments were mainly placed in countries such as the
United States, Argentina, and Turkey; and, within the Empire,
in the old settlement colonies of Canada, Australia, New
Zealand, and also in India; but only to a minimal degree in the
newly acquired tropical colonies. The drive abroad of surplus

capital could, therefore, not be the main reason for the acquisition of colonies between 1884 and 1900.

Since Lenin adopted Hobson's data on the acquisition of colonies and linked them with the export of capital, he committed the same mistake. He wrote, 'The necessity of exporting capital also gives an impetus to the conquest of colonies, for in the colonial market it is easier to eliminate competition, to make sure of orders . . . by monopolist methods (and sometimes it is the only possible way).'[263] This statement was incorrect not only because of the geographical discrepancies mentioned, but also for the simple reason of chronology. As has been seen, Lenin dated the beginning of the formation of finance capital to the turn of the century. Finance capital could not, therefore, have been responsible for the acquisition of colonies in Africa and Oceania which had taken place in the two preceding decades. On this point, Lenin also contradicted himself. For in another passage he stated that the annexation of colonial territories was mainly completed at the turn of the century. It must be added, however, that Lenin's notion of imperialism is thus only partially shaken, for it was defined as the domination of finance capital over colonies *and* non-colonies (semi-colonies and neighbouring industrial powers).

It must have already been clear in Hobson's and Lenin's time that, by isolating capital export as one single factor, a comprehensive explanation of the total phenomenon of imperialism could not be given. Russia, Japan, Italy, and Portugal were powers poor in capital, certainly with no surplus capital; even though they had to import capital, they none the less pursued imperialism. Portugal is an excellent example of a country which indulged in an essentially 'non-economic imperialism'.[264] Russia was the greatest debtor on the French capital market; French capital financed the beginnings of her industrialization, her whole railway network, and her imperialist policy in the Far East.[265] While pushing towards Tunisia, Tripoli, and Abyssinia, Italy possessed no surplus capital at all; at the most she had surplus national energies and, in the case of Tunisia, surplus population which she could export. She played a small role in constructing the Baghdad railway, but with capital originating in Greece.[266] Japan's imperialism in Korea and China was attributable to demographic pressure, to the passion of a nationalist military caste for prestige, and to the striving for sources of raw material. Even in the German case, which Lenin used first and foremost in his discussion of finance capital, recent research on the origins of the First World War has underscored the extent to which German imperialism in the Balkans and in the Near East suffered from a lack of capital in its competition with the other powers.[267] There was insufficient German capital to finance the major imperialist venture of the Baghdad Railway; other capital, the bulk of it from France, had to be invited in.

b) *Lenin and Monopoly Capitalism*

How about the formation of monopolies in the production and banking sector, a central element in Lenin's theory of imperialism? In fact, it was only in Germany and the United States that the cartels and trusts were formed after the turn of the century. This development, however, had nothing to do with Germany's acquisition of colonies. The volume of US acquisitions in 1898 was the most modest of all industrial powers; yet it was wholly unrelated to the export of capital, because the US had to import capital herself (from Britain). Cartelization in Britain before the First World War was only in its infancy.[268] There was the Salt Union of 1888, the United Alkali Company of 1897, and some other combinations in the steel, textile, and shipping industries. But they never dominated the market and never went beyond the experimental stage.

Cum grano salis, Lenin's dictum, 'Tens of thousands of large-scale enterprises are everything; millions of small ones are nothing',[269] may be appropriate in the case of Germany, but when applied to France it turns matters upside down. Among the great industrial powers, it was France where the concentration of production was least advanced. Until World War I the family enterprise was the typical manufacturing unit. According to Henri Sée, there were 2.44 million workers to about one million plants in 1911.[270] The size of the colonies acquired was inversely proportional to the size and speed of industrialization: the Third Republic acquired more colonies than the Second Empire, whereas gross industrial production between 1873 and 1913 increased by only 4.3 per cent on the average, as against 5 to 6 per cent in the years 1849 to

1866. In foreign trade, France under the Second Empire still occupied second position in the world after Britain; after 1871 she was quickly surpassed by Germany and the United States. In contrast to Germany, her pattern of production did not show much adaptability. Luxury and semi-luxury commodities, which were hardly suitable for colonial trade, still formed the bulk of her exports.

As for the formation of finance capital, it is again somewhat applicable to Germany. The contrary is the case for France, however, where industrial and bank capital did not amalgamate. Industrial capital existed independently of the large banks and was employed by industry for internal investments and hardly for export purposes.[271] However, bank capital, which was abundant, was exported. Lenin therefore spoke of France's 'usury' or 'bondholders' imperialism'[272] and unintentionally made it obvious that large-scale imperialism could not be pursued with usurers and bondholders. The patchwork and unorganized character of French imperialism is also evident in the fact that capital export and foreign trade were not synchronized. As for the other industrial powers, the negotiation of loans going abroad was usually linked to the granting of trade benefits to the lender country. In France the export of goods and the export of capital went their separate ways.[273] Thus Russia was France's greatest debtor, but only her tenth best trading partner prior to the war. The Balkan countries used the capital received from France for purchasing arms from Germany. Lenin erroneously, it seems, regarded France as the best illustration of the connection between investments and trade when he wrote: 'The export of capital abroad thus becomes a means [to France] for encouraging the export of commodities.'[274]

Many other such examples could be cited. In Britain, too, there was no amalgamation of industrial and bank capital. Again, industry used its capital for reinvestment purposes, and it was primarily bank capital that was exported.[275]

4.   TRADE WITH THE COLONIES

To the best of present-day knowledge, in which direction did the foreign trade and capital export of both Britain and France go? Did the colonies, especially the newly acquired ones, play a significant part in determining this direction?

a) *Britain*

The pattern of Britain's trade with her colonies was fairly homogeneous between 1880 and 1910–13.[276] Whereas about one-fourth of British exports went to the Empire at the beginning of the 1870s, that share after 1880 was approximately one-third. In ten-year intervals, it amounted to 34.5 per cent in 1882, 33 per cent in 1892, and 39 per cent in 1902. The high percentage in 1902 at the end of the Boer War was ephemeral; thereafter, there was a marked decline, and in 1910 it amounted to 30 per cent.

The increase of the share of one-fourth in the seventies to one-third since the eighties can only to a small degree be ascribed to the new colonies; rather, it was mainly due to an intensification of exports to the old colonies. In 1910 India–Ceylon, Australia–New Zealand, Canada, and South Africa received 26.6 per cent, with the remainder of the colonies receiving only 3.4 per cent of British exports. Egypt's share decreased from 2.8 per cent on a yearly average in the five years between 1870 and 1874 to about 1.4 per cent in the decades between 1880 to 1910. Although the Empire expanded by about one-third after 1880 the new territories absorbed only an infinitesimal fraction of British exports. Exports from Britain to the whole of Africa (including the non-British colonies but excluding South Africa) ranged from 5 to 6 per cent in the decade prior to 1914.

The value of the export of British products to the Empire increased by one-half, from £109 million to £159 million between 1902 and 1910, that is, after the end of the period of new colonial acquisitions. The export to third countries, however, went up much more rapidly. It more than doubled, from £174 million in 1902 to £375 million in 1910.

The share of the British possessions in British imports was, on the average, considerably smaller than their share in British exports. It ranged from one-fifth to one-fourth in the period after 1880: in 1892 it amounted to 23 per cent, in 1902 to 19 per cent, in 1910 to 25 per cent. The value of imports from the British Empire increased from £107 million to £170 million between 1902 and 1910; and of imports from third countries from £422 million to £508 million in the same period. The breakdown between the Dominions and the old colonies on the one hand and the new colonies (Egypt excluded) on the other shows a share of 23 per cent and 2 per cent respectively for the year 1910. Egypt supplied 3 per cent of the imports. British imports from the whole of Africa (excluding South Africa) amounted to 8 per cent in the pre-war years.

Hobson's analysis and assessment of British trade in 1902 were completely to the point: 'Of the trade with British possessions the tropical trade, and in particular the trade with the new tropical possessions, was the smallest, least progressive, and most fluctuating in quantity.'[277]

b) *France*

France's trade with her colonies in the period between 1882 and 1913 shows a somewhat different pattern.[278] The share of all her colonies, including the protectorates, in her volume of exports increased continuously, from 6.7 per cent in 1882 to 10.9 per cent in 1913, and the share in her volume of imports from 4.7 per cent to 9.3 per cent. That is, total trade with the colonies increased from 5.7 per cent to 10.2 per cent. (The value of France's total trade increased from 10.7 million francs to almost 20 thousand million francs between 1882 and 1913.) The growth is to some extent due to trade with the territories acquired after 1881.

The North African territories of Algeria, Tunisia, and Morocco occupied a special position in France's colonial trade. In 1908 their trade with France came to the same amount as that of the other colonies. Afterwards it grew more quickly than the trade with the other colonies. In 1913 the value of French trade with Northern Africa amounted to 1.4 thousand million francs, while trade with the remaining colonies amounted to 0.6 thousand million francs.

A comparison between France's colonial trade and the trade with her industrial neighbour Germany is particularly revealing. The colonies had been forced to give up their tariff autonomy since 1892, whereas Germany (after 1879) and France (after 1892) had protected themselves with tariff walls. France's trade with Germany grew by about 125 per cent (from about one thousand million to 2.25 thousand million francs) in the period between 1901 and 1913, as against 41 per cent (from 417 million to 588 million francs) with regard to the colonies, with the exception of the North African possessions. These figures show that France's colonial trade was of relatively small importance in her over-all trade.

The foreign-trade pattern of the French colonies presents a striking peculiarity which ran exactly counter to the expectations of the colonialists and the neo-mercantilists: the commercial intercourse of most of the colonies was smaller with the mother country than with third countries. In 1901 the total trade of the French colonies with the mother country amounted to 416.9 million francs; with third countries, it was 388.1 million francs. For 1913, the corresponding figures amounted to 588.5 million francs and 822.5 million francs respectively. Trade with third countries had thus increased much more rapidly than that with France. If, however, the three North African protectorates are included for 1913, the proportion shifts in favour of France.

The same peculiar structural feature — a relative decrease in the trade of the colonies with the mother country compared to their trade with third countries despite political control — can also be observed with regard to the German and British colonies. Whereas the German colonies carried on 35.2 per cent of their trade with Germany in the decade between 1894 and 1903, the corresponding share went down in the subsequent decade (1904–13) to 26.6 per cent. As for Britain, the share of trade of the politically almost independent Dominions with the mother country increased slowly but steadily, whereas the share of the crown colonies and also of India decreased. Between 1854 and 1863 Britain's share in India's over-all trade amounted to 52.1 per cent; for the period 1893–1904, it had gone down to 44.5 per cent.

The export direction of some of the more important raw materials from the French colonies is worth mentioning. The iron ore mined in Tunisia and Algeria was almost exclusively shipped to Britain, Germany, and the United States. Coal was mined only in Indo-China, where most of it was consumed; only a fraction was shipped to France; a larger part was exported to Japan. The nickel ore found in New Caledonia and the chromium produced there were exported to the United States, Australia, Britain, Holland, Belgium, and Germany. Of the more important minerals, only the phosphates mined in Northern Africa went primarily to France.

These observations, and there are many more that could be made, show that trade for the most part did not follow the flag, as the colonial enthusiasts demanded, but rather the price-tag.

5. PROTECTIONISM

Contemporaries (among them Lenin) as well as later scholars have explained the supposed connection between protectionism and colonial acquisitions in this seemingly logical formula: industrialization requires protective tariffs; the protective system contributes to over-production; and the producers demand the acquisition of colonies in order to be able to market their over-production. Jules Ferry wrote: 'The protective system is a steam engine without a safety-valve unless it has a healthy and serious colonial policy as a corrective and auxilary measure.'[279] Hobson wrote in his 1902 work on imperialism: 'Just in so far as an Imperialist is logical does he become an open and avowed protectionist.'[280] In his book on classical imperialism, Heinz Gollwitzer summarized that not all imperialists were protectionists, but that all protectionists were imperialists.[281]

The trade data cited above should make it obvious that Gollwitzer has over-simplified. The first part of the proposition is correct: Britain, the imperialist power *par excellence*, adhered to the principle of free trade, as did Belgium and Holland. Germany and the United States, on the other hand, introduced protective tariff systems first and then pursued colonial imperialism. In France, however, the most important protective law, the *Loi Méline*,[282] came into force in 1892 when part of the colonies had already been annexed under the free-trade system.

a) *France's Protectionist Policy*

The *Loi Méline* represents a clear challenge to the accuracy of the second half of Gollwitzer's statement. In subsequent years, the Méline tariff developed into a double-edged sword.[283] It stipulated that the colonies would have to renounce their tariff autonomy introduced in 1866. As regards trading with third countries, both the metropolis and the colonies formed a common tariff area. This did not mean, however, that commercial intercourse between France and the individual colonies was duty-free. In accordance with mercantilist principles, only the export of French industrial and agricultural products to the colonies was free, whereas the imports from the colonies were, as a rule, subject to the normal customs tariffs. The treaties governing state loans granted to the colonies for starting public works often contained a clause specifying that such projects were to be carried out by French firms and that the necessary building materials were to be transported by French ships. In the beginning the colonial markets seemed indeed to serve as the safety-valve for an economic steam-engine running at excess pressure, just as Ferry claimed.

Year by year, however, it became increasingly evident that the colonial markets were not really much needed. It is true that France's total imports decreased slightly after 1892; this was probably caused not so much by the Méline tariff as by the 1893–4 world-wide depression. By 1895 imports were again on the rise. In the minds of the protectionists, the tariff barriers for goods exported by the colonies to France were still not high enough. They were worried about the competition of those branches of industry being established in the colonies which used cheaper labour and were not required to pay trade taxes as high as in France. They were also worried about the colonies satisfying an ever greater proportion of their needs abroad. The *Parti colonial*, which was devoted to the development and promotion of the colonies, opposed the protectionists' demands for higher tariff protection. The struggle was waged for years between these factions until 1910, when the 1892 tariff on such colonial products as coffee, tea, and cocoa was abolished with effect from 1 January 1914.

b) *The Colonial Opposition in the French Chamber*

It is by no means correct to say that the economic balance-sheet of colonial policy has been critically exposed only through the analysis of later scholars. Colonial committees in the parliaments of the industrial powers scrutinized with the utmost accuracy the profit and loss accounts of colonial ventures. Most of the charter companies supported by Germany and Britain went bankrupt sooner or later. The end of the German Colonial Company for South-West Africa came in 1889, four years after it was founded by Lüderitz. The German East Africa Company folded in 1891, and the

New Guinea Company struggled along until its demise in 1899. Only the Jaluit Company made profits. The Imperial British East Africa Company had to give up its charter in 1895,[284] and the Royal Niger Company followed suit in 1899. The Reichstag and the House of Commons sanctioned the indemnification of the bankrupt trading companies not for economic reasons, but out of a sense of prestige and nationalist rivalry. A dissertation from Henri Brunschwig's school which analysed the account books of the forty charter companies installed in the French Congo after 1899–1900 stated that in 1914 a total of thirty-six had vanished from the scene.[285] In 1887-8 the expenditure of the Belgian king for his Congo Free State exceeded receipts tenfold; in 1893–4, expenses still ran three times as high as receipts.[286]

After the second half of the 1890s, the financial aspect of colonial policy was examined closely in the French Chamber.[287] Adolphe Turrel, the Chamber's rapporteur for the colonial budget of 1896, furnished an account of the colonial expenses of 1894 with more than just a trace of sarcasm. The foreign trade of the French colonies (excluding Algeria and Tunisia), he wrote, had amounted to 476 million francs. The largest share had gone abroad. The value of the trade with France was 213 million francs; France had exported goods to her colonies worth 95 million francs and had bought goods from them worth 118 million francs. The trade balance, therefore, closed with a deficit of 23 million francs. But that was not all. French exports to the colonies were earmarked first of all for the needs of the colonial administration and the army, and did not therefore represent an absolutely profitable trade. The colonial budget for 1894 had amounted to 80 million francs. Turrell summed up France's trade relationship with the colonies by stating: 'On the trade France does with its colonies as a whole, France loses 23 million francs a year: to achieve which result the country spends 80 million francs.'[288]

In the following years the Chamber's rapporteurs struck the balance in the same way. In 1899 Gaston Doumergue summarized his statements on colonial policy as follows: ' . . . our colonies are a heavy burden for France and . . . this burden is not sufficiently compensated for by the benefits it receives for trading with them'.[289]

During the debate Doumergue was supported by d'Estournelles de Constant, who had been an ardent expansionist in
earlier years.[290] His remarks reveal the deeper causes of
colonial expansion. He distinguished two stages of colonial
policy: 'First comes the joy of conquest; and then is presented
the bill for payment.'[291] Colonial policy has led to unfortunate
international complications (the Fashoda settlement coming
only a few months earlier) which had been glossed over light-
heartedly. 'We are being drawn along in an irresistible process,
like that of Time, by the mere force of a colonial expansionism
which has got out of control.' It had been asserted that France
could not help pursuing a colonial policy, that she would
have to imitate others regardless of the cost. Economically,
however, France's colonial expansion was impossible to
reconcile with her low birth-rate and with her production
capacity. Most of the territories annexed were deserts or
regions inhabited by savages who would buy European goods
of only the poorest quality and who would, in any case, satisfy
their needs through illicit trading with France's rivals. In harmony with Hobson's demands for social reform, d'Estournelles
demanded that French capital be invested at home: 'You ask
us to colonize China: I ask you to colonize France . . . If you
want France to put herself in a position where she can, in
every way, copy overpopulated countries like Britain and
Germany, the first thing you will have to do is to produce
children.'

Similar profit and loss accounts were presented year after
year to the French Chamber and in the same way to the
German Reichstag and to the British Parliament. The colonial
budget and the colonial credits applied for by the government,
however, were always granted without great cuts. The economic arguments of a Ferry no longer went down with the
deputies, who seemed more persuaded by nationalistic slogans.

c) *Protectionist Agitation in Britain*

In the case of French imperialism, the notion that protectionism had an essential impact on colonial expansion must be
called a myth (Henri Brunschwig). As for British imperialism,
however, matters are not so simple.

It is quite obvious that the political élite in Britain took a
greater interest in economic questions in the period after the

1870s than before. Political calculations ('the official mind') were strongly influenced by economic factors, but were also based on other considerations. The *fundamental cause* of the heightened influence of the economy on politics lies in the fact that the British Empire, in contrast to the French colonial empire, was essentially a commercial empire which had occupied, since the second half of the eighteenth century, a quasi-monopoly of the world market, thanks to its technological and economic predominance. Finally, Britain, due to her special economic structure, depended on commercial relations with other continents (necessity to import food!) much more heavily than the other great powers. The *more immediate* reason for the increased importance of the economic element in politics was that Britain's monopoly was threatened by new and forceful competitors, in the subjective opinion of many (but not all!) contemporaries, the tendency of each competitor to exclude all others from the markets was considered particularly repugnant.

It was especially the imperialists among British politicians — that is, the Conservatives and the Liberal Unionists — who clamoured for the introduction of tariffs as a response to the protectionist policy of other governments. As a rule, they demanded the introduction of a common customs tariff for the whole Empire towards third countries and preferential tariffs within the Empire. As far back as 1872 Disraeli hinted at this demand in his speech at the Crystal Palace. In 1881 the 'National Fair Trade League' came into being and publicly fought for the introduction of countervailing duties, that is, for retaliating against the tariff measures by other countries. The 'Imperial Federation League', founded in 1884, had a greater appeal to the public, however, because it won over leading politicians in its campaign for consolidation of the Empire.

Fearing what measures others might take and thinking in terms of rivalry — these were the elements that encroached on the economic sphere. They are factors previously mentioned, in attempting a political–historical definition, as constitutive of classical imperialism. The same considerations were voiced by Charles Dilke, who wrote that British policy should be reconsidered when Germany and France had secured to themselves those regions which did not yet belong to the European nations. The expansion of these two powers meant that large markets were in danger of gradually being closed to British commerce by paper annexations and subsequent tariff measures.[292] (France in subsequent years actually did introduce high differential tariffs in her colonies, but in the German colonies tariffs were, as a rule, lower.)

Salisbury repeatedly pointed to the dangers of the commercial policy of the other powers and called for appropriate measures. On 14 February 1895 he demanded that business firms in the new African territories be supported because British trade was obstructed everywhere by tariff walls. In France, Germany, and the United States protectionist views were increasingly asserting themselves, with the effect of excluding British commerce wherever political control had been established.[293] On 24 May of the same year Salisbury stated in *The Times*: 'If we mean to hold our own against the efforts of all the civilised powers of the world to strangle our commerce by their prohibitive finance, we must be prepared to open new markets to ourselves among the half civilised or uncivilised nations of the globe.'[294] Among British politicians, it was Joseph Chamberlain who most energetically fought for an imperial customs tariff.

In some cases it can be proved that considerations relating to commercial and customs policy had a basic impact on British colonial imperialism, in others it cannot. In all those territories that were for Britain of strategic value *vis-à-vis* India — for example, Africa from Egypt to the Cape Country, Upper Burma, and Tibet — the economic motive, if it existed at all, was of secondary importance. Rivalry with Russia in Central Asia (Afghanistan) and in Persia was primarily due to this strategic motive.

The remark by Salisbury in a conversation in 1897 with the French ambassador, 'Unless you were such passionate protectionists, you would not find us so greedy of territories',[295] is pertinent above all to West Africa. British policy before and during the Berlin Congo Conference was animated by the desire to remove the restrictions that threatened or had actually been imposed on British trade by France, Portugal, and Belgium. One economic decision by the Conference — the creation of a free-trade area in Central Africa and of freedom of trade in the Congo — was in reality a victory for the

British viewpoint, with the effect that the renunciation of the British–Portuguese treaty of 1884 did not count all that much.[296] However, Britain's request that the free-trade principle also be applied to Gabon, Guinea, and Senegal was not heeded by the Conference. The extension of political control by Britain in the West African hinterland in subsequent years was caused by the fear of being hamstrung by the commercial and customs practices of her French rival. During the Anglo-French negotiations leading to the treaties of delimitation of 1889, 1895, and 1898, the British persistently asked for tariff reductions. They did succeed in preventing the imposition of high protective tariffs for Senegal and the French Congo from being applied as well to Guinea, the Ivory Coast, and Dahomey.[297]

The influence of the tariff factor on British colonial expansion must not be overestimated. The struggle was mainly waged for 'trade facilities', for 'a fair field and no favour', and for the 'open door'.[298] If extending political control for that purpose was deemed absolutely necessary, as it was in West Africa, this was done. In the majority of cases the government did not accede to demands by economic pressure groups or consular agents to broaden political control.

Since Britain ultimately adhered to the traditional free-trade principle, the corresponding principle of non-intervention in the domestic affairs of the underdeveloped territories remained operative. The British government mainly concentrated on the task they had pursued during the free-trade period before 1880, that is, of providing British trade with security, protection, and information. Canning's policy of non-intervention in South America and of commercial equality with regard to other nations was still applied under Edward Grey. In China Britain resorted to delimiting spheres of influence only when Russia had preceded her. After 1898 the claim on the Yangtze area became a major element in Britain's Chinese policy. On 9 June 1898 the British representative in Peking was informed by Salisbury: 'While preferential advantages are conceded to Russia in Manchuria and to Germany in Shantung, these or other Powers should also be offered special openings or privileges in the region of the Yang-tsze.'[299]

6. BRITISH CAPITAL EXPORT

Britain's main interest in China at that time was no longer in trade, as in earlier days, but in investing capital. According to Hobson's and Lenin's views, the export of capital was the central feature of European imperialism. How is this to be judged? Hobson started with the correct observation that, in so far as Britain was concerned, the income derived as interest from capital export exceeded the share of profits derived from trade by the end of the century. Britain had changed from being the 'workshop of the world' to being first banker of the world. As mentioned above, Lenin drew the wrong conclusion from this fact that capital in Britain had already reached the stage of finance capital.[300]

According to Eugene Staley, capital export of the leading industrial powers had developed in the following pattern:[301]

	England	France	Germany	USA	
1870	1.006	.513	—	—	mill. £
1885	1.602	.678	.390	—	mill. £
1900	2.485	1.068	.983	.103	mill. £
1914	4.004	1.766	1.376	.513	mill. £

The irregularity of capital exports reflects the fluctuation of over-all economic development. The downswing at the outset of the 1870s corresponds to the general economic crisis, as does the decline in the 1890s. The sharp upswing after 1902 is attributable to the termination of the Boer War.

The fact remains that the sum of British overseas investments steadily increased after the 1880s. This increase paralleled colonial expansion. That both factors were not causally linked to the extent assumed by Hobson has already been discussed in the context of the geographic targeting of investments.[302] Alexander K. Cairncross's survey lends added precision to this statement.[303]

In 1870 the share of the British Empire in absorbing investments amounted to somewhat more than one-third (£270 million), while the remainder went abroad (£515 million). After the economic crisis of 1873 the share of the Empire rose gradually and assumed a slight lead after the start of the 1880s. In 1885 it amounted to £675 million, compared to £625 million in foreign investments. Until 1890, colonial

The annual rate of Britain's overseas investments is shown in the following chart: [304]

Figure 1: British Overseas Investments, 1870–1913
Source: Imlah, *Economic Elements*, pp. 72–5; Mommsen, *'Nationale u. ökonomische Faktoren'*, p. 651.

loans actually appeared as an alternative in view of the difficulties of those years in the home market, and could therefore be linked to contemporary British imperialism ('consolidation of the Empire'), but not in the way Hobson had interpreted it; these loans were not placed in the newly-acquired territories but in the old Dominions.

At the beginning of the 1890s the chances of placing investments within the Empire were again temporarily unfavourable. The economic crisis subsided in 1896, after which investments were evenly placed in the Empire and in third countries. Preference was given to Russian railway stocks and South African gold and diamond stocks. Although the official statistics show foreign-government loans in stronger demand on the British money market than Empire-government loans for the period between 1892 and 1902, the total sum of British investments in the Empire at the turn of the century was probably higher than the corresponding sum in third countries. Following the Boer War, however, the pattern changed. The flow of capital to the Argentine[305] and to the United States rose dramatically. According to a contemporary estimate, as much as 55 per cent of all British overseas investments was placed in the Americas in 1909. The share of the Empire approximates to 47 per cent in 1913 (£1,780 thousand million compared to £ 2 thousand million in third countries). According to a calculation drawn up by Sir Herbert Frankel, an average of about 5 per cent of total investment went into the newly acquired African colonies, which made up most of the territories annexed after 1880, in the years 1905 to 1914[306] — a percentage that devastatingly refutes Hobson's line of argument.

Generally speaking, the contemporary view that the rate of profit was more favourable in overseas investments than in home investments is held to be accurate.[307] But a distinction between investments in the Empire and those in third countries again results in a refutation of Hobson's thesis. The profit for the years 1905–9 has been calculated to average 3.61 per cent in home investments, 3.94 per cent in the Empire, and 4.97 per cent in foreign markets. Domestically, the profit-margin could vary between 2.88 per cent in British consols and 5 per cent in railway bonds. The profits from overseas railway shares ranged between 3.87 per cent in railway construction in India and 4.7 per cent in Europe.

If the British investor preferred Empire investments to those in other countries, he did so primarily because of the higher safety margin, but perhaps also because of the nationalist interest in a consolidation of the ties between the mother country and the colonies. Charles Dilke cited this latter aspect as one of the causes of the interest taken in Empire investments: 'This vast sum is lent at a comparatively low rate of interest largely on account of the political connection that exists.'[308] In some cases, as will be shown, capital was even systematically mobilized by the government with nationalist appeals.

Another theme in Hobson's critique of imperialism (and, to a certain extent, also in Lenin's) appears naive today: that overseas investments benefited only a parasitic groups of investors, and were detrimental to the economy as a whole.

Cairncross and Samuel B. Saul in particular have described the multiplying effects of British investments: they intensified over-all global trade and thereby promoted British commerce and stimulated Britain's home market.[309] Due to the construction of railways in the United States, in the Argentine, in India, Canada, and Australia–New Zealand, financed mainly by British capital, freight charges for imported food and raw materials were cut considerably. Cheaper transport costs for overseas grain, for example, was one reason for the sudden drop in world corn prices at the beginning of the 1890s. This was indeed harmful to corn producers in Central Europe, but it benefited the consumers. The investments promoted British imports as well as exports by linking the granting of loans to trade advantages, and by generally promoting the economic development of the recipients of capital, that is, by increasing their demand and by improving their purchasing power.

Finally, another important aspect of British capital export must be mentioned briefly. The City of London as well as sectors of commerce and industry looked on the nationalist imperialism at the turn of the century with scepticism or even rejected it. These were the staunch adherents of the traditional free-trade doctrine who regarded not just the Empire, but the entire world, as their field of investment and their market. To the financial circles, a reckless imperialism appeared to be both costly and a danger to peace. The *Investor's Review* of 1896 sharply attacked the government's South African policy.[310] It might be very nice, said the *Review*, to talk in great swelling language of the 'glorious Empire', but striving for glory would not pay, and the burden of Empire lay more heavily with each passing year on the backs of the British people. Britain's fortune depended on her magnificent foreign trade and her huge overseas investments. These could be maintained only if peace was secure. Preparations for war would undermine British strength slowly but irresistibly.

The Boer War confirmed such views. The economist Sir George Paish wrote about the ebbing of British investment and the advance of French and German capital during the conflict: 'They invested, whilst we have been at war.'[311] Following the end of hostilities, British capital increasingly turned to territories outside the Empire – to South America and the United States. The parliamentary election of 1906 brought to power the Liberals, who were advocates of free trade and, to some degree, 'Little Englandism'. The voters meted out a sweeping rebuff to jingoist imperialism and to Chamberlain's protectionist aspirations.[312]

7.   FRENCH CAPITAL EXPORT

France's export of capital presented a pattern different from that of British capital export. To begin with, it should be determined whether there were contemporaries who stressed, in the manner that Hobson did, the importance of acquiring colonies for the export of French capital.

In his great speech in the Chamber on 28 July 1885 Jules Ferry stated: 'For wealthy countries colonies are places where capital can be invested on the most favourable terms.'[313] Ferry probably took this view from Pierre Paul Leroy-Beaulieu, who was a colonial propagandist as well as an economist. [314] Addressing himself to the connection between capital export and the acquisition of colonies, the latter had argued in his book, *De la colonisation chez les peuples modernes*, that it was more advantageous to export capital to one's own colonies than to totally foreign countries.[315] Lenin stated that 'in France it was precisely the extraordinarily rapid development of *finance* capital, and the weakening of industrial capital, that, from 1880 onwards, gave rise to the extreme extension of annexationist (colonial) policy'.[316]

These statements are not supported by the available statistical data.[317] The geographic distribution of French capital export changed in some respects after 1880 as compared to the preceding decades. As Rondo E. Cameron has shown, the greater part of France's capital went to the South and South-East European countries – from Portugal to Turkey – in the three decades between 1850 and 1880, and was aimed at covering the deficit of those governments and developing their system of transportation. It was France's capital that financed or took part in financing the construction of almost the entire railway network of Continental Europe, excluding Germany, Denmark, and Scandinavia. Even after 1880 French capital still ranked above that of the other industrial powers in Portugal, Spain, and Turkey; but a sizeable share now went to South America, and an even larger share was chanelled into Russia. A total of 71.1 per cent of France's foreign capital, which, according to estimates, amounted to 28 thousand million francs in 1900, was invested in Europe (25 per cent in Russia alone and 16 per cent in Spain–Portugal), and the remainder (28.9 per cent) was placed overseas. The overseas amount breaks down as follows: 10.7 per cent in the British colonies in Africa and Egypt, 10 per cent in the Americas (South America, the United States, and Canada), 2.9 per cent in China, and 5.3 per cent in the French colonies. The corresponding figures for 1914 are: of a total sum of 45 thousand million francs, 61.1 per cent was invested in Europe (Russia, 25.1 per cent, Spain–Portugal, 8.7 per cent), and 38.9 per cent in the overseas territories (British colonies in Africa and Egypt 7.5 per cent, the western hemisphere 17.7 per cent, China 4.9 per cent, and the French colonies 8.8 per cent).[318]

The export of capital from the metropolis to French colonies actually did increase gradually between 1900 and 1914 (by which time Morocco had been added), yet it played a minor role in France's total exports. To a much larger extent than his British counterpart, the French investor preferred European stocks. Colonial loans were difficult to place. The commitments of capital lagged behind colonial activities. Delcassé deplored this fact in the Chamber on 4 November 1899: 'I wished our capital had the same confidence in our own overseas territories as that offered, often in a careless manner, to foreign enterprises.'[319] It was Delcassé who, after 1901, encouraged the Banque de Paris et des Pays-Bas to grant loans to the Sultan of Morocco, who had searched in vain on the London and Paris money-markets.

In 1905 France invested about twice as much capital (three thousand million francs) in the non-French territories of Africa as in her own African possessions (except Algeria–Tunisia).[320] The results of the most recent research on French investments in French Africa south of the Sahara are unequivocal: 'French high finance did not, to all intents and purposes, show up between 1870 and the First World War when French West Africa was created and exploited.'[321] The French Congo did, indeed, attract a number of colonial companies, but they all had modest capital resources[322] and most of them soon went bankrupt. Only the companies active in the upper Congo area, exporting caoutchouc and ivory, kept alive for a longer time.[323]

From these data it must be concluded that, from the economic standpoint, investment in French industry, which was less developed than that in Britain, Germany, and the United States, would have benefited France's great-power status more than the creation of a largely unproductive and costly colonial empire.[324]

8. THE ROLE OF PRESSURE GROUPS

Remaining to be examined is the core of Hobson's theory of imperialism (and also of Lenin's when referring to colonial imperialism), that is, the dominant role of the so-called financial oligarchy which, owing to its monopoly position, was supposed to have determined not only the economy of a country, but also its policy. It is useful to quote once again Hobson's rhetorical question: 'Does any one seriously suppose that a great war could be undertaken by any European State, or a great State loan subscribed, if the house of Rothschild and its connexions set their face against it?' There is also Hobson's terse pronouncement: 'The final determination [in imperialist policy] rests with the financial power.'[325] A corresponding statement in Lenin's book reads, 'It is not difficult to imagine the solid bonds that are thus created between British finance capital (and its faithful "friend", diplomacy) and the Argentine bourgeoisie, and the leading businessmen and politicians of that country.'[326]

Such contentions that governments, in pursuing their imperialist actions, were the captives of economic pressure groups, especially of the sinister financial clique, appears absurd in the face of previously cited data underscoring the importance of the economic factor in imperialism. This is not to say that groups did not exert pressure on the governments concerned. Indeed, the reverse thesis, that governments were completely free from pressure by economic interests, and devoted themselves to imperialism free from all economic worries and plans, is equally absurd. Each imperialist action must be investigated to determine the influence of economic pressure. Consequently, if a common denominator for the relationship between the economy and imperialism is to be established, general formulas will have to suffice. As examples:

the economy and politics influenced each other in a two-way relationship; or, the traditional motives for colonial expansion were strengthened by new economic factors (the export of excess production, the pressure of investments abroad). It was, therefore, the new over-all situation of the economy that created the need for a stronger consideration of economic factors by politicians, not the individual interest of any particular group.[327]

The sources on British imperialism offer an overwhelming mass of evidence showing that political leaders in the age of imperialism displayed the traditional strong aversion to the idea that political views should be subordinated to special economic interests. The British ambassador in St. Petersburg, Sir Robert Morier, wrote to Rosebery on 22 April 1886: 'No rule has been more absolutely insisted upon in the dealings of Her Majesty's Missions abroad than this one, that, unless there is denial of justice, or treatment of British subjects engaged in mercantile transactions contrary to Treaties or to the spirit of Treaties, no assistance shall be rendered to further private interests.'[328]

The government, whose highest goal is the welfare of the nation, regarded it as its duty to pave the way for commerce, to grant it protection in an emergency (in breaches of contract), or in cases of discrimination, but in all other respects to allow it to develop according to its own laws.[329] With regard to attempts to subsidize the British shipping-line to East Africa, the Chancellor of the Exchequer wrote to the Foreign Office in 1889: 'It has been and is My Lords' conviction that it is unsound commercial policy to seek to assist the British enterprise in its struggle with foreign rivals, out of the pocket of the general taxpayer.'[330] The continued application of this principle appeared to be amply justified by the history of British commerce. When the City of London tried to press the Salisbury government to intervene in the South American republics during the political and economic crises of 1890-1, the Prime Minister replied that he was not willing to relinquish the principle of non-intervention which had been in operation since Canning: 'We have been pressed . . . to undertake the part of arbitrator, of compulsory arbitrator in quarrels in the west of South America . . . We have been earnestly pressed, also . . . to undertake the regeneration of Argentine finance.

On neither of these subjects are Her Majesty's Government in the least degree disposed to encroach on the function of Providence.'[331] When the British government in 1898 abandoned the principle of non-intervention in the instance of China, it did not do so primarily because of the railway interests; it sought, rather, to equalize international competition in a situation where other powers, especially Russia, had tried to obtain privileged positions in the Chinese economy.

Looking at the individual colonial acquisitions of the industrial powers after 1880, it would appear at first sight that capital-investment interests were decisive in bringing about intervention or annexation at least in the North African countries of Egypt, Tunisia, and Morocco, and in the Transvaal as well. In each of the three Islamic regions, the ruler was deeply in debt to British and French creditors. And much British capital had been invested in the Transvaal. A detailed analysis of the motives, however, clearly indicates otherwise. With regard to the occupation of Egypt, the foreign-policy and strategic motive of securing the Suez Canal was definitely predominant. Establishing the Tunisian protectorate fulfilled a promise made to France at the Congress of Berlin as a compensation for Cyprus; it was meant to forestall an Italian occupation and to round off the Algerian territorial possession. The French claim to Morocco was made to ward off German claims. The Transvaal was annexed in order to be able to maintain the predominance of the Cape Country in view of the separatist tendencies of the Boer Republic and its friendly relations with Germany. Undoubtedly, interested sectors of the home economy welcomed and even demanded intervention, especially in Egypt and the Transvaal. But their influence alone would not have been sufficient to induce the government to make such a momentous political decision. They only helped to strengthen the essentially political motivation.

In numerous instances the government may have made use of economic pressure groups as a pretext, as a means, or as justification for interventions which usually could not be motivated economically.

Ferry's imperialism in North Africa and Indo-China is sometimes regarded, on the basis of self-evidence, as predominantly founded on economic motives. But rather the contrary is true. The existing evidence is from the time after his resignation on a colonial question, not from the beginning or during the course of his imperialist policy. His great speech of 1885 in the Chamber and his preface to the Tonkin book of 1890 are to be considered primarily as a justification of his colonial policy, for which a suspicious Chamber was no longer ready to foot the high bill, and as an appeal to the economy to engage itself more strongly in the colonies so that one day the expensive colonial policy would finally pay off. Besides, the economic motive quoted by Ferry (colonies as an outlet for over-production, surplus capital, and social difficulties) must not be isolated from the other motives mentioned simultaneously. While he was minister, Ferry was a pragmatist and opportunist in colonial matters. It was only after his resignation that he framed a homogeneous colonial doctrine.[332] Gabriel Hanotaux explicitly rejected the idea of embroidering his imperialist foreign policy with economic motives and even regarded doing so as unworthy.[333]

Chamberlain's frequent and well-advertised praise of the economic value of the colonies must be interpreted in a similar way. Central to his ideas on imperialism was the political concept, tinged with social Darwinism, of a powerful 'imperial federation' unchallenged by other powers. The economic argument served as a justification for sceptics and as a means to his lofty goal. Chamberlain in 1903 told an intimate friend: 'I do not pretend to be an economic expert . . . You must provide the economic arguments.'[334]

Rosebery was of the opinion that cohesion of the Empire was not possible if it depended on national–economic elements alone: 'Empires founded on trade alone must irresistibly crumble.'[335] Imperialism, he believed, was based on a great imperial idea ('a larger patriotism') and on a great vision of the future.

Marchand sharply condemned 'the colonialists advocating a "rational" commercial exploitation'; they betrayed France's colonial mission and considered colonial expansion only as an occasion for speeches and banquets.[336]

To Rhodes, the material wealth to be extracted from South Africa was not the real goal: 'The highest object has been to me the greatness of my country.' And: 'My ruling purpose is the extension of the British Empire.'[337]

The case of Uganda provides strong evidence of how the

economic argument was exploited to mobilize business interests and to rouse a public from its indifference. In his 1893 book, *The Rise of Our East African Empire*, Lugard wrote that it was not only a Christian sense of obligation that spoke in favour of keeping Uganda; commercial advantages were also at stake. The underlying reason, of course, was to safeguard the line of communication to India from that flank.

As far back as 1885 the African expert of the British government, Sir Percy Anderson, had complained: 'The truth is that we [the Foreign Office] not only do not neglect the Manchester interests, but have to stir Manchester up to look after its interests.'[338]

There is also evidence that both Bismarckian colonial imperialism and capitalist imperialism during the two decades and a half prior to the First World War exploited capital for political objectives to a much greater extent than merely doing the bidding of financial cliques. When Bismarck obtained colonies for Germany during 1884-5, he constantly urged Bleichröder and other bankers to foster in the business community a stronger interest in Africa and the South Seas. Business leaders, however, never allowed feelings of nationalism to overwhelm their cool calculation. Quick profits could not be realized in the insecure colonial market. Consequently, business did not wish to get involved. The lack of interest and the scepticism of business are well expressed by the coal industrialist Emil Kirdorf, who would not support Germany's African policy with even 'one ton of coal'.[339]

In the Balkans and the Near East, German imperialism suffered from a dearth rather than a glut of capital, as Fritz Fischer's research has recently shown.[340] In the instance of Serbia, Raymond Poidevin has pointed out that Germany lost more and more political terrain to France, as the latter invested greater amounts of capital. So as not to fritter away resources, German capital export was, for political reasons, concentrated primarily in Romania and in Turkey for the construction of the Baghdad Railway. The political control of capital export is evident in the 1913 business report of the *Disconto Gesellschaft*: 'If accepting a foreign loan appears politically expedient . . . , the present situation of the money market [i.e. the scarcity of capital] must not alone act on the decision.'[341]

The loan policy of both Germany and France towards Russia clearly suggests that capital export was subordinated to politics. Bismarck turned off the credit tap in 1887 in order to exert political pressure on Russia. However, the measure turned out to be a boomerang, because the Paris money-market was now opened to Russia's requests. French loans prepared the political alliance between France and Russia and became an important instrument in the French foreign-policy aim of tying Russia to an anti-German position.

9.   THE LIMITS OF THE ECONOMIC THEORY OF IMPERIALISM

The examination of the economic theory of imperialism as advocated by Hobson and Lenin, and its confrontation with historical facts, have exposed so many major weaknesses that it appears useless as a universal explanation of classical imperialism. The major mistake which Hobson, Lenin, and their followers made was not that they isolated the economic factor from all other elements when explaining imperialism; they do, indeed, acknowledge the force of non-economic factors. It was, rather, that they singled out from the complex economic sphere a supposed compulsion to export capital and proclaimed it to be the decisive motive. It is true that Lenin may have claimed, in contrast to Hobson, that his theory was linked both to colonial expansion and to the intensification of the antagonism of the imperialist powers among themselves. Against this claim, however, it can be argued that, if France's export of capital to Russia was 'usury' or 'bondholders" imperialism, then the considerable investments which Britain placed in the United States and which France channelled towards Britain, etc., could just as well be termed imperialism. Where is the demarcation-line to be drawn between those foreign investments that are imperialism and those foreign investments that are not? Is the decisive criterion the monopolistic use of capital? Did that exist in a fairly pure form, after all? It hardly did, not even in the colonies belonging to the powers, to say nothing of the non-colonial, technologically backward territories.

Another major mistake of the advocates of the economic theory of imperialism was that they regarded their assumption that financial magnates manipulated the governments as self-evident and not requiring concrete proof. An undocumented theory of a sinister conspiracy of omnipotent financial tycoons seems to be useless even as a scientific hypothesis. At bottom it is an article of faith, a dogma. For Leonard Woolf, the connection between capital and governments exists in the shape of 'invisible wires' between bankers, a few aristocrats, among them the Archbishop of Canterbury, and the Foreign Office.[342] Parker T. Moon anticipates the result of his study on imperialism, hoping that the reader will observe the constant leering over the shoulders of the diplomat by the exporting merchant, the manufacturer, the concession hunter, the missionary, and the admiral.[343] For Thomas Kemp, the Leninist way of looking at things is the best way to understand imperialism; he, too, regards it as a matter of course that an 'inner ring of financial manipulators and speculators' is omnipotent in economic as well as in political affairs.[344] George W. Hallgarten reduces the motives of imperialism mainly to the personal ties between politicians and business.[345] For John Strachey, the pressure to export capital remains 'the prime mover for the modern imperialist process'; after all, there undoubtedly was export of capital and there was acquisition of colonies. And 'only the intentionally blind will deny a connection between them'.[346]

The connection existed in some cases, and in others it did not. It cannot, therefore, be taken as a passe-partout to define imperialism. The stage of economic development which each of the great industrial powers had reached by 1880 or 1900 was disparate, as shown in the case of France's industrial backwardness *vis-à-vis* Britain, so much so that it cannot be generally considered as the stage of monopoly capitalism. The intensity of the economic factors varied widely in the case of each of the imperialist powers. It was highest in the case of Britain and lowest — only marginal, in fact — in the case of Russia. It varied even with regard to each single imperialist action of the powers, so that a generalization of their impact on imperialism would do violence to historical reality.

V. The Social-Economic Theory of Imperialism

1. APPLICATION AND ORIGIN

The social-economic theory of imperialism enlarges the economic aspects of imperialism by adding the social dimension. Some of its advocates tie imperialism by definition to industrialization. Imperialism, that is, has been a reflex to the revolutionary effects of industrialization and a means to solve the numerous economic and social problems resulting from it.

In scholarly discussions the term social imperialism has been interpreted in two different ways. From the Marxist and neo-Marxist (and also liberal-leftist) point of view, it is used in an incriminatory and polemical fashion. Those who see social revolution as the final goal of human history judge social imperialism negatively. Imperialism, in other words, was never a goal in itself and was only of functional importance. It was intended to distract from the difficult social question resulting from the rise of the mass proletariat. Primarily, social imperialism has served a domestic function.

According to the non-Marxist view, social politics and the expansionist policy of imperialism are seen as interdependent on principle and the priority or functionality of one field *vis-à-vis* the other is not presumed. In historical analyses, however, in so far as they have been undertaken in this direction, social politics appears rather as a function of imperialism, although the inverse relationship is seen and acknowledged. Accordingly, imperialism is regarded as an end in itself and the solution of the social question has only to contribute to its realization.

Moreover, scholarly work on social imperialism is still in its infancy. For the time being, even a tentative judgement cannot be offered on the importance of this element in the interpretation of imperialism.

The origins of the social-economic theory of imperialism go

back to the first half of the nineteenth century. It the 1830s, the 'colonial reformers' of the Bentham school pointed to the connection between the methods of production of industrial capitalism and overseas colonization.[347] Britain was the first country in this period to have passed the take-off stage towards industrialization and was now in the stage of industrial maturity. She was also the first to experience the consequences of this process: demographic explosion, over-production of industrial goods, and formation of surplus capital. The colonial reformers struggled against the indifference of *laissez-faire* liberalism towards the British Empire and pointed to the Empire's capacity of absorbing the surplus of population, of the production of goods, and of capital. By founding new colonies and by opening up the old ones (particularly Australia and New Zealand), Britain could counter and prevent the dangerous consequences of this process — the increase of the industrial proletariat subsisting on minimum wages, the sharp price fluctuations, and the decline of profits of investment capital. 'Open new channels', wrote Edward Gibbon Wakefield in 1833, 'for the most productive employment of English capital. Let the English buy bread from every people that has bread to sell cheap. Make England, for all that is produced by steam, the workshop of the world. If, after this, there be capital and people to spare, . . . find room for both by means of colonization.'[348] In the same way, John Stuart Mill pointed to the value of the colonies as regions for absorbing surplus capital and the sons of the governing class unable to find work in Britain.

The decisive question of whether the official policy-makers acted on the demands of the colonial reformers, that is, whether they opened up the existing colonies and acquired new ones in order to solve the economic and social-economic problems mentioned, can hardly be answered in the affirmative. Robinson and Gallagher, indeed, have pointed to the British 'free-trade imperialism' of those decades and its peculiarities: that British foreign-trade policy overseas had contented itself with 'informal' control if possible and had only turned to direct domination if no other alternative seemed feasible.[349] But everything depends on whether *laissez-faire* trade policy, which the government pursued according to the principle of political non-intervention, can be termed free-trade or informal imperialism, and, above all, whether it can be connected in each case to the acquisition of colonies of that time. If the *laissez-faire* principle is acknowledged to be the main feature of British foreign-trade policy — and characterizing free trade is meaningful only if based on this principle — calling it imperialism (which always implies domination) appears questionable. It would be queer terminology indeed to speak of a 'laissez-faire imperialism'.[350] That would be a *contradictio in adjecto*: a foreign-trade policy based on *laissez-faire* must in its essence be anti-imperialist.

It is difficult to connect each of the British colonial acquisitions of the free-trade period with the interests of British commerce or with the socio-economic situation. Territories were acquired in order to provide security to foreign trade in the existing Empire by means of consolidating control over the possessions and by expanding their frontiers. Creating a 'fair field and no favour' was the radius of action beyond which British foreign-trade policy did not venture. The acquisition of Hong Kong, it is true, seems to have been a violation of this principle of political non-intervention. Hong Kong served as a port of reshipment and as a base for the British China trade, but was not intended to be a lever or a starting-point for imperialist domination of China. The acquisition of Macao by Portugal was due to the same motive, to which it is even more difficult to impute imperialist intentions. Macao could certainly not have been used as an outlet of over-production, since industrialization had not even begun in Portugal.

Similarly, it would be misleading to describe as imperialist or social-imperialist Britain's powerfully expanding trade in the Near East, especially after the commercial treaty of Balta-Liman of 1838 with Turkey. The British government regarded it as necessary to promote British foreign trade in a country which levied the lowest import and export duties of the time, just as the Turkish government considered it their task to narrow the large technological and industrial gap between Turkey and Europe by purchasing British industrial and investment goods.[351]

When the advocates of the social-economic theory of imperialism point to the demands of the colonial reformers of the Bentham school, they wish to draw attention to their perspicacity and the anticipatory character of their reflections regarding classical imperialism after 1880. It is just as impossible, however, to prove a direct and massive impact of these colonial reformers on British Empire policy of their time, as it is to ascertain a direct influence, surpassing all other motives, of the social-economic situation on the imperialist activity of the powers after 1880. Nor can the simultaneity of the imperialism of the individual nations or the dramatic imperialist movement be fully explained. This is not to preclude the fact that the social-economic situation influenced imperialism to a degree varying from one case to the other, to a higher degree, perhaps, than has hitherto been admitted. But to regard social imperialism as the passe-partout for explaining the phenomenon of imperialism, as Hans-Ulrich Wehler has recently done, is widely overshooting the mark.

Hobson, who was a liberal, mentioned the domestic aspect in his comprehensive explanation of imperialism. He denounced not only the parasitic character of British imperialism, but also its tendency to undermine the 'old English liberties'. Imperialism, he argued, threw into question the viability of the British system of parliamentary government; it called for the strengthening of the power of the executive to the detriment of the legislative; and it sought a society that was homogeneous and, as much as possible, militarily oriented. Hobson regarded such demands as an escape from the responsibility for domestic reforms. Postulating the primacy of foreign policy, the primacy of imperialism would only conceal the extent of social wrongs. It could only benefit the governing and wealthy classes who desired to maintain the status quo and thus blocked the just demands of the lower class for a redistribution of national income and for social and political improvements.[352]

When exposing the domestic aspect of imperialism, Hobson had his eyes on, more than hiterto presumed,[353] the autocratic–paternalistic government of the Indian Empire, praised at the time by high-ranking colonial officials as a model for governing Britain. He was also sensitized by the campaign started during the Boer War for higher 'national efficiency' which was regarded as a prerequisite for the survival of the British Empire amidst the competing world powers.

Hobson was moved to expose wrongs out of a genuine

impulse for social reforms. The same urge to expose appears in Lenin's 1917 book on imperialism with regard to the predicted world revolution. Lenin, however, did not systematically discuss the phenomenon of social imperialism. Referring to ideas which Hobson had articulated, he labelled as bribery the attempt of the imperialists, the financiers, and the capitalists to win the workers over to imperialism. The imperialists diverted a portion of their monopolistically high profits for the purpose of splitting the workers. A minority among the workers, a labour aristocracy,[354] was won over in that fashion. This minority thereby opportunistically betrayed the real interests of the working class and hence the struggle against capitalism.[355] In a more advanced stage, which Britain, according to Lenin had already reached, opportunism would change into 'social chauvinism'. Workers already bribed by the imperialists would advocate the same political demands as did the bourgeoisie. Since even in Germany leading members of the Social Democratic Party supported imperialism, Lenin called them 'social imperialists', in other words, 'socialists in words and imperialists in deeds'.[356]

2.   HANS-ULRICH WEHLER'S MODEL OF DEFINITION

Only recently has the theory of social imperialism been developed in detail in one of the two senses mentioned. In an ambitious attempt, Hans-Ulrich Wehler believes he has been able to prove that Bismarck's foreign-trade and colonial policy, the motive of which has baffled historians for generations, was essentially social imperialism.[357]

What has been said above about the motives of Lenin's book on imperialism, to which Wehler in some respects feels indebted, also applies, *cum grano salis*, to Wehler's book on imperialism, which affects to produce a political impact. Inspired by Max Horkheimer, Wehler hopes to contribute through his book to 'a radical improvement of human existence'.[358] He believes he is able to expose the mainspring of Bismarck's mechanism of ruling, and of the egregiously repressive and manipulative character of his policy towards the working and middle classes, which strove to share power. By way of this exposure, Wehler hopes to 'educate politically', as Theodor Mommsen had demanded. He explicitly regards his approach as 'politically motivated', that it is aimed at elucidating one of the major questions of our age, the situation of the developing countries.[359] Deliberately polemical, Wehler brushes aside the relevant literature already published on Bismarck as apologetic, orthodox, or vulgarly Marxist (George W. F. Hallgarten). With the theory of social imperialism, he makes the ambitious claim that he can persuasively explain the imperialism of Bismarck as well as of Britain and France.

This claim matches the one recently put forward ty Dieter Senghaas, who has called for the abolition of traditional 'scholarly imperialism' (*Wissenschaftsimperialismus*) in historiography dealing with relations between the industrial powers and the developing countries. Senghaas would eliminate the role of the intuitive approach to history, which unilaterally represents the interest of the European powers, by unsparingly laying bare the technique as to how these powers rule the Third World.[360] It rather seems to be a case of replacing one 'scholarly imperialism' — even granting the existence of such a phenomenon — in favour of another by arbitrarily scrapping the endeavour to discover the numerous motives of a historical process without succumbing to the temptation of suspecting manipulation, machinations, or whatever by certain wire pullers, sinister conspiratorial groups, or the American 'super-metropolis'. Since evil is omnipresent in human history, and since it is only human to mitigate or arrest its effects by developing utopian schemes, the justifiable attempt is made to get hold of it or to personify it, and quite recently also to 'structuralize' it in order to better understand it. But in doing so, one quickly resorts to demonizing social groups or persons in history — the Conservatives or Bismarck, for example — who, in a terrible over-simplification, are assigned responsibility for the wrong path history has taken in their wake.

Wehler starts by setting up a political-science model, a 'critical theory' (claiming that only by doing so can 'historical research on imperialism do justice to the political necessities of our present age and sharpen a critical consciousness of the problems of the "Third World"').[361] Its applicability and solidity are then tested by taking Bismarck's overseas policy as a case in point. At the end of his analysis Wehler sees the four criteria fulfilled, by which the value of the 'critical theory' is tested — its informative value, its capability of being verified through facts, its explanatory force, and its universal applicability to the history of those decades. Social imperialism, he concludes, is the key to Bismarck's overseas policy; the latter must be regarded solely as a function of domestic, social, and economic policy.

The framework of the model is provided by the economic-trend period of 1873 to 1896 discovered by modern research on business cycles. According to the theory of trade cycles, an economic-trend period (Walt W. Rostow) or a long wave is the phase of the expansion and contraction of the economic development between 1790 and 1914, each comprising two to three decades, especially the movement of the general level of commodity prices, in the period between 1790 and 1914. According to Rostow, the movement of prices in Britain in this period of one century and a quarter can be divided into the following upswing and downswing phases: 1790-1815, 1815-50, 1850-73, 1873-98, 1989-1914.[362]

With the aid of these phases, in which not only the price level is analyzed, but also variables such as formation of capital, wages, volume of production, and foreign trade, Rostow tries to classify the secular process of industrialization by meaningful subsections taken from economic history and not from political history (e.g. the dates of the rule of sovereigns). Other scholars, e.g. Hans Rosenberg, have also tried to make use of this method of dividing periods for investigating the general history of that period. They ask the question: cannot the political behaviour of governments be better explained in certain respects by taking trade cycles into consideration than by simply examining it according to purely political data?[363]

The downswing period after 1873 was both a phenomenon of the British economy and, with some variations, of the international economy in general.[364] It can be divided into several medium-wave cycles, each of which represents a movement of depression and of prosperity. The economic contraction occurs in three periods: between 1873 and 1879, 1882 and 1886, and 1890 and 1894. The two intermediate spaces (1879-82, 1886-90) are phases of expansion. The downswing phase ending in the years after 1894 turns into a cycle of prosperity lasting until 1914 which again can be divided into minor cycles.

The trend period after 1873 is characterized by partially

violent disturbances in the growth of production, by symptoms of stagnation in consumption, and by a decline or even breakdown of commodity prices resulting from an oversupply of commodities. The growth rate of the economy as a whole slackens compared to the preceding trend period, that is it does not decline. Profits and the expectation of profits on the part of the producers drop, especially during the movements of depression; unemployment rises rapidly at times. On the other hand, nominal and real wages increase sharply; the purchasing power of the consumers is raised.

From the standpoint of industry, the trend period after 1873 has been called the 'Great Depression',[365] a term which tenaciously survives. It conveys a one-sided total impression of economic development, however, and so is misleading. It evokes inadmissible associations with the international economic crisis after 1929, which had by far stronger consequences in the over-all economy and deeply affected all social classes.

Before constructing his model, Wehler starts with methodical reflection that seems plausible at first sight. If scholars generally attribute to the international economic crisis of 1929 and to the subsequent period of depression great importance for the political history of the 1930s, then it is also justified to employ the economic crisis of the post-1873 period as a chronological unit for historical research. Since, moreover, the economic depressions of the two decades after 1873 were an international phenomenon and coincided with the first phase of classical imperialism, the question imposes itself as to whether the two phenomena were not interconnected.[366]

Wehler defines imperialism as 'the direct-formal and indirect-informal domination . . . , which the occidental industrial countries, under the pressure of industrialization with its specific economic, social and political problems and due to its comprehensive superiority, have extended across the less-developed regions of the earth'.[367] Imperialism is thus connected to industrialization with its uneven, crisis-ridden growth and includes the presumably limitless field of informal (non-military and non-political) rule. Imperialism becomes social imperialism when a government, pressed by the classes by which they are supported and for fear of social revolution, intends 'by way of imperialist expansion to regain economic prosperity, and in doing so to maintain the social and political status quo and to block the process of emancipation'.[368]

Such a social imperialism was pursued by Bismarck, Wehler argues. His colonial policy of 1884–5 is only one section from his overseas policy which Bismarck pursued before and after that date. The latter served three functions: in economic policy, in domestic policy, and in social politics.

Contemporaries were fully agreed (there was 'an ideological consensus')[369] upon the causes of the disturbances arising after 1873 in the growth of the economy and upon the means of combating them. In the economy and in the business world, among analysts of trade cycles, in the parties, and in the bu-reaucracy there was complete agreement that a way out of the problems of the disproportionate growth[370] in industry could be found in economic expansion beyond the national borders, that is, by exporting commodities and capital. Bismarck recognized the independent working of economic forces resulting from industrialization and reacted to them in a pragmatic way by officially promoting foreign trade. He did this by expanding German consulates, by granting credits, by encouraging the establishment of overseas banks, and by subsidizing steamship lines. Stimulating foreign trade, creating new outlets for export goods overseas, among other things, represented an anticyclical economic policy. In this 'pragmatic policy of expansion'[371] Wehler sees the economic function of Bismarck's imperialism.

As for domestic policy, imperialism served the function of continuing along the road pioneered by the Prusso-German revolution during the wars of unification. This revolution from above had made it inevitable that Germany's industrialization would be accomplished within the setting of the conservative, neo-feudalist, authoritarian state. Since, however, new social forces in the working class assailed this setting, and since these assaults resulted in ever greater tensions, imperialism, especially colonial imperialism, was extolled to the whole nation as the great goal by which to ease class strife. By using imperialism as a means of integrating the nation, Bismarck had in particular waged the election campaign of 1884 and had apparently effected the successes of the 'governmental' parties. He had 'manipulated' colonial enthusiasm after 1883 for his electoral and party purposes in the same way as he had done in 1879 with the 'Red Spectre'.[372]

The social–political function of imperialism is closely connected with this domestic one. Bismarck recognized social imperialism as a means of ruling the nation by which the progressive forces pressing for emancipation could be diverted abroad. Machiavelli had already described this technique, and Napoleon III had applied it during his Bonapartist dictatorship. Diversion of social tensions overseas via imperialism was the means by which the traditional social and power hierarchy in the industrial age could be conserved.

Wehler is so prepossessed by the discovery of this 'critical' theory of imperialism that, before having investigated its applicability to Bismarck's overseas policy between 1862 and 1890, he applies it, among other things, to Britain's and France's policy of expansion. He thinks he is justified in applying it universally because of the world-wide effects of the disturbances in economic growth after 1873. He also finds justification in a few relevant contemporary remarks.

As to Britain, Wehler points to the reflections of the 'Philosophical Radicals' around Wakefield and John Stuart Mill. Since, however, they cannot alone be called upon to testify to social imperialism after 1873, a remark from the Prime Minister of New Zealand, Sir Julius Vogel, from 1879 is quoted: as soon as Britain loses her overseas territories she will become 'the theatre of a fierce war between workers and the upper class'. [373] As further evidence, he quotes a remark made in 1895 by Cecil Rhodes, then Prime Minister of South Africa, a statement already evaluated by Lenin: 'If you want to avoid civil war, you must become imperialists.' Wehler does not seem to have discovered any relevant remark from such leading British politicians as Disraeli, Salisbury, Rosebery, or Chamberlain.

As for France's supposed social imperialism, relevant passages are selected from Ferry's speech of 1885 in the Chamber and from the preface to his book *Le Tonkin et la mère-patrie*. Ferry's 'safety valve' analogy in reference to France's colonial policy has already been discussed. Social peace in the industrial age, he had said, was also a question of finding outlets for exports. Since the needs of the European consumers were satisfied, new consumers in other parts of the world must be found unless one wanted to lead modern society to ruin and to conjure up a 'settling of social accounts' of unforeseeable consequences for the beginning of the twentieth century.[374]

3.   GERMAN COLONIAL POLICY

Wehler's main objective, however, is to prove the functionality of German imperialism for domestic, economic, and social
politics by confronting his critical model with Bismarck's
overseas policy. This will be briefly outlined before the British
form of social imperialism is discussed. Reviewing French
social imperialism is unnecessary in the present stage of research, because a critical analysis of Ferry's relevant remarks
— the only support for Wehler's postulate — shows them not
to be a predominant motive, but only one of many motives
behind France's imperialism. Moreover, Gilbert Ziebura, in an
essay on the economic and social-economic aspect of French
imperialism, has come to the conclusion that 'the colonial
expansion of the 1880s was not primarily the consequence of
the depression and of the beginnings of protectionism';[375] that
the proclamations of Leroy-Beaulieu, Ferry, and their disciples
that colonial policy is an outgrowth of industrial policy, etc.,
had proved to be a *fata morgana*; that 'the social-economic
basis of France's imperialism before 1914 was small and therefore fragile'; that 'the element of social imperialism was hardly
relevant'; that 'social tensions and conflicts . . . appeared
rather in phenomena such as Boulangism, which was the exact
opposite of imperialism';[376] in short, that neither the classical
economic nor the new social-economic theory of imperialism
is of great value for explaining France's colonial expansion.

Wehler deserves thanks for having compiled a mass of contemporary comments which impressively characterize the
consensus about the diagnosis of the stagnation and disturbances of economic growth after 1873. He does not examine
with the same intensity the question of whether the consensus
was as great about the therapy of the fluctuations of growth,
i.e. about imperialism, or whether there was outspoken dis-
sension about it (for example, among the Conservatives, the
left Liberals, and the Social Democrats). Wehler states once
in parentheses that German economic expansion was not
only directed overseas into the less-developed regions, but —
admittedly, first and foremost — to the developed industrial
countries; and that this expansion did not assume 'an imperialist character, or control which the term imperialism necessarily implies'.[377] At this point the term imperialism, in its

informal aspects, is becoming vague. What are the criteria which neatly establish that increased interchange of products with a partner of the same or of a comparable stage of industrial development is not imperialist; with a region that is not yet industrialized imperialist? Is technological superiority the criterion? Does it imply control and subjection?

Despite the redeeming formula that not every foreign-trade policy is imperialism, Wehler inflates the term social imperialism in his analysis to such an extent that it covers government-promoted trade and export, including formal colonial control, as well as such domestic aspects as the protectionist policy begun in 1879; the cartel between industry and big estate owners brought about simultaneously; the breach with liberalism and the corresponding conservative civil-service policy; the anti-Socialist law and social politics; as well as government intervention in the economy in the form of attempted state monopolies. Bismarck undertook all these 'Bonapartist' measures not only to tackle the economic, social, and political problems of a dynamically developing society, but also to freeze the social status quo, to keep the workers outside the limits of the constitutional order as framed in 1871.[378] Accordingly, social politics is not regarded as the attempt to integrate the workers into the existing system, but as a measure to keep them from demanding emancipation by dangling before them 'the prospect of becoming state-paid pensioners', — to bribe them, as Lenin put it.

In defending his idea of imperialism and social imperialism, Wehler will be able to retreat — as Marxist critics of imperialism are similarly wont to do — behind the impregnable citadel of 'informal imperialism'. However, the postulated preponderance of the social-economic factor can be indirectly questioned by criticizing formal imperialism, that is, the acquisition of German colonies in 1884–5. For, according to Wehler's interpretation, the acquisition of colonies can only be the manifest aspect of the total phenomenon of imperialism, which in reality is indissoluble.

When analyzing the motives directly linked to Germany's colonial expansion contained in the narrative of Wehler's book, the upshot by no means conveys the priority of the social-economic factor, as Wehler assumes in his 'critical theory', which he develops in the beginning, and as he claims at the end when attempting to classify the various motives. He mentions most of the factors contributing to Germany's colonial acquisitions already cited: from the complex of foreign policy and power policy, of social psychology, and from the economic field.

Wehler rightly keeps pointing to the favourable circumstances in 1884–5 in foreign policy[379] without which Bismarck could not have obtained European (in reality, British) recognition of Germany's numerous colonial claims in Africa. Following the occupation of Merv by the Russians in 1884 and their advance towards Afghanistan, Anglo-Russian relations became critically tense and led almost to the brink of war. People in Britain feared that a struggle over India would break out. In January 1885 the British expeditionary force under Gordon Pasha was annihilated by the Mahdis.

A thorough analysis of German documents should be undertaken in order to discover whether the British occupation of Egypt in 1882 was not really the key to Bismarck's African policy. An enlightening new perspective from the German side might either supplement or refute the findings of Robinson and Gallagher that, in the last resort, power–political motives were decisive for Europe's scramble for Africa. At any rate, Britain's precarious position in Egypt was a convenient means of pressure for Germany's policy towards Britain. Secretary of State Herbert von Bismarck in August 1884 stated that the 'Egyptian bone of contention' was 'positively a godsend for our policy'.[380] As late as the Franco-British Entente of 1904, Germany was brandishing the 'Egyptian baton' towards Britain. Moreover, Egypt in the two decades after 1882–4 was probably the centre of gravity of Europe's African policy in general, at least north of the Zambezi.

There is no doubt that Britain's much constricted manœuvreability favoured, perhaps even made possible, Germany's acquisition of colonies in 1884–5 under conditions that resembled those in 1898. At that time Britain was in an embarrassing situation, preoccupied with an explosive confrontation with Russia because of East Asia, with France because of Fashoda, and with the Boers in South Africa; it was because of these preoccupations of Britain that Germany gained a foothold in China and in the South Seas.[381] The importance of German–British relations for Germany's African policy is also underlined by the fact that Britain's greater liberty of action after 1885 caused Bismarck to be more easygoing in African matters. Bismarck now clearly subordinated his colonial policy to his relations with Britain. He considered good ties with Britain and the continuance of Salisbury in office 'a hundred times more valuable than the whole of East Africa' or than 'twenty marsh colonies in Africa'.[382] Bismarck termed Carl Peters's plans of acquiring a German 'giant colony' in Central Africa 'criminal' and called on Salisbury to run Peters out of Zanzibar by force of arms! He continued pouring water into the 'colonial wine' of German colonial enthusiasts. 'Contente estote', he assuaged the German consul in Zanzibar, 'we have more African possessions than we are able to digest for the time being and also more friction with Britain than is useful.'

This subordination of the German colonial policy to the relations with Britain finally culminated in the Heligoland-Zanzibar treaty of 1890, in which claims to African territories several times the size of the German Reich were given up in return for a tiny island in the North Sea. Bismarck's plans, however, to give up the desert colony of South West Africa 'as worthless, or for use as an object of compensation'[383] did not materialize. Finally, the adjustment of colonial policy to European policy becomes evident in the fact that Bismarck in 1884–5 wanted to go hand in hand with Ferry in West Africa and thereby exploit Britain's dilemma for a German–French 'colonial entente'. 'There are more protectorates than we are able to protect', he noted down in the documents in the summer of 1885, '. . . I wish a conciliatory attitude in everything that is not related to Alsace.'[384]

Wehler also acknowledges the motive factors of rivalry, of prophylactic annexations, and of the exogenous 'suction effects', those working from the African scene, for Germany's African policy. The occupation of the Cameroons was preceded, similar to that of Tunisia before 1881, by 'a war of the European consuls'. Woermann's motives for hoisting the flag could be explained, according to Wehler, by the fear of other European powers advancing in East Africa.[385] Woermann was afraid of the activity of the British consul Hewett as well as of the French manifestations in Equatorial Africa and from Dahomey. In South West Africa, also, German policy had started to 'precede commercial interests in order to ward off the Anglo-Cape-Country rival'.

The psychological factor which exerted some influence on Germany's colonial policy is by no means omitted by Wehler either. With regard to Carl Peters, the German Cecil Rhodes, he even puts it clearly in the foreground.[386] Peters's uncontrollable ambition and his striving for personal power had definitely passed the threshold to a pathological desire to show off. His rude nationalism and social Darwinism had made themselves felt in a maniacally exaggerated self-assertion and missionary zeal. A great colonial empire was to him an absolutely necessary attribute of a European great power. Anticipating the ideas of Max Weber and of the neo-Rankeans, Peters described the German colonial movement as 'the national continuation of the German desire for unity'. The economic motives which certainly existed in his colonial propaganda were subordinated to the vision of a world power and to the idea of Germany's civilizing mission.

Finally, Wehler repeatedly points to the remarkable reserve of the German economy and of banking circles in African affairs.[387] To be sure, enthusiasm about a German India in Africa, a boundless overestimation of the future economic prospects of the African market, and the hope of alleviating the economic depression in Europe by opening up Africa 'with its dense population capable of consuming much' are to be found again and again in remarks, memoranda, and the like relating to the economy. However, after cool calculation, and with the impact of a broad influx of information from Africa after 1885, as well as the inglorious fate of the numerous colonial companies, such expectations evaporated like thin veils of mist. 'Finance capital', Wehler notes, 'observed even during the second depression [1882–6] a cautious reserve and preferred secure investments to the insecure result of competition overseas.'[388]

The German Foreign Office had to press the banks time and again to enter the colonial business. This indicates that the government sought to justify in economic language their colonial policy before the public, that is to say, in the *Reichstag*. Bismarck was unable to counter the leftist Liberals' derision of the lack of interest by private capital and business even by showing them a successful profit and loss statement or forecasts of such. He dropped a hint to the British government to the effect that he would welcome Britain's provision of capital, which 'our people are almost completely lacking' for the purpose of 'opening up German East Africa'![389] Imperial Commissioner Göring in May 1887 stated that since the German Colonial Society for South West Africa was going bankrupt, there would hardly be other 'German capitalists who, from pure enthusiasm, would give money for such colonizing enterprises'.

Assuming that Bismarck had the degree of enthusiasm attributed to him by Wehler for using the colonies as a palliative for the difficulties besetting the German economy, his disillusionment came as early as 1885 and increased in subsequent years. In October of 1885 Bismarck sharply rejected the offer put forward by Flegel, a traveller to Africa, and by the German Colonial Society to prepare a 'permanent economic occupation' of the Benuë area in West Africa: 'On no account do I wish a renewal of tensions with Britain on colonial matters.' Flegel's expedition was 'to be cut off for the following year'.[390] When native uprisings in East Africa caused grave trouble to the German East Africa Company, Bismarck wanted 'rather to give up all our East African colonial ventures than agree to a military advance of the Reich into the interior'.[391] However, faced with the alternative of renouncing East Africa and leaving the territory for Britain to occupy, he decided instead on a costly colonial campaign from the same considerations of prestige that can be seen in British and French imperialism. Herbert von Bismarck put this prestige factor in the following terms: 'Since we have entered the field of colonial enterprises and have reserved, by way of international treaties vast African territories to German influence, a complete retreat would hardly be feasible without loss of political reputation abroad.'[392] Besides, domestic motives may have played a part in securing the cohesion of the cartel parties in 1887, as well as the consideration that the anticolonial parties should not be offered a weak spot for propaganda exploitation.

Bismarck, having repeatedly admitted that the participation of German financiers in colonial enterprises reflected 'rather the character of a favour towards current trends of public

opinion and official influence', no longer wanted to have anything to do with the 'colonial . . . fraud'.³⁹³ Addressing
Ambassador Schweinitz, he cursed Samoa and Africa. Eventually he went about Europe seeking to peddle Germany's
colonial possessions. Initially he considered handing them
over to the Admiralty. Then he offered them for sale to Crispi,
the Italian Prime Minister, who declined the offer with thanks
and riposted with a corresponding counter-offer. In the
autumn of 1889 Bismarck tendered the administration of the
colonies to the Senate of Hamburg. To Mayor Versmann, he
remarked that it was his 'business . . . to keep the peace for
Europe; if I do that I am paid. I can no longer stand on other
niceties . . . In short, the Foreign Office will get rid of the
colonial matters or it will get rid of me.' If commerce did not
show interest in the colonies, they should rather be given up
just as the Great Elector had done.³⁹⁴

In view of this mass of evidence on Bismarck's disillusionment, there is no reason to revise radically the present view
of historiography on Bismarck's colonial policy, which he
cogently expressed in a conversation with the German
African explorer Eugen Wolf on 5 December 1888: 'Your Map
of Africa is very nice, but my map of Africa is in Europe. Here
is Russia, and here is France, and we are in the centre; that's
my map of Africa.'³⁹⁵ Wehler passes a corresponding judgement: 'At the end of the Bismarckian era, however, a striking
incongruity had developed between the hopes of the ideological consensus and the actual value of the colonies . . . When
drawing up a total economic account up to 1914, low profits
which some colonial companies and shipping lines had made
did not match the millions and millions of expenses which
the administration and the suppression of uprisings had cost
the German Empire up to that time.'³⁹⁶ The economic foundation of Germany's status as a great power was not constituted by the colonies, as the colonial enthusiasts had dreamt,
but 'solely [!] by Germany's industrial economy and foreign
trade with the other industrial nations'.

What then remains of social imperialism and of the primacy
of the social-economic factor and of domestic policy in Bismarck's formal imperialism? At the most it may have played
a part in the period of colonial acquisitions itself, that is, in
1884–5, perhaps to a larger extent than has hitherto been

assumed by historians. Yet to postulate it for the whole Bismarckian era from 1862 to 1890 and to reduce it to the informal variety of foreign trade — which was primarily carried on with the industrial partners, even after the introduction of protective tariffs in 1879, and not with the undeveloped regions of the world — appears to be a grotesque exaggeration. The establishment of tariff walls for a time did give some branches of German industry a leg forward, but it did not essentially affect imports and exports with the best trading partners. The support of industry and big estate owners, which was directed against the industrial proletariat, should be called, as hitherto, a policy of rallying the conservative forces, or cartel policy (*Sammlungs-, Kartellpolitik*), but not social imperialism, notwithstanding the fact that colonial policy and the expansion of trade relations were linked to these domestic conflicts temporarily and as an accompanying circumstance. If social imperialism had been prominently in the foreground or less conspicuous in the background as a decisive motive, Bismarck would have employed it all the more after 1885, when the domestic situation actually deteriorated. In those years, however, Bismarck was anti-colonial; that is, he was anti-imperialist and anti-social-imperialist.

If the economic-policy function of German imperialism is examined in a wider chronological framework than is done by Wehler, his statement that the policy of expansion served as an anticyclical corrective suffers.

Caprivi, Bismarck's successor, made a large-scale attempt to radically reorganize foreign-trade policy amidst an economic and agricultural depression. Since he was aware that the feudal nobility, which had been the staunchest supporter of the Prussian crown, was now entering the field of demagogy (establishment of the Agrarian League) and felt engulfed by the materialist spirit of the age, he considered its loyalty to the king doubtful. He regarded 'a revolution on an agrarian basis as not impossible and, for the time being, more dangerous than a social democratic one'.[397] The answer to the question, 'Is it worthwhile for the state to make sacrifices in favour of this class?', was to Caprivi unequivocal. He furnished it in foreign-trade treaties with numerous European countries which aimed at promoting the export of German industrial goods and the import of foreign foodstuffs, and which, therefore, could not help hitting hard at the grain producers east of the Elbe. Promoting industrial exports to the detriment of one social class, the big estate owners, was, as it were, social imperialism, but certainly not in the sense regarded by Wehler, who prefers, obviously, a one-sided application to only the working class.

Caprivi had no more than four years at his disposal to implement his attempt at reorganization. Three years later, in 1897, the era of German *Weltpolitik* was inaugurated, consisting of a fresh start in colonial policy, of naval armament, of revoking foreign-trade policy in favour of the large estate owners, and of a renewal of the policy of rallying the conservative forces. But this imperialism coincided with a trend of rapid economic growth and cannot, therefore, be regarded as an anticyclical economic policy. The domestic and social-political ingredients of German imperialism were now becoming more prominent. The policy of rallying the big estate owners, the middle classes, and industry against the Social Democrats (not against the workers as a whole) was now more closely connected to *Weltpolitik* than it had ever been in the Bismarckian era. *Weltpolitik* was to be pursued as a great task rallying the whole nation. The term social imperialism as a means of social and national integration (Wehler's 'crisis ideology' and 'diversionary strategy') is fully justified in this respect.

But again, one must beware of exaggeration. Right from the start, the policy of integration suffered from strong intrinsic contradictions and soon petered out, whereas colonial policy and now also naval policy were soon becoming independent and were continued with vigour. But just as in the period after 1884–5, there was no increased interest among German industrial or finance-capital circles in the German colonies, apart from completely marginal pressure groups. This was recently pointed out by Helmut Boehme, who usually is Wehler's ally in stressing the social-economic development of German history in the second half of the nineteenth century. In a very businesslike manner the coal industrialist Emil Kirdorf, already mentioned, refused to support the policy of integration even with 'one ton of coal' for Africa. To German heavy industry and to the banking world the African territories were 'colonial empires lying on the moon'.[398] German capital did not go to Africa, but to the Balkans and to Turkey where it competed with the capital of other European powers.

4. WALT W. ROSTOW'S THEORY OF ECONOMIC STAGES

Before reverting to the connection between imperialism and the economic-trend period between 1873 and 1896, another way of classifying the economic development of Europe should be mentioned which is structured differently from the Marxist diagnosis of the stages of capitalist development or from the classification into business cycles used by Nikolay D. Kondratiev, Arthur Spiethoff, and others. Intentionally opposing the Marxist theory of capitalism, Walt Whitman Rostow developed a 'dynamic theory of production' according to which the process of industrialization is divided into five stages of growth.[399] The pre-industrial period is called by Rostow the stage of the 'traditional society'. Its economic productivity is changeable, but changeable only beneath a certain limit drawn by the existence of primitive technical devices. The second stage, comprising the late seventeenth and the early eighteenth centuries in Western Europe is a period of transition, in which the preconditions for the beginning of economic growth are developed by technical inventions and by changes in the methods of production.

The decisive breakthrough occurs in the third stage, which Rostow calls the stage of economic take-off. It is the industrial revolution. An important criterion is not only the speed of technological developments in industry and agriculture, but also the formation of capital used for investment purposes. The rate of investment and savings may rise from 5 per cent of the national income to 10 per cent. A few leading sectors of industry develop with a high rate of growth. As they are chained to other sectors, their progress accelerates the growth of the whole national economy. A precondition is the coming forward of political and social forces, willing to make use of the technological means for an industrial development and to push aside the conservative forces of traditional society. The take-off period is usually limited to two or two and a half decades. In Britain it was between 1783 and 1802, in France between 1830 and 1860,[400] in the United States between 1843 and 1860, in Germany between 1850 and 1873, in Japan between 1878 and 1900, and in Russia between 1890 and 1914.

The take-off period is followed by an interval of sustained, if fluctuating, growth. The rate of investment is now 10 to 20 per cent of the national income. Almost all branches of the economy are being industrialized, and technology is being refined. After about four to five decades the stage of maturity has come about. Rostow offers the following dates: 1850 for Britain, 1900 for the United States, 1910 for Germany and France, 1940 for Japan, and 1950 for Russia. After a phase varying from one industrial country to another, the stage of mass consumption sets in which is irrelevant to a discussion of classical imperialism.

Rostow is not quite explicit on the point that the stage of the development to maturity is not simply identical with the second industrial revolution in the last quarter of the nineteenth century. This was characterized by the shifting of the industrial centre of gravity from railway construction, based on coal and iron, to the machine-tool industry, based on steel, and to the chemical and electrical industries. There are, to be sure, strong national differences in this relocation.

Rostow's theory of the stages of growth undoubtedly constitutes a simplification of the process of economic changes. Its usefulness is therefore rated low by some scholars. Refined investigations have made it possible to point to the fact that the rate of effective investment of 5 to 10 per cent in the take-off period, as assumed by Rostow, cannot be confirmed in some cases. On the other hand, if the theory is accepted as a whole, it can be said that a conclusive link between the classical imperialism of the industrial countries and the stages of take-off or maturity does not exist. Britain's (formal) imperialism commenced when the stage of maturity had long been passed. Germany's and France's imperialism started in the midst of their stage of maturity.

5.   THE ECONOMIC-TREND PERIOD OF 1873 TO 1896

The theory of trade cycles, too, is not uncontested. What applies to Rostow's theory of economic stages, i.e. that statistical source material is very fragmentary for the purpose of verifying it, equally applies, to a large extent, to the trend period after 1873. Wehler unduly overemphasized some of its features in order to fit them so much the better into his theory of imperialism.

Since the trend period affected, with variations, all the industrial countries, and since the primary concern here is British imperialism for which, as well as for German imperialism, Wehler postulates the priority of the social-imperialist element, its importance to British imperialism shall now be briefly examined.

To begin with, the term 'Great Depression', used by contemporaries and sometimes also used by Wehler (although in quotation marks), is misleading. It should be banished from scholarly debates because it too easily evokes associations with the world depression of 1929 and after, which hit all economic sectors very hard, whereas the most important feature of the trend period after 1873 is precisely its extreme irregularity in the individual economic sectors. When passing an over-all judgement on the psychological effects, it is by no means unimportant to keep in mind that the rate of economic growth between 1870 and 1873, especially in 1873, was extremely high, and that the development of these years can therefore be regarded as a cyclical overheating, which in Germany was aggravated by the abundant French reparation payments. In this respect, the slump in economic growth must be considered as a healthy cooling of a chronic overproduction.

Simplifying matters somewhat, the cause of the slackening of business can be attributed to the natural end of the railway boom. Railways could not be built indefinitely. Another decisive factor was the innovative capacity of technology (Bessemer and Siemens processes), the ensuing lowering of production and distribution costs (cutting of transportation charges through railways and steam navigation), the rise in productivity, the growing international competition.

The distortion of the price structure by the extraordinary boom year of 1873 is well illustrated by the price of coal and pig iron.[401] The price of coal per ton (London) dropped from 32s. to 18s. between 1873 and 1878. But the latter was also the price of the sixties, and it maintained the level of 16s. to 19s. in the period 1879 to 1896 as well as in the trend period after 1896 until the World War, with the exception of the two boom years 1900 and 1901. The cost of Scottish pig iron averaged 54s. 6d. between 1867 and 1871; in 1873, however, it was double that amount, i.e. 117s. 3d., and in 1876–7 it fell back to 54s. 6d. The downward trend was reversed as early as 1888.

The following remarks summarize, with reference to Britain, the most important features of the trend period after 1873, especially with regard to their irregularity.[402]

The course of wholesale prices in Britain between 1850 and 1896–1914 is shown in Figure 2. It becomes obvious that

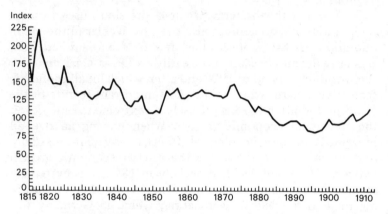

Figure 2: Wholesale Prices in Britain from 1815 to 1913 (1900 = 100)
Source: Saul, *The Myth of the Great Depression*, p. 12.

comparing the curve with an oscillation or an undulation means considerably harmonizing it. It is especially noticeable, when looking at the trend period between 1850 and 1873, that to consider solely the trough of 1850 and the peak of 1873 is misleading. The price structure in the fifteen years after 1855 is, in a simplified graph, a horizontal line or a plateau rather than part of an amplitude. However, the price recession after 1873 is continuous for fourteen years. After that, prices go up again until 1891, then they fall until 1896 to even below the level of 1887. Apart from the exceptional years of 1870–3, it can be said that the recession had already started in the middle of the sixties. And in some branches of the economy, e.g. in heavy industry as a whole, to which the theory of imperialism attributes a key role, the price recession is reversed as early as the beginning of the 1880s. According to the statistics of the Board of Trade, the index number for coal and metals amounts to 66.7 for the five years from 1876 to 1880 (1871–5 = 100); 60.7 for 1881–5, 61.5 for 1886–90; and 63.6 for 1891–5.

When considering Britain's terms of trade between 1850 and 1896–1914, the term 'Great Depression' is even less appropriate than with regard to price development.[403] After the end of the Crimean War the index rose in Britain's favour; it jumped between 1871 and 1873, especially because of the very high prices for coal and iron. After that it slumped correspondingly until the end of the 1870s, when it had reached the same level as ten years earlier. From the beginning of the 1880s until 1914 it rose rather steadily, with the exception of an unusual upward tendency between 1908 and 1910. The early increase within the trend period of 1873 to 1896 was essentially influenced by the relatively stable price of exported coal and by the sharp decline of prices of imported wheat. Thus the upward tendency began in the middle of the trend period of 1873–96 and continued afterwards.

The annual rate of growth in Britain's industrial production is to be treated with caution as regards its total average rates.[404] It cannot simply be said that it declined after 1873 as against the period before that. The rate of growth in the sixties is distorted above all by the cotton industry suffering from the effects of the American Civil War, to some extent also by the building trade. The following table takes this fact into account. The first column shows the rates of growth without the building trade; the figures excluding both sectors are bracketed.

Average annual real growth rates of British industrial production (excluding building; in brackets are figures excluding building *and* cotton industry):

	Total	Per head
1847–53 – 1854–60	3.5 (3.0)	2.4 (2.1)
1854–60 – 1861–5	1.7 (3.5)	0.6 (2.3)
1861–5 – 1866–74	3.6 (2.8)	2.4 (1.3)
1866–74 – 1875–83	2.1 (2.1)	0.9 (0.6)
1875–83 – 1884–9	1.6 (1.6)	0.2 (0.0)
1884–9 – 1890–9	1.8 (2.0)	0.4 (0.4)
1890–9 – 1900–7	1.8 (2.0)	0.2 (0.3)
1900–7 – 1908–13	1.5 (1.5)	−0.2 (−0.3)

The table shows that the slowdown is noticeable already after the middle of the 1860s; moreover, that the rate increases again in the middle of the trend period of 1873 to 1896 and falls again after its close, that is, in the new period of economic prosperity. If the rate of growth is calculated on a per capita basis, the year 1873 likewise does not mean a genuine dividing-line, and in the second trend period after the turn of the century there is not just a slowdown of the growth rate, but an actual contraction.

Applying the term 'Great Depression' to the development of wages is downright absurd. With a view to the German situation, Hans Rosenberg writes that the 'Great Depression' 'was accompanied by nothing less than a revolutionary increase of the level of real wages',[405] and he quotes the opinion of a contemporary political economist in 1888: 'This crisis has been much more a crisis of the rich than of the poor.' The price recession benefited the bulk of the wage and salary earners so that to them the period was one of prosperity, not of depression. Only when prices increased during the trend period after 1896, did real wages stagnate again.

A similar view applies to the situation in Britain.[406] Taking 1850 as 100, the index increased by 30 in the following twenty-three years. In the same period after that, however, it climbed by 46 to 176. In the upswing period after 1896 it moved up and down several times and even dropped to 169 in 1913. Thus, apart from the steep increase in the years of the Boer War, it fell slightly in this period. In the trend period between 1873 and 1896 there were minor irregularities in the development of the index (a slight downward and upward tendency) only in the years 1876 to 1882 and 1890 to 1892 (a decline from 166 to 164). For the remainder the index went up continually.

In its findings published in 1886, the Royal Commission on the Depression of Trade and Industry referred several times to the favourable development of the level of real wages of the workers. 'The workmen were getting all the profit,'one entrepreneur said, 'the iron manufacturers none.'[407] The Commission's report summed the situation up in the following terms: 'We have shown that while the general production of wealth in the country has continuously increased, its distri-bution has been undergoing great changes; that the result of these changes has been to give a larger share than formerly to the consumer and the labourer, and so to promote a more equal distribution.'

The development was not only beneficial to the worker in

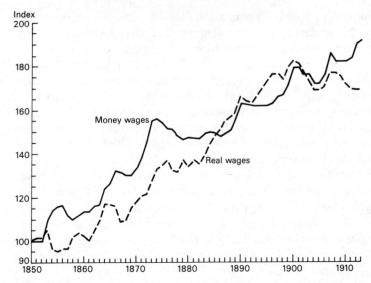

Figure 3: Money and Real Wages in Great Britain, 1850-1913 (1850 = 100)
Source: Saul, *The Myth of the Great Depression*, p. 31.

terms of wages, but also in regard to working hours. According to the Commission's report, weekly hours dropped by three to four hours in the fifteen years before 1886.

Compared to today's material standard of the workers, labour conditions of the period a century ago may appear deplorable or inhuman. The fact that there was continual material improvement, however, is as indisputable as the relative high safety margin of industrial peace. Social unrest, marked by a high frequency of strikes, became generally noticeable only in the boom period after 1896. The number of unemployed, however, seems to have been higher in the trend period after 1873 than before or after that time-frame. The most recent estimates for Britain show an average of 7.2 per cent compared to 5 per cent for the period 1851-73 and 5.4 per cent for the period 1896-1914.[408] But again, 1873 is no turning-point. Up to 1878 the number of unemployed was below average. In 1879 it amounted to 10 per cent, in 1888 it had dropped to 4.5 per cent, and between 1892 and 1895 it increased again.

To employers, indeed, the economic development after 1873 must not have appeared particularly favourable. In its report the Royal Commission did mention an expansion of goods turnover, but the diagnoses of the chambers of commerce resulted in near-unanimous opinions, using terms such as 'overproduction, decline of prices and profit rates', to some extent also in complaints about sharper foreign competition and tariff discrimination. The subjective mood of business, however, is in general more appropriately characterized by terms such as discontent and ill-humour rather than the one-sided alarmist language used by Wehler ('traumatic and shock experiences').

The decisive question is: to what extent did discontented business, or, to phrase it without psychological nuance, to what extent did over-production of goods and the formation of surplus capital push abroad, especially into the colonial regions; in other words, how much did they cause an imperialist policy? Again, the answer cannot be supplied in generally applicable terms.

From the 1873–96 trend data provided above about British exports, it can be seen that exports to the British possessions stagnated from 1880 to 1896, but that exports to third countries increased slightly as a whole and increased sharply in the years 1885 to 1891. Total exports to the crown colonies even declined slightly, although it was precisely in this period that they were extended in number and volume. There is nothing essential to be added to Hobson's judgement on the small commercial value of the newly acquired colonies, unless one seeks to refine it by pointing to what has already been said in another context, that trade with an underdeveloped area was more active before the occupation than after it. Although it would be extremely difficult to compile relevant comparative figures from European colonial acquisitions of that period as a whole, a few characteristic examples can be mentioned. As Kautsky has already pointed out, British trade with Egypt declined after the occupation of 1882.[409] Total trade of German East Africa decreased by about one-third in the four years after it was proclaimed a protectorate in 1891 (from 16.5 to 10.9 million marks — Germany's share from 1891 is unknown — for the year 1895 it amounted to 2.4 million marks).[410] France's exports to Tunisia declined from a total value of about 30 million francs in 1884 to about 5 million francs in 1887.[411]

Likewise, the pattern of British foreign investments is irregular for the period 1873-96. The growth of the total sum of capital investments as depicted in Figure 4 says scarcely anything about a connection with the trend period. More revealing is the pattern of annual exports of new capital investments. (Compare Figure 1.) The export of capital ranges from 10 million to 100 million pounds per year. The curve is so irregular that an analogy is difficult to be seen between the periods of depression (1873-9, 1882-6, 1890-4) or upward movements (1879-82, 1886-90) and a decline or increase of capital exports. Investment operations declined between 1873 and 1877 and between 1890 and 1894, but between 1877 and 1887 they rose in a fluctuating manner.[412]

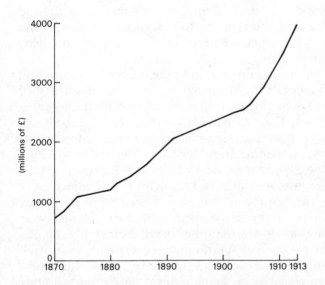

Figure 4: Total Overseas British Capital Investment, 1870–1913
Source: Imlah, *Economic Elements*, pp. 72-5; Mommsen, 'Nationale und ökonomische Faktoren', p. 630.

Indeed, comments from business and banking urging more governmental action in colonial affairs were not lacking during the crises of 1884-6 and 1892-4, as Rostow and, most recently, Wolfgang J. Mommsen have pointed out. In the above-mentioned report of the 1886 Commission, the Manchester

Chamber of Commerce made the following suggestion: 'The opening of new markets and development of those already partially open to Great Britain should be assisted by the Government in every practical way.'[413] In Africa new markets ought to be opened, and in Burma the railway link with western China should be established quickly, it was argued. In the years following the collapse of the IBEA, the government were urged to take over Uganda in order to help overcome the economic crisis by means of railway construction.[414] A general, uniform influence of economic forces associated with the depressions on Britain's imperialist actions, however, cannot be identified in the trend period 1873-96. The prevailing mood of the representations made by the chambers of commerce to the Royal Commission of 1886 appears to have been the hope that the old markets in America, India, and China would have the capacity to absorb more goods, rather than the desire to open *new* markets as a means of resolving economic difficulties.

More attention should be paid to the functional connection between imperialism and social policies on the basis of Wehler's research. However, it is not convincing to argue, in the first place, that Bismarck's overseas and foreign-trade policies were generally subordinate to his predominating social-conservative ideas from 1862 or from 1879 to 1890. Nor, secondly, is it persuasive to claim that Bismarck's social conservatism was as static as assumed or determined by a polarized, friend-or-foe relationship. Social integration may have been one of the decisive motives when colonies were acquired in 1884-5. On the other hand, Bismarck's comprehensive and progressive social-insurance system was in itself refutation of the assertion that his social policy was fundamentally repressive or, in Lenin's view, 'opportunistic'. Only by equating the workers with the Social Democrats could one arrive at such conclusions.

Bismarck's interest in social legislation diminished markedly at the end of his tenure. However, despite massive set-backs, there were many fresh attempts and several pioneering successes in the protracted process of integrating the workers. Much more typical of German history after 1897 than Bismarck's social imperialism was the idea of rallying all 'state-supporting (*staatstragenden*) classes under the standard of

Weltpolitik in a struggle against Social Democracy. This does not mean that Wilhelmine imperialism can only be seen as a function of domestic politics. It also developed a momentum of its own in its more natural field of activity, foreign policy. Indisputably, the government's policy of integration bore an essentially social-conservative stamp. At the same time, however, social-progressive forces demanded, and to a modest degree achieved, social development as a necessary equivalent of imperialism and, vice versa, the utilization of imperialism for the national and social unity of the nation. These forces included the Academic Socialists (*Kathedersozialisten*), the Association for Social Politics (*Verein fur Sozialpolitik*) under Gustav Schmoller, and Liberal Imperialists such as Friedrich Naumann, Paul Rohrbach, and Walther Rathenau, as well as members of the government, including Count Arthur von Posadowsky-Wehner and Bernhard Dernburg.

6. BRITISH SOCIAL IMPERIALISM

a) *Origins*

Social imperialism became effective in Britain, not in Wehler's sense of a manipulated, social-reactionary strategy of diversion, but as a combination of social reform and expansive imperialism. In view of the special preconditions of Anglo-Saxon history and British imperialism, one could even speak of a primacy of imperialism in this reciprocal relationship. This is because social reform, to the extent that it was advocated or at least influenced by imperialists who were in government positions, was more frequently pursued as a function of imperialism than the other way round. Moreover, because British imperialism was defensive in nature, it is illogical to speak of a priority of domestic policy with regard to social imperialism. When overseas imperialism is to be employed as a diversion from domestic problems, it must first be created, that is, it must proceed offensively. There already was a British Empire in 1880; the central concern was to maintain it against competition from emerging (colonial) empires. It was for the purpose of sustaining the Empire, among other reasons, that the domestic base was to be consolidated.

The origins and functions of British social imperialism were first investigated by Bernard Semmel. Its intellectual origins have recently been analysed by G. R. Searle, and Robert Scally has dealt with the party-politics aspect.[415]

British social imperialism has many facets because its advocates came from all political parties (with the exception of Manchester Liberalism, which clung to a dogmatic anti-imperialism): from the Conservatives, above all from the Liberal Unionists, and finally from the Fabian Socialists. Its programme consisted of the maintenance and consolidation of the British Empire *and* a comprehensive social reform. When implementing this programme, the social imperialists split into two groups. The dividing-line went right through the Unionists. The breach resulted from disagreement over whether Britain should create a customs union and a preferential tariff system within the Empire to counter the protectionist tendencies of the other powers, or whether the traditional free-trade system should be maintained in harmony with the increasing interdependence of international trade and so preserve the unrestricted freedom upon which the British money-market, in its predominant position, depended. The advocates of the first proposition gathered around the Colonial Secretary Joseph Chamberlain. Supporters of the second approach at the turn of the century recognized Lord Rosebery as their political leader; after his resignation from political life a collective leadership was formed and consisted of Herbert H. Asquith, Richard B. Haldane, and Sir Edward Grey. After the elections of 1906 the latter group determined the course of the new Liberal cabinet.

The deeper cause of British social imperialism can be traced to the revolutionary upset in the European balance-of-power system wrought by the solidification of a power bloc in Central Europe during the German wars of unification (the inseparable link to other attempts at defining imperialism, especially the first, mentioned above, now begins to be evident), and the corresponding shift in Britain's formerly singular power status.

Gauged by quantitative criteria, the erosion of the British colonial, economic, and especially industrial monopoly proceeded at an alarming pace after 1870 in the eyes of the entire British public. The gap between Britain's former supremacy and the emerging centres of power on the Continent and in North America narrowed with each passing year. In absolute figures, Britain's decline set in as early as the mid-nineteenth century. According to Eric J. Hobsbawm, Britain in 1850 still produced two-thirds of the world's coal, about one-half of the iron and cotton, and two-fifths of the ironware.[416] By 1870 she was still unchallenged at the top of the list of major export countries, with her export volume exceeding the combined total of the next ranked countries, France, Germany, and Italy. By then, however, the phenomenal rise of Germany and of the United States had begun. And in the 1890s these two countries surpassed Britain in steel production. Britain's share in the production of manufactured goods declined from 37.1 per cent to 25.4 per cent between 1883 and 1913, whereas Germany's corresponding share rose from 17.3 per cent to 23 per cent in the same period, and that of the United States from 3.4 per cent to 11 per cent.[417] The steadily growing military power of the Continental countries caused a reorientation in Britain's defence policy. In 1889 the two-power standard was established so that the British Navy would have superiority over the second- and third-strongest challengers. Britain's demographic development was above all compared to German statistics. The population of the United Kingdom rose from 26 to 41 million persons between 1870 and 1900; the German population, however, increased from 41 to 56 million in that same time-frame.

The relative decline of the British position was gauged both in quantitative and qualitative categories. Again, keen attention was fastened on Germany, but with ambivalence. Germany was both the model to emulate and the opponent to combat and eventually settle final accounts with. Britain's admiration of Germany together with her Germanophobia show that the ingredients of British social imperialism were motivated in foreign-policy terms. Recommended for imitation were the organization of the German army and her system of legislation, as well as the German educational system with its integration of the modern sciences, especially the natural sciences. In fact, British social imperialists demanded a total overhaul of society. They questioned the efficiency of Britain's governing institutions, based as they were on parliamentary control, local government, and the proficiency of a civil service that was chiefly recruited from the public schools and the traditional universities. The social imperialists also called for a reform of the system of political leadership and the educational system; a reorganization of the defence institutions, especially the top organs of the army; and the extension of the public health service. The reformist cries were made in the name of a more tightly organized society. The demand was raised for 'national efficiency', for an invigoration of the social structure.

It is again remarkable that this outcry was touched off by an event in foreign policy, the Boer War, which revealed the country's weaknesses. A similar consequence was noticeable during the years of the Crimean War. The catastrophe during the winter of 1854 in the Sevastopol war theatre led to a passionate debate over the worthiness of the parliamentary system of government.[418] A 'strong man', a new Pitt, it was argued, should be placed at the helm of government who would organize the conduct of the war unfettered by constitutional institutions. The power of the nobility came under attack. There was a demand that incompetent persons at the top of the administration and the army be replaced by individuals selected exclusively according to their ability and independently of social status. The 'Administrative Reform Association' was established with the aim of reforming the Civil Service and reorganizing the system of government. During the Boer War a similar institution came into being under the same name and with similar objectives. Even more important than this association in the 'quest for "national efficiency"'[419] were the social imperialists of various affiliations.

During the 1870s under Disraeli's leadership, there was already an obvious desire to pursue imperialism simultaneously with social reform.[420] In his Crystal Palace speech of 1872, Disraeli proclaimed three important goals of the Tory Party: the maintenance of the old institutions, the consolidation of the Empire, and the improvement of the living conditions of the people. The great electoral victory of the Tories in 1874, due mainly to new voters from the lower middle class and from the workers, showed the attractiveness of combining imperialism and social reform. It also revealed the crisis of confidence in British liberalism and its principle that the state should not intervene in the relations among social classes or in international relations.

Still, there was no organizational link and no reciprocal dependence between imperialism and social reform either under Disraeli in the 1870s or under Salisbury in the 1890s. These two elements had not yet become a central issue of the government's policies. Nor was there a doctrine or theory of social imperialism in those years. Things changed, however, when the Boer War broke out and plunged the British people into a deep crisis. Its psychological effects were similar to those of the Crimean War, or those after the battle of Adowa in Italy, or, much more recently, of the Vietnam War in the United States. Britain's position as a pre-eminent world power seemed shaken to its foundations when the Boers defied the colonial giant with skilful guerrilla tactics. It was necessary to deploy almost half a million British soldiers and colonial troops, more than twice the total Boer population, including women, children and the elderly.[421] Back home the British were determined to 'learn the lessons of the war'. This slogan, used by the Prince of Wales on 5 December 1901, was echoed throughout the country. The newspapers printed his speech under the headline, 'Wake up, England!' It was a slogan calling for reflection, a sense of unity, and reform. The ailment was diagnosed as Britain's seemingly weak posture towards the world. (On the Continent there was talk of a collapse of the British Empire and of an ensuing war of succession.) And the disease needed to be radically cured, both in the structure of the government and in society. The nation was to be invigorated from within so that it could act vigorously abroad with the other great powers in the coming years of the new century — particularly towards a Germany that was bristling with strength.

b) *The Liberal Imperialists*

The demand for a better organization of national life, for 'national efficiency', was raised by social Darwinists such as Benjamin Kidd and Karl Pearson, by the Liberal Imperialists under Rosebery's leadership, by the Fabians under Sidney and Beatrice Webb and George Bernard Shaw, and finally by the Empire tariff reformers under Jospeh Chamberlain's leadership. The slogan of 'national efficiency' symbolized the reaction against the liberal spirit of *laissez-faire* and muddling through which was regarded as one of the reasons for the decline of the British Empire in the quarter-century prior to that time. In more sanguine terms this would mean the physical recovery of the nation, especially of the inhabitants of the slums; the education and training of the young people according to the achievements of modern science and technology; a government beyond partisanship; a condition of military and naval preparedness; modernizing industry and the economy in order to reach the level of the highly organized German system; and finally, the unification and strengthening of the Empire.

Rosebery's social-imperialist credo is well expressed in his speeches made during the Boer War. Some years before (in 1895), he had defined his Liberal imperialism in the Albert Hall as 'first, the maintenance of the Empire; secondly, the opening of new spaces for our surplus populations; third, the suppression of the slave trade; fourth, the development of our commerce, which so often needs it'.[422] Now, after the experience of the Boer War, he was demanding as a condition for maintaining Britain's status as a world power 'an imperial race — a race vigorous and industrious and intrepid'.[423] An 'imperial race' could not be raised in the slums of Britain's cities. An improved hygiene, improved sanitary conditions, and a public health service were preconditions for strengthening the Empire. Combating alcoholism, improving housing conditions, reforming the schooling and training system — all these measures were regarded as absolutely necessary in order to realize the idea of 'efficiency'. The latter was defined by Rosebery in a speech in Glasgow on 10 March 1902 as 'a condition of national fitness equal to the demands of our Empire — administrative, parliamentary, commercial, educational, physical, moral, naval, and military fitness — so that we should make the best of our admirable raw material'.[424]

Rosebery entertained the hope of forming a government from both parties — 'a sort of coalition Government', as he noted on 17 March 1901 in his diary,[425] 'formed of the best men of both parties'.[426] He thought he could remain aloof from party strife and from political wrangling, 'plough my furrow alone', as he put it,[427] hoping he would be approached, as was Pitt, to steer Britannia's ship through the hazards of war. The call never came, however; the war soon drew to a close, and, in the final analysis, Rosebery had conducted himself all too passively. He was not the man to prepare his own advent to power on the lower levels of party toil.

Nevertheless, in the spring of 1902 Rosebery organized the Liberal League[428] as a non-partisan organization (comparable in some ways to Friedrich Naumann's National Social Association in Germany), whose most prominent members were Herbert H. Asquith, Robert B. Haldane, and Sir Edward Grey. The League's programme provided for the promotion of imperialism as well as of social reform. With the end of the Boer War some months later, however, the poorly patched-up party differences came to the fore again; the Liberal League had too small a basis to be able to work as a third force in party politics. But the quest for 'efficiency' did not stop. It now acquired a markedly anti-German bias.

c) *The Socialists*

The programme of social imperialism had also attracted the Socialist Fabians since social reform played a prominent part in it. At the end of 1902 Sidney and Beatrice Webb founded a small debating society bearing the characteristic name 'the Coefficients'.[429] Apart from the two Fabians, it consisted of half a dozen Liberal Imperialists – among them Haldane, Grey, and Halford J. Mackinder, professor of geography, who was regarded by many as the 'comer' of the Liberal Party – and, finally, of a few prominent Conservatives. The Coefficients considered themselves to be the brain trust for preparing the establishment of a Social-Imperialist Party. The brain trust, however, soon dissolved over the question of free trade or Empire tariffs which Joseph Chamberlain discussed in public after 1903.

The views of the Fabians about imperialism had already been circulated in 1900 in the middle of the Boer War, in a pamphlet written by Shaw.[430] He took great intellectual delight in surprising the orthodox Socialists, who believed in fighting against the Boer War as a war of capitalism and in supporting the Boers as its victims, with his views. Shaw spoke pure social Darwinism when he claimed that the best justification of the war was that small nations like the Boer Republic were anachronistic 'in the new world of the twentieth century', which was to be the century of great empires.

In 1901 Sidney Webb drew up a programme for a party of

'National Efficiency' that could have come from Rosebery as well. It consisted of items such as slum clearance, reform of the health service and of housing conditions, relief of the poor, educational reforms, and reorganisation of the government, particularly of the War Office. Introducing a certain standard of sanitary measures was regarded by Webb as 'the minimum necessary for breeding an even moderately Imperial race'. How could an efficient army be enlisted 'out of stunted, anaemic, demoralised denizens of the slum tenements of our great cities?'[431] The future battles of the Empire for economic prosperity would already be lost in the school class-rooms.

These themes and reform proposals, the implementation of which was regarded as the precondition for maintaining and strengthening the Empire in order to withstand the international competition, especially that of a Germany which was growing distressingly powerful, were the main items of the domestic debate in the decade and a half after the turn of the century and, as will be shown, were at the centre of activity of the new Liberal cabinet after 1906.

With these highbrow public relations, the Fabians could hardly reach the mass of the workers. However, the Socialist journalist Robert Blatchford succeeded in doing just that.[432] In 1891 he founded the weekly paper, *The Clarion*, which became the most successful weekly in Britain before the First World War. As a devout 'Imperial-Socialist', he managed to drive home to the workers in plain language that the struggle for the unity and homogeneity of the British people as well as of the Empire was more important than the international class struggle of the Socialists. 'The masses must be better educated, better governed, better trained and better treated, or the Empire will go to pieces . . . when the poor rot, the Empire is rotten. We cannot make soldiers and sailors out of weeds . . . If the Empire is to stand we must have a healthy, and an educated and a united people.' This was one of his messages which he repeated again and again. He also kept conjuring up the 'German menace'. Germany, he said, was striving for world domination and she was therefore aiming at the destruction of the British Empire. Against this, British traditional policy must be strengthened: 'The extension of the Empire and the maintenance of the balance of power in Europe.'

Blatchford, the Fabians, and the Liberal Imperialists saw the future of greater Britain safeguarded only in the continued existence of the free-trade system. Working together with certain sections of the economy they scored a victory for the free-trade idea over the clamour massively raised since 1903 by Joseph Chamberlain and his followers for an Empire customs union.

d) *The Tariff-Reform Campaign*

Although it requires simplification, it is correct to say that capital and enterprise were economic antipodes in the debate waged over free trade and protectionism.

It has already been mentioned that at the turn of the century, the rate of profit accruing from the export of capital was considerably higher than the corresponding rate of profit accruing from the export of commodities. This shift of emphasis effected by free trade was regarded by the advocates of free trade such as Rosebery and Mackinder as a natural development. They thought there was an analogy in the early phase of industrialization when agriculture was pushed into the background by industry. Mackinder, who after 1903 became an advocate of protectionism, pointed to the connection between the growing importance of capital export and the extension of the Empire three years before Hobson's book on imperialism: 'It is for the maintenance of our position in the world, because we are the great leaders, that we have been driven to increase our empire.'[433] Using social-Darwinist arguments, Mackinder justified British imperialism and, because a prosperous export of capital depended on it, the necessity of maintaining the free-trade system. He regarded the exported capital as the most important weapon in the 'struggle of nationality against nationality', in the 'struggle for Empire in the world'.

Besides capital export, to which must be added the insurance companies engaged in international business, there were the shipbuilding industries, the international forwarding agencies, and the cotton industry which thought their prosperity was safeguarded only by free trade. The trade unions, too, advocated the continuation of the free-trade system because they feared a rise in the prices of food imports as a consequence of protectionism.

The protectionist group of the social imperialists around Joseph Chamberlain had a hard battle to fight against these interests. However, their social-imperialist credo was not devoid of effective arguments. Back in the early eighties the National Fair Trade League had agitated in favour of establishing protective walls. But the resistance put up at that time by the advocates of free trade had been much too strong for the supporters of protectionism to be able to enlist effective support. Chamberlain learned a lesson from the failure of the propaganda of the League, which was dissolved in 1891, by closely tying the Tariff Reform League, founded in 1903, to the cause of imperialism — hoping in this way to win over the masses of the workers.

The attempt to curry favour with the workers and the desire to keep them from entering the Socialist camp may be reminiscent in many respects of German social imperialism. To some of the leading members of the Tariff Reform League, above all to those who were primarily concerned with the interests of the industry to be protected, the appeal to their imperialist views was but a means to an end, that is, to implement protectionism. Chamberlain, the initiator of the tariff-reform campaign, was primarily concerned with the Empire, however. On the other hand, his social reformism was genuine because he did not regard it as a means to his imperialism: during his tenure as mayor of Birmingham the wealthy middle class were afraid of him because of his far-reaching measures of socialization. Even after the Liberal Unionists had seceded from the Liberal Party, he pressed for continued social reforms. In 1897 the government enacted an accident-insurance law that was partly due to him. In subsequent years he fought above all for an old-age and infirmity-insurance bill.

The Tariff Reform League founded in 1903 regarded as its task 'the defence and development of the industrial interests of the British Empire'.[434] This objective was to be realized by introducing a preferential tariff system within the Empire and by establishing a customs union of the members of the Empire. But only a part of the Liberal Unionists advocated the programme.[435] Industry, with the characteristic exception of the shipbuilding and cotton industries, strongly supported the second item.

The two measures were intended to transform the Empire

into a self-sufficient economic unit. The argument that British industry and the British Empire were dependent on each other for their very existence and were to be protected against foreign competition was aptly expressed in a speech which Lord Milner delivered in Montreal in 1908: 'By buying its wheat, so far as possible from Canada rather than from the Argentine, the United Kingdom will be helping to build up the prosperity of the Dominion. By buying china and earthenware, or glass-ware, or cutlery, from the United Kingdom rather than from Germany or Belgium, Canada is giving employment to British instead of to foreign hands.'[436]

The notion that protecting British industry also meant protecting jobs, that is doing away with unemployment, was a recurrent theme in the publicity campaign of the Tariff Reform League among the workers. 'Tariff Reform Means Work for All'; 'Every Vote for Free Trade Means Work for the Foreigner and Want for British Workers'; 'Why allow goods made by blackleg labour to come to this country free of duty and rob the British workers of employment and wages?' These were the slogans used in millions and millions of pamphlets, brochures, speeches, and suchlike and hammered into the people.[437]

The campaign, however, had one flaw. Introducing protective tariffs would necessarily lead to higher prices for food imports. The workers' bread would get more expensive. The opponents of the League accordingly called the protective tariff the 'stomach tax'; memories of the period before the repeal of the Corn Laws, of the 'hungry forties' were conjured up. Chamberlain's compensatory hint that the tariff receipts would be chanelled into old-age insurance did not go down with the workers. They were more concerned with their stomachs than with the glory and grandeur of the British Empire.

The social imperialists thus split into two camps over the question of how to finance social reform. Whereas those fighting for protective tariffs wanted to draw the money from the tariff receipts, the Liberal Imperialists, supported by the Fabians, intended to provide it by raising taxes, especially direct taxes. The electoral victory of the Liberals under Campbell-Bannerman and Asquith in 1906, which forced the government of the Tories and Liberal Unionists to resign, decided the issue about tariff reform and free trade for the time being,[438] but it was carried on for years and necessitated two elections in 1910.

The Liberals at once inaugurated comprehensive modern legislation, making use of reform proposals from the period of the Boer War (Education Act of 1902, reorganization of the Committee of Imperial Defence of 1904).[439] A central item continued to be the demand for raising an 'imperial race'. The Secretary of State for War, Haldane, introduced changes in the army. The General Staff was reorganized on the German model and the organization of a territorial and reserve army was commenced. An education bill aimed at reducing the influence of religious denominations in education and a licensing bill satisfying most of the demands of teetotallers still failed due to the resistance of the House of Lords, dominated by the Conservatives. A bill providing for old-age worker-pensions was enacted in 1908. In the same year the eight-hour day was introduced for miners. In order to meet the costs of the old-age-pensions bill and of naval armaments, Lloyd George in 1909 brought in a budget providing for higher taxes, among them a liquor tax and a land increment tax, as well as new land taxes. It was designed to intensify the struggle against alcoholism, and at the same time called upon the wealthy class to make higher financial sacrifices. The bills were passed after bitter conflicts with the House of Lords. In 1909 the Housing and Town Planning Act, and in 1911 the National Insurance Act (health and unemployment insurance), modelled upon the German social-insurance system, were passed.

The quest for a 'national government' was also begun during the Boer War and was continued in later years. In 1910 Lloyd George initiated coalition talks with the Conservatives, thereby resuming directly Rosebery's earlier position. They were successful only during the war, however, when a truce seemed imperative. During May of 1915 Lloyd George was able to form his first coalition government; this was replaced in December of the following year by a cabinet which was not composed according to party politics but based solely on the capabilities of its members.

However tedious the search for 'national efficiency' turned out to be, it was not without success. The social imperialists were instrumental in demanding a reform of the social legislation as the prerequisite for the maintenance and strengthening of the Empire.

The research on German social imperialism of the Wilhelmine period, which has not been extensive enough at all, would be well advised to take into consideration the results of the research on British social imperialism. The partiality shown in researching Bismarck's social imperialism could thus be avoided.

VI. Summary

When the word imperialism is applied to the expansion of the Western industrial powers into the world's underdeveloped regions in the decades between 1880 and 1914, there should be clarity as to the *content* of the *term*. At one end of the scale of possible definitions, imperialism is limited to mean direct political–territorial control of the industrial powers over nations that are inferior in various respects. At the opposite end is the use of the term in referring to limitless fields and all sorts of domination and control, among them indirect rule. Alongside and between these two extremes there are many preliminary and borderline types of imperialism. In this intervening variety — for example, in the relations of the industrial powers with Latin America, with the Ottoman Empire, and with China in the decades before and after 1880 — a distinction must be made between the imperialism that was a possible option and a tendency, and the imperialism that sprang from absolute necessity.

The recently introduced term *informal imperialism* seems, indeed, to free the researcher from having to choose between the two extreme definitions, since it covers all the intermediate forms. It also has the advantage of removing the partially unhistoric distinction between an anti-imperialist age, which is associated with British history (the early and mid-Victorian ages), and an age of expansion (after the 1870s and 1880s); this it does by emphasizing the continuity of British colonial and Empire history throughout the entire nineteenth century. Unfortunately, informal imperialism so inflates the definition of imperialism that no contours or distinctions are left; it also applies the term indiscriminately, both in regard to British history and in other contexts. Above all, one of its preconditions, which is that the state continually intervenes in order to open and control new overseas markets for an expanding trade, is not yet adequately verified. According to the most recent research, in particular that by Desmond C. M. Platt, both the state and the economy regarded expansion in the older, established markets abroad — in Europe, the United States, and the white-settled colonies — as more important than involvement in insecure regions. Informal imperialism in those regions, in other words, was a secondary phenomenon and not the main characteristic of British Empire policy before and after 1880.

Classical imperialism on the political–territorial level can be interpreted with particular forcefulness in the cases of Britain and France. The division of Africa, which was the most spectacular event in the general movement of expansion after 1880, appears to be a particularly appropriate example if one is in search of the motives for this expansion. The existence of a British and a French colonial empire was the basic element of post-1880 imperialism when stressing the factor of continuity in European overseas expansion. Another set of preconditions was the existence of trading stations and naval bases on the coasts; the missionary endeavours and geographic exploration; and finally, the technological revolution.

Such factors were not merely preconditions, fundamental elements, or instruments of imperialism. They were also highly independent motive forces. Britain's struggle against slavery in the early nineteenth century resulted in the founding of colonies or in colonial involvements on the West and East African coasts. The missionary societies, which took a leading part in the anti-slavery campaign, sought to resocialize the slave-herds both with Bible instruction and with practical training. There is the example of the missionary societies in Uganda, which exerted such pressure that Britain declared the area a protectorate. The geographic exploration of the Congo basin by de Brazza and Stanley inspired in the minds of Europeans the notion of a new eldorado and resulted directly in competition by various European powers for the heart of the dark continent. The security of the Suez Canal, the construction of which was the most celebrated technical feat of the period along with the building of the transcontinental railways, was the main reason for Britain's occupation of Egypt in 1882. In turn, Britain later had to cope with Egypt's security as other European powers sought to intervene in East Africa.

The occupation of Tunisia by France and of Egypt by Britain directly linked the traditional Eastern policy of the

European powers with their new imperialist policy in Africa. Just as the Eastern balance of power had been integrated into the European power equilibrium in the first half of the nineteenth century, so was the colonial balancing-act to emerge as a corollary ingredient. Europe's acquisition of colonies can thus be regarded as the direct continuation of the traditional great-power politics of the preceding centuries. The Eastern Question, originally a bilateral question directly affecting only Russia and Austria, was Europeanized after 1833 when Britain took a direct interest in it. In an analogous way, the colonial question, which at the outset was of concern only to Britain and France, became internationalized when the new nation states, Germany, Italy, and others, began to be involved. At the Berlin Congress of 1878, the powers established a colonial stock exchange through which in subsequent years colonies were traded. The Berlin Congo Conference of 1885, the partition treaties of the 1890s following the Conference, the two Ententes of 1904 and 1907, and the two Morocco Conferences of 1905 and 1911 represent the most conspicuous colonial trading operations.

The motive that seems to have had most significance in giving imperialist expansion its major boost was the *rivalry* that developed among the powers. The aspect of rival competition is most conspicuous in the documents of the imperialist politicians. It assumed major proportions in 1882 when Egypt was occupied. Wherever the interests of several powers converged — as in the Congo area, on the Upper Nile, in Samoa in the last two decades of the nineteenth century, or in China at the turn of the century — rivalry was at its keenest. Along with such international zones of tension were several regions where bilateral rivals vied.

Earlier research on imperialism investigated only the motive forces originating with the industrial powers in imperialist endeavours. More recent study has drawn attention to the local impulses caused either by the pioneers of imperialism — the missionaries, merchants, adventurers, and soldiers — or by the resistance of the colonial peoples. The occupation of the Western Sudan by French military forces, for example, was carried out against the will of the metropolis and despite the resistance of the Islamic empires of the Sudan; it also gainsaid any economic calculation whatsoever.

France's far-flung territorial plans in Western Africa lead from the political–territorial concept to the second major item in the interpretation of imperialism, that is, *nationalism*. The latter was manifest in Britain in the active foreign policy of Disraeli who, once the balance of power on the Continent began to shift, initiated a re-evaluaton of the existing Empire in order to consolidate Britain's world status. He was supported by similar efforts in the sciences, especially in historiography, which pointed to the greatness and sublimity of the creation of the Empire, in literature, and in journalism. Jingoistic exaggeration of pride in the Empire and its vulgarization in the newly created mass-circulation press and in the imperialist mass associations illustrate that nationalism historically was both a motive force of imperialism, in that it reacted to the power–political changes in Europe, and an instrument susceptible of being manipulated in the pursuit of imperialist foreign-policy or domestic objectives.

Nationalism had a stronger impact on French imperialism than on the British version. It was decisively influenced by the national catastrophe of 1870-1. Following the period that was necessary for consolidation of domestic policy and abstention from foreign activism, France took the occasion of the Congress of Berlin of 1878 to attempt a fresh debut on the great-power stage. The desire for rehabilitation and for recuperating the status of a major world power could best be satisfied by colonial expansion. Algeria, already subjugated, was the staging point for expansion in Northern Africa. Britain's move in Egypt — which to French nationalist sentiment was like a second Sedan — released a colonial fever in the metropolis. Its origins and effects can best be studied in the way the Congo treaty between de Brazza and the African chief Makoko was received by the French public.

The genesis and development of the Fashoda crisis of 1898, the most explosive emergency of imperialism, must also be primarily traced to the peculiar roots of French nationalism. The crisis was set in motion by the traditional calculations of power politics: the French seizure of areas on the Upper Nile, Egypt's lifeline, was intended to compel Britain to a negotiated settlement of the Egyptian question. In its last dramatic phase, the crisis assumed proportions in which the honour and dignity of both antagonists as great powers were involved.

The prestige of imperialist rivals was concentrated here as no-where else. French diplomacy was judicious, however, and an imperialist war did not break out over Fashoda. On the contrary, the incident eventually culminated in the colonial entente of 1904.

Crises of imperialism such as Fashoda, the Spanish–American War, and the Boer War were interpreted by contemporaries in *social–Darwinist categories*. The slogans of natural selection and of the struggle for existence and the survival of the fittest, which Darwin had applied only to evolution in the animal world, were applied to human society in the first phase of popularization; later the doctrine of evolution was even applied to relations among nations. Military armaments, economic expansion, and social integration were regarded as necessary preparations for the great struggle among countries. History, with its panorama of rising and declining empires, the contemporary spectacle of coloured peoples surrendering to white domination; and Spain's abandonment of the colonial scene offered an apparently plausible confirmation of this 'eternal' natural law of the evolution of nations. The course and the result of the Spanish–American War and of the Boer War led, at the turn of the century, to the widespread notion that three or four world empires would soon divide the world among themselves.

Almost all the statesmen of that time moulded their ideas of international relations from such an evolutionist pattern. Ferry placed before the French nation the choice between abdication or rebirth (by way of colonial acquisitions); Salisbury spoke of the dying and living nations; Hanotaux regarded the acquisition of colonies as the most visible sign of the vitality of a country as did Asquith, who interpreted European expansion 'as normal, as necessary . . . a sign of vitality in a nation as the corresponding processes in the growing human body . . . we might control and direct it . . . we could not arrest it'.

This notion of a natural law, of a possibly controllable but irresistible dynamism, is also at the basis of the *economic theory of imperialism* as it was most effectively developed by Hobson and Lenin. It is based on the dogmatic assumption that imperialism is economically determined; all non-economic motives could not be considered as independent, but would eventually have to be subordinated to this basic economic motive. The common starting-point of their theory is the maddening pace of production in the capitalist economy. According to Hobson, surplus goods and especially the excess flow of capital push towards foreign outlets because the domestic market cannot absorb them, thanks to the prevailing social and fiscal policy. He regarded the export of capital as the main motive power of imperialism and the investor as the omnipotent person pulling the strings of international relations.

Hobson saw imperialism as capable of being tamed by redistributing wealth. Lenin, however, welcomed imperialism as the highest stage of capitalism, which would bring about its own ruin because of numerous inherent contradictions. The main characteristic of imperialism for Lenin was the process of concentration in the production of goods and in banking. Although capitalism in contrast to its earlier anarchical form of production, displayed the capacity to organize itself, it obtained only a respite in doing so. The imperialist powers, under the domination of finance capital, would wear out their forces during their struggle for a redivision of the world and would thereby clear the way for Socialism.

The interpretations of imperialism by Hobson and Lenin, with their topical and revolutionary objectives, were not meant to be scientific explanations, but rather instructions for action. The fundamenttal weakness of these two approaches is that they single out of the total phenomenon of imperialism *one* important factor — the difficulties facing the economic growth of the industrial powers and the attempts at solving them — and proclaim this single element itself as the total phenomenon. Their theories are scarcely applicable or verifiable in major cases, most markedly in the instance of Africa. When analysing numerous economic factors — the formation of monopolies and of finance capital, the export of commodities and capital, protectionism, and the importance of economic pressure groups, for example — the result indeed is that traditional power politics and motives of trade expansion in the decades after 1880 are seen as having been reinforced by, but not replaced by, new economic factors, especially over-production's thrust abroad. Here too, as on the level of power politics, the rivalry of the powers, in the sense that preventive imperialism no longer calculated rationally, played

an important part. Many contemporary critics and opponents
of imperialism were guided by rational economic calculations.
Had such imperialist actions as the division of Africa been
similarly approached in a critical light, the cost would have
been calculated as greater than the profit, and so they would
never have been undertaken.

Another theory, one considerably more refined but in the
end also extreme and one- or two-dimensional, has been introduced most recently. This definition sees imperialism as a
corrective device of economic policy for harmonizing uneven
economic growth, as a means of national integration, and as a
strategy to divert social tensions. Although thus viewed in a
palpably social–reactionary perspective, *social imperialism*
can also have applications less kindred to the class struggle. It
can even have a social-progressive tenor. It was precisely
British imperialism, as it was discussed in theory and pursued
in practice after the turn of the century, that viewed social
reforms as the prerequisite to maintaining a strong position
amidst the vigorous world empires that were emerging. The
unity between social reform and consolidation of the Empire,
with the former a condition of the latter, was postulated
both by the Liberal Imperialists around Rosebery and by the
Socialists. There was also an attempt in Germany after the
close of the 1890s to arrive at a synthesis of social progress
and vigorous *Weltpolitik*. This failed, however, despite
renewed efforts undertaken by the government and the
National Social Association around Naumann.

It is rather the reactionary and repressive meaning that has
recently been introduced into the debate on imperialism. An
attempt has been made to interpret the whole of Bismarck's
policy, in which the spectacular colonial expansion of 1884–5
was only the visible peak, in this version of social imperialism.
On the surface, the effort to apply the findings on economic
development in the trend period of 1873 to 1896 appears
useful for explaining the policy of the Bismarckian state,
especially its overseas policy. The difficulties of economic
growth may have, structurally speaking, played a more
prominent part in Bismarck's overseas policy and in his social
politics occasionally than has hitherto been supposed. But the
lofty theoretical claim to have found in the social–imperialist
model the passe-partout for Bismarck's foreign-trade and

overseas policies — as well as for the imperialist policies of Britain, France, and the United States — is fulfilled only to a small degree when it comes to analysing Bismarck's imperialism. A social imperialism defined in such terms seems hardly applicable to British imperialism, and at any rate is not its essential feature. It is even less applicable to French imperialism, especially in view of the most recent research. The result of its verification in the two classical cases of imperialism does not, however, belittle the heuristic value of the social-economic approach.

The complex phenomenon of imperialism cannot be adequately explained in a one-dimensional approach. An ideal definition of the total phenomenon would include all the motives mentioned in this study and probably more. In reality, however, only a small bundle of factors will have to be considered as decisive for each single imperialist action. It is therefore advisable always to place a qualifying adjective before the term imperialism. When examining the division of Africa, the foremost case-study for a detailed explanation of classical imperialism, one will be generally dealing with the power–political motive which aimed at territorial domination. The economic motive, which aimed at direct or indirect influence, was indeed present and grew in importance after 1880; in numerous imperialist actions, however, it played a secondary role or was absent altogether.

Notes

[1] Fundamental works on the origins and changes of meaning of the term imperialism are Koebner and Schmidt, *Imperialism*; and Kettenbach, *Lenins Theorie des Imperialismus*.

[2] See Stokes, 'Late Nineteenth-Century Colonial Expansion', pp. 296, 298. For Lenin's interpretation of imperialism, cf. pp. 100–7.

[3] See Schmitt, *Der Begriff des Politischen*, p. 11: 'Das Klassische ist die Möglichkeit eindeutiger klarer Unterscheidung'. ('The classical method is the way of distinguishing unequivocally and clearly.')

[4] Cecil, *Life of Salisbury*, iv, p. 310. A new interpretation of Salisbury's imperialism in Africa is: Uzoigwe, *Britain and the Conquest of Africa*.

[5] Nkrumah, *Challenge of the Congo*, p. x.

[6] In fact, Franco-British rivalry in West Africa, going back to the early nineteenth-century, at least to Faidherbe's governorship in Senegal (1845–65), had increased since 1879. The difference between the situation in 1879 and that in 1882 is that in the former an increased *two*-party rivalry was at work. In 1882, however, a strong, *many*-sided rivalry set in. See Brunschwig's attempt to mediate in the debate over dates in '"Scramble" et "Course au clocher"'. A brief summary has recently been provided by Rumpler, 'Zum gegenwärtigen Stand der Imperialismusdebatte, p. 258. The ablest attempt to weigh the many theories advanced to explain the 'scramble' and its beginning is Hargreaves, *West Africa Partitioned*. See also Sanderson, 'The European Partition of Africa'.

[7] Fay, *Imperial Economy*, p. 23. See also Fay, 'The Movement Toward Free Trade', p. 399. Hobson already had tried in his 1902 book on imperialism to distinguish between an 'intensive growth of empire by which . . . control [is] tightened over spheres of influence and protectorates' and an 'extensive growth which takes shape in assertion of rule over new areas of territory and new populations'. He called the latter 'formal "expansion"'. (Hobson, *Imperialism*, p. 223) This distinction, however, does not apply to the entire century, only to the decades after 1880.

[8] Gallagher and Robinson, 'The Imperialism of Free Trade', whence the quotation (p. 13).

[9] An informative survey of the debate is in Eldridge, *England's Mission*, pp. 1–24; also in the collection of essays, *Great Britain and the Colonies*, pp. 1–26; Williams, *British Commercial Policy*, pp. 486–7. See also p. 138 and footnote 351. The most recent surveys of the controversy are Eldridge, *Victorian Imperialism*, pp. 74–83; and Mommsen, *Imperialismustheorien*, pp. 69–74. A very handy collection of essays *pro* and

contra is *The Robinson and Gallagher Controversy*. A mediatory view is taken by Cain, *Economic Foundations of British Overseas Expansion*.

[10] Landes, 'The Nature of Economic Imperialism', pp. 510–11.

[11] Regarding the Empire policy between 1815 and 1870–80, they now speak more precisely of Britain's overseas (political and economic) 'influence' rather than of 'informal imperialism': Robinson and Gallagher, *Africa*, pp. 8, 10, 50; also pp. 55, 158, 159.

[12] This becomes even more obvious in the contribution by Robinson and Gallagher to the *New Cambridge Modern History*: Robinson and Gallagher, 'The Partition of Africa'.

[13] Kettenbach, *Lenins Theorie des Imperialismus*, p. 194. The two quotations also come from this source, p. 200 and p. 339 (note 315) respectively.

[14] Pierre Raboisson in 1877 defined the terms colonization and colonialism as 'the effective action of a state on a territory (which it wields in virtue of treaties or conquests) in order to get hold of its products and to assimilate its inhabitants'. See Murphy, *Ideology*, p. 213.

[15] This classification derives from the lecture in Baumgart, 'Zur Theorie des Imperialismus'. A new bibliographical guidebook on the history of European colonialism in Africa is Duignan and Gann, *A Bibliographical Guide*. In addition to Brunschwig's periodical review articles on the partition of Africa in the *Revue Historique*, a recent review article is Vinogradov and Naumenkov, 'Sovremennaja buržuaznaja istoriografija'. An extensive new bibliography is in *Studies in the Theory of Imperialism*, pp. 331–76. The most comprehensive up-to-date bibliography is Halstead and Porcari, *Modern European Imperialism*. See also Wehler, *Bibliographie zum Imperialismus* (which is selective and uneven).

NOTES TO CHAPTER I

[16] See Lüthy, *'Die Kolonisation und die Einheit der Geschichte'*; Cain and Hopkins, 'The Political Economy of British Expansion Overseas'.

[17] The standard work is Fyfe, *A History of Sierra Leone*. On the phase dealing with the founding of Sierra Leone, see ibid., pp. 13–126. Two recent surveys are Peterson, *Province of Freedom*, pp. 17–44, and Asiegbu, *Slavery and the Politics of Liberation*, pp. 1–33. On the 1,200 American slaves leaving the British colonies in North America during the American Revolution and resettling, after a brief stay in Nova Scotia, in Sierra Leone, see the new book by Walker, *The Black Loyalists*.

[18] For writings on the activities of the American Colonization Society, see Shick, 'A Quantitative Analysis of Liberian Colonization'.

[19] Regarding the interrelationships of the humanitarian movement, the anti-slavery campaign, and the colonial involvement, as illustrated by Britain's annexation of the Fiji Islands in 1874, see Eldridge, *England's Mission*, pp. 148–56, also McIntyre, *The Imperial Factor*, pp. 221–66, 317–36; Hyam, *Britain's Imperial Century*, pp. 40–7.

[20] See Ward, *The Royal Navy and the Slavers*.

[21] Above all, see Williams, *Capitalism and Slavery*. Information on the controversy which this book caused is in Anstey, 'Capitalism and

Slavery: a Critique'; Asiegbu, *Slavery and the Politics of Liberation*, pp. xiii-xvi; and Temperley, *British Antislavery*, pp. 273-6. The most comprehensive attack of the Marxist and neo-Marxist view that the slave-trade was abolished only when its economic value had markedly declined is Drescher, *Econocide*. See also the collection of essays *Anti-Slavery, Religion and Reform*.

[22] Recent studies are Bethel, *The Abolition of the Brazilian Slave Trade*; Conrad, *The Destruction of Brazilian Slavery*. On the history of Britain's abolition of slavery after 1833, see Temperley, *British Antislavery*. On the effects of France's abolition of slavery in 1848, there is the recent account by Renault, *L'abolition de l'esclavage au Sénégal*.

[23] On this question see Dilke, *Trade and Politics in the Niger Delta*, pp. 84-5; 91-6; also Hargreaves, *Prelude to the Partition*, p. 34. A case-study on the Cameroons is Wirz, *Vom Sklavenhandel zum kolonialen Handel*, pp. 60-91.

[24] Robinson and Gallagher, *Africa*, p. 35.

[25] Brunschwig, *French Colonialism*, p. 10.

[26] Groves, 'Missionary and Humanitarian Aspects of Imperialism', p. 468. See also Hargreaves, *Prelude to the Partition*, pp. 34-41.

[27] The standard account on Livingstone, his missionary work, and its relationship to European colonization is Oliver, *The Missionary Factor*. A large amount of specialized literature is based on it. One of the most recent discussions of the tension between missionary work and colonialism is Hammer, *Weltmission und Kolonialismus*.

[28] Newbury, *British Policy Towards West Africa*, i. p.529; Hargreaves, *Prelude to the Partition*, pp. 76-7. See also Dilke, *Trade and Politics in the Niger Delta*, pp.166-81; Robinson and Gallagher, *Africa*, pp. 29-30; Eldridge, *England's Mission*, p. 143; Brunschwig, *French Colonialism*, p. 12.

[29] Disraeli to Malmesbury, 13 August 1852 (Malmesbury, *Memoirs*, ii, p. 58). On the restricted meaning of this much-cited remark, see Stembridge, 'Disraeli and the Millstones'; see also p. 5-7.

[30] On the tensions between Catholic, Anglican, and Protestant Missions in East Africa, see Hellberg, *Missions on a Colonial Frontier*.

[31] On the missionary work of the 'White Fathers' under Cardinal Lavigerie in Central and East Africa, see the detailed account by Renault, *Lavigerie*.

[32] For the extensive older literature on the declaration of a protectorate over Uganda, referring primarily to the bankruptcy of the IBEA Co., Lord Lugard's propaganda for a continuation of British rule, the split in the British cabinet over the question of retaining Uganda, and Britain's strategic interest in this area as the main motive, see the review article by Baumhögger, '*Dis Geschichte Ostafrikas*', pp. 693-4, 747-51. On Sir William Mackinnon, founder and head of the IBEA Co., see the recent able account by Galbraith, *Mackinnon*. On Lugard's Uganda campaign, see above all Perham, *Lugard*, i, pp. 387-469. On Rosebery's activity in the cabinet, see James, *Rosebery*, pp. 261-8, 274-86. On public opinion in Britain on Uganda, see Low, *Buganda*, pp. 55-83.

[33] Caplan, 'Barotseland's Scramble for Protection'. For another case-

study on the link between missionary work and the foundation of a colony, see Dachs, 'Missionary Imperialism – The Case of Bechuanaland'.

[34] Groves, *Missionary and Humanitarian Aspects of Imperialism*, p. 493. One of the most recent relevant case-studies is Berger, *Mission und Kolonialpolitik* (on the Cameroons).

[35] A more recent collection of biographical accounts is *Africa and Its Explorers*; it contains accounts of, *inter alia*, Heinrich Barth, David Livingstone, Samuel White Baker, Gerhard Rohlfs, Henry Morton Stanley. See the bibliography, ibid., pp. 323–32. For an account of South Seas explorers, see Dunmore, *French Explorers in the Pacific*, another recent collection.

[36] The most recent biography is Marlowe, *Rhodes*.

[37] See Smith, *The Emin Pasha Relief Expedition*, based on unpublished material, for one of the expeditions which the European public followed with great interest. Emin Pasha was Egyptian governor in the Equatorial Province. The various search expeditions led to many complications in Anglo-German relations.

[38] Stengers, 'L'impérialisme colonial', p. 475.

[39] Ibid., p. 475, footnote 22.

[40] Garvin, *Chamberlain*, iii. p. 219.

[41] Kanya-Forstner, 'Military Expansion in the Western Sudan', p. 415.

[42] With regard to French imperialism, the India myth played a role especially in the extension of French influence in Indo-China, which was seen as a compensation for the loss of French India in the eighteenth century. Murphy cites some relevant quotations in *Ideology*, pp. 46, 54.

[43] Stengers, 'L'impérialisme colonial', p. 490.

[44] Kanya-Forstner, 'Military Expansion in the Western Sudan', p. 418.

[45] See Kanya-Forstner, *The Conquest of the Western Sudan*, p. 66, footnote 2. Decimated by two centuries of slave-trade and chronic domestic troubles, the population of what was later to become French West Africa was estimated to be just slightly over ten million inhabitants, or two inhabitants per square kilometre. See Ganiage, *L'expansion coloniale*, pp. 316–17.

[46] Louis, 'The Berlin Congo Conference', pp. 171–2.

[47] Seeley, *The Expansion of England*, p. 61.

[48] The standard history of the Suez Canal is Farnie, *East and West of Suez*; a detailed bibliography is on pp. 759–98.

[49] Naval stations, from which colonies were founded in the interior, were established as follows: Aden, 1869; Zeila, 1874; Berbera, 1884 (from which British Somalia was formed); Obok and Djibouti after 1867 (French Somalia); Assab, 1869 (the Italian colony of Eritrea, from which stemmed Italy's foothold in Abyssinia).

[50] Figures are in Hoffman, *Great Britain and the German Trade Rivalry*, p. 63, footnote 79.

[51] Blake, *Disraeli*, p. 577.

[52] Langer, *European Alliances*, pp. 255–6.

[53] Soleillet, *Voyage à Ségou*, pp. xv–xvi.

[54] Murphy, *Ideology*, pp. 70–5.

[55] Among the much-discussed canal-construction schemes of the

time, it was the Panama Canal along with the Suez Canal which exerted a direct influence on imperialism (US rule over Panama). The involvement in the South Seas of the European powers, especially Germany, is attributable in part to the anticipated building of the Panama Canal. See the quotation from the *'Grenzboten'* of 1895 in Wehler's *Bismarck und der Imperialismus*, p. 391.

[56] See Langer, *The Diplomacy of Imperialism*, pp. 103-10, 573, 574; also Sanderson, *England, Europe and the Upper Nile*, pp. 9-11. A more recent monumental study of the history of the Nile, its geographic exploration, and its significance for European politics in the nineteenth century is Zaghi, *L'Europa davanti all'Africa*.

[57] Prompt, 'Soudan Nilotique', pp. 105-7. While it is true that the supply and transportation of building materials would have presented great problems, its technical feasibility might be considered in the light of the fact that the first Aswan dam was built between 1892 and 1902 (with the Nile itself used for transporting construction materials), and initially could hold 1.2 thousand million cubic metres; after its elevation in 1912, it could contain 2.3 thousand million cubic metres. By way of comparison, the largest reservoir in West Germany, the Rurtal Reservoir, has a capacity of 205 million cubic metres.

[58] Italy pledged in the Anglo-Italian treaty of 15 April 1891 that, should Kassala be occupied, Italy would not erect any structure in the Atbara that could materially influence its flow into the Nile. The text is in Hertslet, *The Map of Africa by Treaty*, iii, p. 950.

[59] Sanderson, *England, Europe and the Upper Nile*, pp. 143-4.

[60] See Brunschwig, *Le Partage de l'Afrique noire*, p. 31; also Girard, 'From Sea to Sea', pp. 250-61.

[61] Cited in Renty, *Les Chemins de fer coloniaux*, i, p. i.

[62] On the Trans-Siberian Railway, see Borzunov, *Transsibirskaja magistral'*.

[63] A more recent study is Young, *British Policy in China*. The relevant literature is found on pp. 327-45.

[64] The older literature is in Fischer, *Krieg der Illusionen*, p. 425, footnote 2. The most recent account is Mejcher, 'Die Bagdadbahn'.

[65] Cited in Millin, *Rhodes*, p. 138.

[66] See especially Murphy, *Ideology*, pp. 75-93; also Newbury and Kanya-Forstner, 'French Policy and the Origins of the Scramble'.

[67] For their activity, see also Kanya-Forstner, *The Conquest of the Western Sudan*, pp. 60-72. There exists as yet no definitive study on Freycinet's colonial policy.

[68] Newbury and Kanya-Forstner, 'French Policy and the Origins of the Scramble', p. 262.

[69] Ibid., p. 263. See also Kanya-Forstner, *The Conquest of the Western Sudan*, pp. 65, 68 105, 265.

[70] Newbury and Kanya-Forstner, 'French Policy and the Origins of the Scramble', p. 264.

[71] The various expeditions to the Upper Senegal area in 1881-2 were not even able to feed on the land and were frequently exposed to hunger. There were no prospects of trading whatsoever; only arms trafficking

seemed to yield some profit. Negative reports to this effect were received with indignation in Paris and were refuted by investigating committees that, as in duty bound, had to trumpet the economic benefits of the conquests. See Kanya-Forstner, *The Conquest of the Western Sudan*, pp. 109-10.

[72] Ibid., pp. 15, 56, 174, 198, 263-4.

[73] Sébillot, *Le Transafricain*. See also *Die Eisenbahnen Afrikas*, pp. 201-10; Meyer, *Die Eisenbahnen im tropischen Afrika*, pp. 9-13.

[74] See Robinson and Gallagher, *Africa*, p. 331. For a different interpretation, see Sanderson, *England, Europe and the Upper Nile*, p. 165.

[75] The older literature is in Langer, *The Diplomacy of Imperialism*, p. 117, footnote 43.

[76] Rostow, *The Stages of Economic Growth*, pp. 2-3.

[77] See, in a wider framework, the more detailed account in Baumgart, *Vom Europäischen Konzert zum Völkerbund*, pp. 19-23, 31-3, 36, 114-8.

[78] A characteristic example is the French foreign minister, Gabriel Hanotaux (1894-8), who regarded economic considerations in his colonial policy as detrimental. Along with the desire of regaining for France the status of a great power and France's 'civilizing mission', the idea of the balance of power played a decisive part in his doctrine of imperialism. Looking back at the Congress of Berlin, he wrote: 'European politics bow to Germany's preponderance. The others can only look for faraway compensations: a new era sets in, the era of world politics.' And, with general reference to Europe's colonial expansion: 'The European Concert presided over the period of colonial expansion.' See Grupp, *Theorie der Kolonialexpansion*, pp. 41-3, 50-3, 70-3. The quotations are on pp. 42 and 71.

[79] Vogüé, *Le Maître de la mer*, pp. 234-6. See also Brunschwig, *French Colonialism*, pp. 173-4.

[80] Waddington to Harcourt, Paris 21 July 1878, in Ganiage, 'The Tunisian Affair', p. 51. See also Ganiage, *Les Origines du protectorat française en Tunisie*, pp. 494-520; Rosenbaum, *Frankreich in Tunesien*, pp. 12-13; 190-1.

[81] Andrássy to Haymerle, 2 February 1878, in Ganiage, 'The Tunisian Affair', p. 44.

[82] See Baumgart, *Vom Europäischen Konzert zum Völkerbund*, pp. 19-23, 31-58.

[83] Hertslet, *The Map of Africa*, iii, pp. 983-4; 865-7; ii, pp. 711-12. How Brunschwig (*Le Partage de l'Afrique noire*, p. 85) counts 249 treaties for Britain and France is not clear.

[84] Fieldhouse, *The Colonial Empires*, p. 209.

[85] See Hammond, *Portugal in Africa*, pp. 360-4; Axelson, *Portugal and the Scramble for Africa*, pp. 1-83; Latour da Veiga Pinto, *Le Portugal et le Congo*.

[86] Hertslet, *The Map of Africa*, ii, p. 660 (No. 198).

[87] Ibid., p. 817 (No. 251).

[88] Cambon to Delcassé, London 11 October 1903, in *Documents diplomatiques française*, 2e série, iv, p. 16 (No. 7).

[89] Guillen, 'The Entente of 1904', p. 363.

[90] See Baumgart, *Deutschland im Zeitalter des Imperialismus*, pp. 78–9, 104.

[91] Brunschwig, 'Anglophobia', p. 5.

[92] The volume of Europe's colonial acquisitions in the period 1800–78 is remarkable in view of the prevailing doctrine of the costly burden of the colonies. It was 6,500,000 square miles, compared to 8,653,000 square miles in the period from 1878 to 1914. See Fieldhouse, *The Colonial Empires*, p. 178.

[93] Newbury and Kanya-Forstner, 'French Policy and the Origins of the Scramble', p. 268.

[94] Newbury, *British Policy Towards West Africa*, ii, p. 179 (No. 18).

[95] Regarding the attempt to dissuade the IBEA Co. to give up Uganda, Harcourt, Chancellor of the Exchequer, stated: 'Similar enterprises in these regions have been disastrous failures. The Congo is bankrupt. The Germans have met with severe repulses. The Italians have not been more fortunate. Everything warns us against this ill-omened international jealousy which is at the root of all this annexing policy.' Galbraith, *Mackinnon*, p. 221.

[96] Newbury, *British Policy Towards West Africa*, ii, p. 180 (No. 18).

[97] Ferry, *Le Tonkin*, pp. 37–8. The ensuing quotation, ibid., p. 51.

[98] Stengers, 'L'impérialisme colonial', p. 473. The ensuing quotation is taken from Stengers, 'King Leopold and Anglo-French Rivalry', p. 157.

[99] On this point see Zaghi, *I Russi in Etiopia*.

[100] See the most recent account on this subject by Kennedy, *The Partition of the Samoan Islands*; Kennedy, 'Anglo-German Relations in the Pacific and the Partition of Samoa' (with the older literature).

[101] Along with the study referred to in footnote 99, see the article by Marcus, 'Imperialism and Expansionism in Ethiopia' (pp. 455–61 with the older literature); also Menelik's biography by Marcus, *Menelik*; and Rubenson, *The Survival of Ethiopian Independence*, pp. 288–410.

[102] See e.g. the protest which the British Chancellor of the Exchequer, Sir William Harcourt, levelled against Australian aspirations towards Samoa on 8 December 1894: 'These colonial gentlemen expect us to quarrel on their behalf with the great military Powers of Europe, and to add millions to our expenditure, to which they refuse to contribute a single farthing and leave the whole burden to fall on the English taxpayer.' (Robinson and Gallagher, *Africa*, pp. 416–17.)

[103] *The Concept of Empire*, p. 310 (No. 83). For Britain's concern to safeguard future economic needs by means of her colonial policy, see Wrigley, 'Neo-Mercantile Policies'.

[104] This phenomenon has been termed the 'turbulent frontier'. Galbraith, 'The "Turbulent Frontier"'.

[105] Morison, 'Colonial Rule', p. 52. In much the same vein the Russian foreign minister, Alexander M. Gorchakov, had written in 1864 about British-Russian rivalry in Asia that the leaders of both nations were being 'irresistibly forced, less by ambition than by imperious necessity, into this onward movement where the greatest difficulty is to know where to stop'. See Gillard, *The Struggle for Asia*, p. 2.

[106] Two recent books dealing with this question are Schölch, *Ägypten*; Nersesov, *Diplomatičeskaja istorija egipetskogo krisisa.*

[107] A brief survey can be found in, among others, Ganiage, *L'Expansion coloniale*, pp. 81-101. On the ensuing remarks see Erusalimsky, *Kolonial'naja ėkspansija*; Schreuder, *The Scramble for Southern Africa.*

[108] Robinson and Gallagher, *Africa*, have used a wide range of source material to examine the motive for the occupation of Egypt. The forces of resistance working from Africa — from the Africans themselves and not from the Europeans on the spot — are becoming more and more evident in numerous relevant investigations of the last decade. The influence of these forces on classical imperialism must be rated higher than has hitherto been done. In view of the details now available on this African 'resistance movement', the traditional view that this resistance was always doomed to failure from the start, appears to be an oversimplification. It caused much more trouble to the Europeans than has been admitted; trouble came not only from the Mahdis of Khartoum, the Abyssinians of Adowa, but also from the Hottentots. On this subject, see the various contributions in the collection of essays: *Colonialism in Africa*, i, pp. 199-219, 293-324; *Problems in the History of Colonial Africa*, pp. 41-82; *Expansion and Reaction*. Regarding Africa, see the contributions by J. J. Miège, ibid., pp. 103-15; Henri Brunschwig, ibid., pp. 116-40; Ronald Robinson, ibid., pp. 141-63. A recent case-study is Dunn, *Resistance in the Desert.*

[109] Marshall Lyautey once described it in the following terms: '*A resolute course* — therein lies the whole secret of efficient colonial action. To seize the initiative, to think and act without waiting for orders "from above" which never come, or are given only in the negative, in the building of our magnificent colonial empire, this "from above" had always to be met with the *fait accompli*.' Kanya-Forstner, *The Conquest of the Western Sudan*, p. 14, footnote 3.

[110] The significance of the claim by the European powers, as laid down in the Berlin Congo Treaty of 1885, to the *hinterland* beyond the coastal strip already occupied, *and* of the demand for *effective occupation* of this hinterland as a means and as an impulse for imperialism, has been previously underrated in the debate on imperialism. This claim to the hinterland worked as an impulse in so far as each power was interested in extending its hinterland, its sphere of interest, as far as possible and in ruling it effectively so that other powers could not push into this hinterland from other directions. This was evident again and again in the numerous negotiations on delimitations. See Brunschwig, *Le Partage de l'Afrique noire*, pp. 161-3; Touval, 'Treaties, Borders, and the Partition of Africa'. On the occupation of the hinterland of the Slave Coast, see the new account by Obichere, *West African States and European Expansion*, pp. 19-28, 49-50. On the occupation and delimitation of Nigeria see the most recent account by Hirshfield, *The Diplomacy of Partition.*

[111] A more recent account is Sieberg, *Étienne und die französische Kolonialpolitik*. In the framework of French colonial policy, see also Cooke, *New French Imperialism*. The book merely describes events without getting at the problems.

[112] *Documents diplomatiques français*, le série, xvi, p. 248 (No. 156).
[113] See Fischer, *War of Illusions*, pp. 310–18, 534. See also Cooke, *New French Imperialism*, pp. 58, 67–8.
[114] Robinson and Gallagher, *Africa*, p. 462.

NOTES TO CHAPTER III

[115] See Baumgart, 'Das Grössere Frankreich', pp. 186–9.
[116] Langer, *European Alliances*, pp. 13–14. For further British comments on the foundation of the German Reich see Hildebrand, 'Grossbritannien und die deutsche Reichsgründung', esp. pp. 37–56; Kennedy, *The Rise of the Anglo-German Antagonism*, pp. 3–37.
[117] The entire text is in Disraeli, *Speeches*, ii, pp. 523–35. For interpretation, see Koebner and Schmidt, *Imperialism*, pp. 109–12; Kettenbach, *Lenins Theorie des Imperialismus*, p. 55; Eldridge, *England's Mission*, pp. 173–80; Smith, *Disraelian Conservatism*, pp. 158–61; Stembridge, 'Disraeli and the Millstones'.
[118] See his 'wretched colonies' letter of 1852, p. 15.
[119] See Ramm, Great Britain and France in Egypt', p. 73.
[120] Cf. Baumgart, *Vom Europäischen Konzert zum Völkerbund*, pp. 47–8 (with the old literature). More recently, Porter, *Critics of Empire*, pp. 36–40; Cunningham, 'Jingoism and the Working Classes'.
[121] It is remarkable that a colonial book by the French journalist Lucien Anatole Prévost-Paradol was published in Paris in the same year under the equally programmatic title, *La France nouvelle*. See Gollwitzer, *Geschichte des weltpolitischen Denkens*, i, pp. 483–9.
[122] The old literature is in Mommsen, 'Nationale und ökonomische Faktoren', pp. 618–19. See also Faber, *The Vision and the Need*, pp. 86–95.
[123] A more recent account is Mogk, *Paul Rohrbach und das 'Grössere Deutschland'* (especially pp. 78–85, 109, 129, 143, 170, 180–3).
[124] Bülow, *Reden*, i, pp. 90–1.
[125] Seeley, *The Expansion of England*, p. 12.
[126] Kettenbach, *Lenins Theorie des Imperialismus*, p. 68. See James, *Rosebery*, p. 158. These authors differ on the dates they give for these statements.
[127] Kettenbach, *Lenins Theorie des Imperialismus*, p. 339, footnote 305.
[128] Hobson, *Imperialism*, p. 215.
[129] Langer, *The Diplomacy of Imperialism*, p. 84.
[130] Semmel, *Imperialism and Social Reform*, p. 57.
[131] Langer, *The Diplomacy of Imperialism*, p. 85. For the relations of the Foreign Office with the press at the turn of the century, see Steiner, *The Foreign Office*, pp. 186–92.
[132] Wernecke, *Der Wille zur Weltgeltung*.
[133] Pelling, 'British Labour and British Imperialism' contains shrewd remarks on this subject, e.g. p. 99: There is no evidence of a direct continuous support of imperialism by the workers. From the detailed account of this subject, Price, *An Imperial War and the British Working*

Class, it emerges that during the Boer War (which lends itself particularly to an investigation of this problem) there was even an anti-war and anti-imperialist attitude among the workers which was, however, poorly articulated and organized. The workers were rather interested in the problem of social reform affecting them more closely. Actually, their attitude seemed to be one more of indifference than either enthusiasm or rejection.

[134] Hobson, *Imperialism*, p. 215.

[135] An extensive treatment of this feature is in the old book by Brie, *Imperialistische Strömungen in der englischen Literatur*. (The nineteenth century is treated from p. 83 onwards.) A new case-study is Raskin, 'Imperialism: Conrad's Heart of Darkness'.

[136] Brie, op. cit., traces further back into history the idea of imperialism in the sense of empire; reference to Carlyle is on pp. 100–13. See also the bibliographic notes on imperial ideas in English fiction in Aziz, *The British in India*, pp. 373–4; regarding Rudyard Kipling, see ibid., pp. 376–7.

[137] Brunschwig, 'Anglophobia', p. 6. See also Graham, *Tides of Empire*, pp. 59–62, 67–8.

[138] A useful collection of sources is in Girardet, *Le Nationalisme français*.

[139] See Gollwitzer, *Europe in the Age of Imperialism*, pp. 54–5.

[140] Anticolonialism of the monarchist right decreased in the 1890s after the alliance with Russia seemed to ease the danger of a German attack. A new collection of sources on French anticolonialism before the First World War is in Ageron, *L'Anticolonialisme*.

[141] Brunschwig, *French Colonialism*, p. 25. See also Murphy, *Ideology*, pp. 19–20; Girardet, *L'idée coloniale en France*, pp. 32–5.

[142] Brunschwig, *French Colonialism*, p. 175.

[143] Ibid., p. 176.

[144] Ibid., p. 177. On Chailley-Bert, see also the essay by Persell, 'Chailley-Bert'.

[145] Brunschwig, *French Colonialism*, pp. 178–9.

[146] In 1880 Paul Gaffarel, professor of history and geography, compared the population figure of the colonizing European nations to that of their colonial population and concluded that for Britain there were seven colonial inhabitants for each 'metropolitan'; in the case of Holland the ratio was 5:1; for Portugal 1:1; for Spain 1:2; and in the case of France 1:6. 'There is no concealing the fact, our inferiority is flagrant and it becomes even more so every day.' See Murphy, *Ideology*, p. 196.

[147] Stenographische Berichte, viii. Legislaturperiode, i. Session 1890–1, vol. i, p. 41.

[148] *Documents diplomatiques français*, le série, iii, p. 330 (No. 349).

[149] Kanya-Forstner, *The Conquest of the Western Sudan*, p. 5, footnote 1. On Gambetta's colonial policy, see the new study by Ageron, 'Gambetta et la reprise de l'expansion coloniale'.

[150] Grupp, *Theorie der Kolonialexpansion*, p. 21, also p. 39.

[151] Brunschwig, *French Colonialism*, p. 175.

[152] Louis, 'The Berlin Congo Conference', p. 170.

[153] On this subject, see Baumagrt, *Vom Europäischen Konzert zum Völkerbund*, p. 47.

[154] For the ensuing remarks, see Stengers, L'impérialisme colonial'. See also Stengers, 'King Leopold and Anglo-French Rivalry', which contains an extensive bibliography; also Brunschwig, *L'avènement de l'Afrique noire*, pp. 133-69; Brunschwig, *Le Partage de l'Afrique noire*, pp. 43-52. The expeditions of Count Pierre Savorgnan de Brazza in Central Africa (identification of the course of the Ogowe River, 1874-9; establishment of Franceville and Brazzaville and the treaties with Makoko, 1880-2; and exploration of the hinterland of Gabon, 1883-5) are dealt with in three volumes of sources edited by Brunschwig and his students: Brunschwig, *Brazza explorateur*, i, ii; Coquery-Vidrovitch, *Brazza et la prise de possession du Congo*. A specialized study on the exploration of the territory on the Upper Congo by de Brazza and on the subsequent exploitation of this area was written by Mazenot, *La Likouala-Mossaka*.

[155] Stengers, 'L'impérialisme colonial', p. 474, footnote 13.

[156] Ibid., p. 473.

[157] Ibid., p. 474.

[158] Ibid., p. 476, footnote 27.

[159] Ibid., The quotation is in Stengers, 'King Leopold and the Anglo-French Rivalry', p. 166.

[160] See e.g. Friedrich von Holstein's entry in his diary about a remark made by Bismarck on 19 September 1884 (Holstein, ii, p. 161): 'All this colonial business is a fraud, but we need it for the elections.'

[161] Sanderson, *England, Europe and the Upper Nile*; Sanderson, 'The Origins of Fashoda'; Michel, *La Mission Marchand*. These three books contain of the older literature on Fashoda. See also the review article by Baumgart, 'Das Grössere Frankreich', p. 198.

[162] See Brown, *Fashoda Reconsidered*.

[163] *Documents diplomatiques français*, le série, xii, p. 280 (No. 192).

[164] Brown, *Fashoda Reconsidered*, p. 39, footnote 29.

[165] *Documents diplomatiques francais*, le série, xiv, p. 388 (No. 258).

[166] Sanderson, *England, Europe and the Upper Nile*, pp. 390, 394; Sanderson, 'The Origins of Fashoda', pp. 286-7, 292, 303.

[167] Brown, *Fashoda Reconsidered*, pp. 99-100.

[168] Cecil, *Salisbury*, iv, p. 42; Lowe, *The Reluctant Imperialists*, ii, pp. 58-9.

[169] Victoria, *Letters*, iii, 1 (12 June 1890), p. 615. In a quite similar way, the French Minister for the Navy in 1869 had informed the Governor of Senegal: '. . . it would be impolitic to abandon the territories we possess'. (Kanya-Forstner, *The Conquest of the Western Sudan*, p. 53, footnote 1; see also p. 85, footnote 1.)

[170] *Documents diplomatiques française*, le série, xi, p. 465 (No. 303).

[171] Sanderson, 'The Origins of Fashoda', p. 289.

[172] Sanderson, *England, Europe and the Upper Nile*, pp. 324, 327, 400; Steiner, 'The Last Years of the Old Foreign Office', p. 59. See also Grenville, *Salisbury*, pp. 128-9, 146-7, 219, 234; Young, *British Policy in China*, pp. 65, 75.

[173] See Andrew, *Delcassé*, pp. 91-108; Brown, *Fashoda Reconsidered*, pp. 120-6; Cooke, *New-French Imperialism*, pp. 93-6.

[174] Under the motto 'Chacun doit grandir ou mourir' ('Everybody must expand or perish'), the urge for unlimited expansion is the central thesis of Schumpeter's theory of imperialism applied to the whole history of mankind. Schumpeter, 'The Sociology of Imperialism'.

[175] Following the Crimean War the German publicist Constantin Frantz spoke of the three coming world empires, Great Britain, the United States, and Russia. His view was probably influnced by Alexis de Tocqueville. See Gollwitzer, *Geschichte des weltpolitischen Denkens*, i, pp. 472-82.

[176] Brunschwig, *French Colonialism*, p. 29. See also Murphy, *Ideology*, p. 209; Girardet, *L'idée coloniale en France*, pp. 31-2.

[177] Seeley, *Expansion*, p. 50. For the quotation, ibid., p. 62.

[178] Dilke, *Problems of Greater Britain*, ii, p. 582. See also Mommsen, 'Nationale und ökonomische Faktoren', p. 661. The quotation on that page is inaccurate and quoted from the wrong page.

[179] See Baumgart, *Deutschland im Zeitalter des Imperialismus*, pp. 45-53; Fischer, *War of Illusions*, pp. 30-7.

[180] Kettenbach, *Lenins Imperialismustheorie*, pp. 199-200.

[181] Brunschwig, *French Colonialism*, p. 80.

[182] Chamberlain, *Speeches*, i, p. 5. The following quotation is taken from Langer, *The Diplomacy of Imperialism*, p. 90.

[183] *The Times*, 5 May 1898. (Speech of 4 May.)

[184] *Documents diplomatiques français*, le série, iii, p. 330 (No. 349).

[185] Brunschwig, *French Colonialism*, p. 80.

[186] On the 'generation of 1898', see Jeschke, *Die Generation von 1898*; Granjel, *La Generación*; Krauss, *Spanien*, pp. 40-99, 241-9; Carr, *Spain*, pp. 524-32; Ramsden, *The 1898 Movement*; Blinkhorn, 'Spain: The "Spanish Problem". It is remarkable that there is no special study of the notion of four world empires, which was widespread around 1898-1900 (due probably to the Spanish–American War and the Boer War). Other evidence is the conversation between Emperor William II and Sir Arthur Bigge, private secretary to Queen Victoria: 'Before very long there will only be four nations: England, Germany, Russia and America — we have seen what has befallen Spain — Italy — well we will say nothing — and as to France — you know more about her than I do as all your springs are passed there.' (Grenville, *Salisbury*, p. 281.)

[187] Langer, *The Diplomacy of Imperialism*, p. 419. On Mahan and his doctrine, see the outline in Wallach, *Kriegstheorien*, pp. 317-27, with bibliography on p. 327. A more recent study is Hanke, *Mahan*.

[188] Berghahn, *Der Tirpitz-Plan*, pp. 179-81.

[189] See Bueb, *Die 'Junge Schule'*.

[190] Berghahn, *Der Tirpitz-Plan*, p. 179.

[191] The most detailed account is Murphy, *Ideology*, pp. 1-40. The figures mentioned in the following remarks are on p. 8.

[192] Gollwitzer, *Europe in the Age of Imperialism*, p. 125. See also Smith, *Disraelian Conservatism*.

[193] See Kendle, *Colonial and Imperial Conferences*, pp. 5-18 (with

the old literature). On the Colonial Society founded in 1868, see Reese, *The History of the Royal Commonwealth Society*.

[194] Brunschwig, *French Colonialism*, pp. 105–34; Andrew and Kanya-Forstner, 'The French "Colonial Party"' (correcting Brunschwig on a few points); Persell, 'Chailley-Bert'. Brief summaries are in Ganiage, *L'Expansion coloniale*, pp. 165–9; Girardet, *L'Idée coloniale*, pp. 68–75; Cooke, *New French Imperialism*, pp. 34–7. The most recent surveys are by Ageron, *France coloniale*, pp. 131–64; Grupp, *Deutschland, Frankreich und die Kolonien*, pp. 11–43. See also the dissertation by Walker, *The 'Comité de l'Afrique française'*.

[195] Brunschwig, *French Colonialism*, pp. 112–13.

[196] According to the findings by Andrew and Kanya-Forstner, the membership amounted to thirty persons in 1890 (see footnote 194); it rose to forty-eight in 1900. Andrew and Kanya-Forstner, 'The French "Colonial Party"', p. 103.

[197] Ibid., pp. 104–5. The figures presented in Brunschwig, *French Colonialism*, p. 117, are somewhat different.

[198] Brunschwig, ibid., pp. 109–10. See also Andrew and Kanya-Forstner, 'The French "Colonial Party"', pp. 107–8 and footnote 51. The latter two authors have recently refuted the assertion that the *parti colonial* had much more political influence than has hitherto been thought, and that it was actually in the hands of big business: Abrams and Miller, 'Who Were the French Colonialists' and Andrew and Kanya-Forstner, 'French Business and the French Colonialists'.

[199] Ziebura, 'Interne Faktoren des Französischen Hochimperialismus', p. 121. As to Étienne, however, a direct influence on the colonial decisions of the French government can be proved in some cases. To speak of a 'vast power of the colonial party and the *Comité de l'Afrique Française*', as Cooke, *New French Imperialism*, p. 97, does, is probably exaggerated.

[200] There is as yet no satisfactory general interpretation of social Darwinism. Even special studies are not numerous. See the review article by Biddiss, 'Racial Ideas'. The most recent surveys of social Darwinism in the Anglo-Saxon countries are Koch, *Der Sozialdarwinismus*; Bannister, *Social Darwinism*; Jones, *Social Darwinism*. A brief study with bibliographic notes is Zmarzlik, 'Sozialdarwinismus'. A one-sided and incoherent interpretation is Wehler, 'Sozialdarwinismus'. The best starting-point for further research would be the collected essays, *Biologismus im 19. Jahrhundert* (especially pp. 73–93, the contribution by Gunter Mann with extensive bibliographic notes). For the problem of the popularization of Darwinism, see the two books by Henkin, *Darwinism in the English Novel*, and Ellegård, *Darwin and the General Reader*. For the racial element in British imperialism, see also the material put together in Aziz, *The British in India*, pp. 273–83. See also *Der Darwinismus* (especially pp. 95–250).

[201] The path for Darwinism was already so well paved through the doctrine of evolution that it could be said with some exaggeration that Darwinism would have been invented without Darwin. See Burrow, *Evolution and Society*; Koch, *Der Sozialdarwinismus*, pp. 24–37;

Biologismus im 19. Jahrhundert, pp. 19-20, 34.

[202] Bolle, 'Darwinismus', p. 238. On Haeckel, see Gasman, *The Scientific Origins of National Socialism*.

[203] Bagehot, *Physics and Politics*, pp. 43, 49.

[204] Bolle, 'Darwinismus', p. 269. See also Brie, *Der Enfluss der Lehren Darwins*, pp. 9-10. Irvin, *Obez'jany, angely i viktoriancy*. Searle, *Eugenics and Politics;* Jones, *Social Darwinism*, pp. 99-120; Bannister, *Social Darwinism*, pp. 164-79.

[205] On Kidd and Pearson, see Semmel, *Imperialism and Social Reform*, pp. 29-52.

[206] Pearson, *National Life*, p. 54.

[207] Bolle, 'Darwinismus', p. 272. (The passage therein is corrected in Baumgart, *Deutschland im Zeitalter des Imperialismus*, p. 41.) The following quotation, ibid., p. 273. For ideas on eugenics, see also *Biologismus im 19. Jahrhundert*, pp. 73-93; Koch, *Sozialdarwinismus*, pp. 113-25. On German social Darwinism, see also Zmarzlik, 'Der Sozialdarwinismus in Deutschland'.

[208] Novicow, *La Politique internationale*, pp. xxiii, 242.

[209] Seidler, 'Evolutionismus in Frankreich', p. 371.

[210] See Brie, *Der Einfluss der Lehren Darwins*, pp. 15-16.

[211] Pearson, *National Life*, p. 62. See also Koch, *Sozialdarwinismus*, pp. 116-18.

[212] Seidler, 'Evolutionismus in Frankreich'.

[213] For the ensuing account, see Seidler and Nagel, 'Vacher de Lapouge', from whence also the quotation, p. 103.

[214] Wyatt, 'God's Test by War', pp. 592, 595.

[215] Barnaby, *Naval Development*, p. 3.

[216] Berghahn, *Der Tirpitz-Plan*, p. 181, footnote 47.

[217] Marlowe, *Rhodes*, pp. 58-9.

[218] Faber, *The Vision and the Need*, p. 59. 'This apparently widely-used phrase can be found in the book *The Races of Man*, published in 1850, by the Edinburgh anatomist Robert Knox: 'Race is everything; literature, science, art — in a word, civilization depends on it.' See Burrow, *Evolution and Society*, p. 130.

[219] Brunschwig, *French Colonialism*, p. 78.

[220] Faber, *The Vision and the Need*, p. 62.

[221] Ibid., p. 87.

[222] *The Concept of Empire*, p. 315 (No. 86).

[223] Faber, *The Vision and the Need*, p. 127.

[224] See p. 72. In Germany, Friedrich Naumann in 1899 spoke of the 'struggles of the rising and declining nations ... So long as the natural instincts of procreation and eating cannot be inhibited, the reasons why there is struggle among nations for existence will prevail.' (Düding, *Der Nationalsoziale Verein*, p. 72. See also ibid., p. 179, footnote 20.)

[225] Because of the inferiority complex resulting from Sedan (1870), Tel el Kebir (1882), and Fashoda (1898) it was not so widespread with French politicians as with German and Anglo-Saxon politicians. Instead, the propelling or motivating aspect of their social Darwinism was probably stronger than its employment as a justification, as a rationale.

NOTES TO CHAPTER IV

[226] A brief survey of the 'classical' Marxist theses on imperialism is in Schäfer, *Imperialismusthesen*, pp. 13–28. A very comprehensive discussion is Hampe, *Die 'ökonomische Imperialismustheorie'*.

[227] See Langer, 'A Critique of Imperialism', p. 178.

[228] On Hobson and his book on imperialism, see Gann and Duigan, 'Reflections on Imperialism'; Porter, *Critics of Empire*, pp. 168–238; Kettenbach, *Lenins Theorie des Imperialismus*; Fieldhouse, '"Imperialism": An Historiographical Revision'; Fieldhouse, *The Theory of Capitalist Imperialism* (a reader; see especially pp. 120–9, 187–94); Kemp, *Theories of Imperialism*, pp. 30–44 (written from a Marxist point of view; a pretty superficial critique); Lloyd, 'Africa and Hobson's Imperialism'; Cain, 'J. A. Hobson, Cobdenism, and the Radical Theory of Economic Imperialism'; Wilson, 'The Economic Rule and Mainsprings of Imperialism'; Hodgart, *The Economics of European Imperialism*, pp. 25–33; Hampe, *Die 'ökonomische Imperialismustheorie'*, pp. 126–9. The most recent surveys are Eldridge, *Victorian Imperialism*, pp. 124–7; Betts, *The False Dawn*, pp. 135–142; Mommsen, *Imperialismustheorien*, pp. 12–19. Note the constraints which Hobson himself placed on his own interpretation of imperialism in Hobson, *Confessions*.

[229] The most recent research on imperialism has quite adequately stressed the significance of these and other forerunners of the economic theory of imperialism, who emphasized more than previously assumed the drive of the industrial system towards overseas expansion. The most detailed account presently is Semmel, 'The Philosophical Radicals'; Schröder, *Sozialistische Imperialismusdeutung*, pp. 7–15. See also the general account on the Philosophical Radicals by Thomas, *The Philosophical Radicals*.

[230] On this point, see especially Schröder, *Sozialismus und Imperialismus*; Kettenbach, *Lenins Theorie des Imperialismus*, pp. 164–79.

[231] Helphand, *Marineforderungen*, p. 35.

[232] Kettenbach, *Lenins Theorie des Imperialismus*, p. 172.

[233] Hobson, *Imperialism*, p. 217.

[234] See, for example, ibid., pp. 173, 179, 185.

[235] Ibid., p. 73. For the next quotation, ibid, p. 81.

[236] Ibid., p. 51.

[237] Ibid., p. 59.

[238] Ibid., p. 57.

[239] Ibid., pp. 17–20.

[240] In his third edition of 1938 (p. 52), Hobson abridged the table and the commentary heavily. The first edition of 1902 (p. 57) should therefore be used.

[241] Ibid., (third edition), pp. 29, 81, 86–8.

[242] See ibid., pp. 142, 184, 220.

[243] Ibid., p. 171.

[244] On Lenin's theory of imperialism, see Fieldhouse, '"Imperialism": An Historiographical Revision'; Fieldhouse, *The Theory of Capital Imperialism*, pp. 130–7; Stokes, 'Late Nineteenth-Century Colonial

Expansion'; Schmidt and Mommsen, 'Imperialism', pp. 214–20; bibliography, ibid., pp. 227–9. Meyer, 'Lenins Imperialismustheorie'; Schröder, *Sozialistische Imperialismusdeutung*, pp. 48–98; Kemp, *Theories of Imperialism*, pp. 63–85 (superficial and uncritical — e.g. p. 85: Lenin's book on imperialism 'comes nearest to being a full and satisfactory treatment of the subject'; for his own view, see p. 4; see pp. 141–7 on Raymond Aron's critique); Brown, 'A critique of Marxist Theories of Imperialism'; Kiernan, *Marxism and Imperialism*, pp. 37–64 (sympathizing with Lenin's analysis, see ibid., pp. vii–viii: '. . . the only serious theory of imperialsim ever put forward'); Arrighi, *The Geometry of Imperialism* (deals with Lenin's dependence on Hobson). The most recent surveys are Hampe, *Die 'ökonomische Imperialismustheorie'*, pp. 45–55, Eldridge, *Victorian Imperialism*, pp. 124–34; Mommsen, (*Imperialismustheorien*, pp. 40–4; Brewer, *Marxist Theories of Imperialism*, pp. 108–22.

[245] Briefly stated, the difference between the earlier and later Socialist interpretations of imperialism is that the Socialist critics of the phase of economic stagnation (1873–96) emphasized the *diagnosis* of the difficulties of industrial capitalism, whereas after the turn of the century colonial imperialism was, due to the new economic prosperity, regarded as a temporarily effective *therapy* for economic difficulties.

[246] See Stokes, 'Late Nineteenth-Century Colonial Expansion'. The applicability of a notion of imperialism excluding the spectacular and dramatic phase of territorial expansion is, of course, very problematic.

[247] For this remarkably late dating of the beginning of the imperialist period, the evident explanation has been offered (e.g Schröder, *Sozialistische Imperialismusdeutung*, p. 55) that Lenin could thus remove the contradiction between his own attitude towards the World War — which was that the working class should not side with any of the belligerent camps — and the position of Marx and Engels on war — which was that the proletariat should side with the camp most useful for its objectives: relevant utterances by Marx and Engels had been made *before* the period of imperialism, which had its own different circumstances.

[248] Lenin, *Collected Works*, xix, p. 85.

[249] Ibid., p. 91.

[250] Ibid., pp. 167, 192.

[251] Ibid., pp. 138, 154.

[252] Ibid., p. 160.

[253] According to a calculation in Sombart, *Der moderne Kapitalismus*, vol. iii, part I, p. 65, European rule extended as follows:

Continent	1876	1900
Africa	10.8%	90.4%
Polynesia	56.8%	98.9%
Asia	51.5%	56.5%

[254] Terms such as rot, decay, etc. belong to the social-Darwinist vocabulary.

[255] Lenin, *Collected Works*, xix, pp. 135, 143, 166, 167, 169, 186, 192, 193.

[256] The latest accounts of Kautsky's critique of imperialism and his conflict with Lenin are in Schröder, *Sozialistische Imperialismusdeutung*, pp. 14, 40-8; Brewer, *Marxist Theories of Imperialism*, pp. 122-6.

[257] Lenin, *Collected Works*, xix, p. 187.

[258] Ibid., p. 100. For the quotation, ibid., p. 101.

[259] For 'organized' capitalism, which is primarily characterized by tendencies towards concentration and centralization in industry and banking and by increasing state interventionism, see the papers presented to the Regensburg meeting of West German historians: *Der Organisierte Kapitalismus*. The term does not appear, particularly because of its vagueness, to materially advance the debate on imperialism.

[260] Fieldhouse, '"Imperialism": An Historiographical Revision', p. 193.

[261] As cited in Lenin, *Collected Works*, xix, pp. 182-3.

[262] See footnote 240.

[263] Lenin, *Collected Works*, xix, p. 156.

[264] See Hammond, 'Uneconomic Imperialism'; Hammond, *Portugal and Africa*; Hammond, 'Economic Imperialism'.

[265] The most recent account is Girault, *Emprunts russes*. On Russian imperialism in general, see Geyer, *Der russische Imperialismus*.

[266] A recent survey of Italian imperialism distinguishing between an earlier phase, which is mainly non-economic and non-social-economic, and a later phase which is more strongly determined by economic factors is W. Schieder, 'Aspekte des italienischen Imperialismus'.

[267] This state of affairs has been impressively described, alongside Fischer, *War of Illusions*, pp. 8-9, 356, by Poidevin, *Les Relations économiques*; see also his brief survey, Poidevin, 'Weltpolitik allemande'; also Zorn, 'Wirtschaft und Politik im deutschen Imperialismus'. Hobson, too, misrepresented the situation of the German capital market when he wrote: 'Germany was in the early 1900s suffering severely from what is called a glut of capital . . . ' (Hobson, *Imperialism*, p. 80). See the remarks by Helfferich in a confidential meeting in December 1909, to the effect that Germany's position in the international finance business was not based on her own (insufficient) capital, but on her intermediary function in the transactions of foreign capital. 'It is especially in our foreign transactions that we work . . . with foreign capital to an extent that an outsider can hardly realize. That is the business secret, as it were, of the German finance world.' (Witt, *Die Finanzpolitik des Deutschen Reiches*, p. 198).

[268] The insufficiently organized structure of British capital has most recently been pointed out in the survey by Medick, 'Anfänge des Organisierten Kapitalismus in Grossbritannien'.

[269] Lenin, *Collected Works*, xix, p. 92.

[270] Sée, *Histoire économique*, ii. p. 306, footnote 4. For the ensuing remarks, see also Ziebura, 'Interne Faktoren des französischen Hochimperialismus', pp. 86-7; Klein, 'Ein zweitrangiger Imperialismus?' pp. 166-82; *Histoire économique et sociale de la France*, vol. 4, part 1, pp. 257-84.

[271] See Kindleberger, *Economic Growth*, pp. 52, 56 (including bibliography therein).

²⁷² e.g. Lenin, *Collected Works*, xix, p. 138.

²⁷³ See Cairncross, *Home and Foreign Investment*, p. 225; Ziebura, 'Interne Faktoren des französischen Hochimperialismus', pp. 90, 116, 117; Klein, 'Ein zweitrangiger Imperialismus?', pp. 182–5. The most important case-studies are: Poidevin, *Les relations économiques* (for Franco-German relations); Girault, *Emprunts russes* (for Franco-Russian relations); Thobie, *Les Intérêts économiques* (for Franco-Turkish relations). See also Bouvier, 'Les traits majeurs', pp. 308–26; Reuter, *Die Balkanpolitik des französischen Imperialismus*, pp. 62–83.

²⁷⁴ Lenin, *Collected Works*, xix, p. 139.

²⁷⁵ On this question, see the most recent account in Medick, 'Anfänge des Organisierten Kapitalismus in Grossbritannien', pp. 64, 70.

²⁷⁶ For the ensuing remarks, see especially Mommsen, 'Nationale und ökonomische Faktoren', pp. 650–1 (including the bibliography); Hoffman, *Great Britain and the German Trade Rivalry*, p. 30, Fieldhouse, 'The Economic Exploitation of Africa' (especially pp. 626, 646–52); Hobson, *Imperialism*, pp. 28–40. On a number of problems relating to Britain's economic relations with her colonies, esp. with India and her African territories (e.g. the concepts of the 'drain of wealth' and of the 'dual economy') see Albertini, *Europäische Kolonialherrschaft*, *pp.* 10–14, 71–3, 390–403.

²⁷⁷ Hobson, *Imperialism*, p. 40.

²⁷⁸ For the ensuing remarks, see especially Ziebura, 'Interne Faktoren des französischen Hochimperialismus', pp. 105–11 (including the bibliography); Brunschwig, *French Colonialism*, pp. 82–96, 187–93; Ganiage, *L'Expansion coloniale*, pp. 300–12, 320–1, 333–5; Clark, *The Balance Sheets of Imperialism*, pp. 11, 14; Albertini, *Europäische Kolonialherrschaft*, pp. 174–6, 228–21, 278–87.

²⁷⁹ Ferry, *Le Tonkin*, p. 42.

²⁸⁰ Hobson, *Imperialism*, p. 67; also p. 106.

²⁸¹ Gollwitzer, *Europe in the Age of Imperialism*, p. 63.

²⁸² A brief survey also outlining the state of research in this field is Kindleberger, *Economic Growth*, pp. 278–80. The most recent study is Smith, *Tariff Reform in France*.

²⁸³ For ensuing remarks, see Brunschwig, *French Colonialism*, pp. 92–4, 96; Ziebura, 'Interne Faktoren des französischen Hochimperialismus', p. 111; *Histoire économique et sociale de la France*, vol. 4, part 1, pp. 218–23.

²⁸⁴ On the Company, see the account in Galbraith, *Mackinnon*. On the Jaluit Company, see Treue, *Die Jaluit-Gesellschaft*; on the New Guinea Company, see Firth, 'The New Guinea Company'.

²⁸⁵ Coquery-Vidrovitch, *Le Congo*.

²⁸⁶ Galbraith, *Mackinnon*, p. 7.

²⁸⁷ The renowned French economist Paul Leroy-Beaulieu, one of those advocating the economic usefulness of colonies, largely withdrew his economic thesis in the second edition of his book, *La Colonisation chez les peuples modernes* (p. 572): 'To view the advantages of colonies solely on the basis of trade statistics is to consider only a part, and probably not even the most important part, of the connexions exerting

so many different and beneficial effects.' Anticolonialism in France in the early 1870s was mainly due to the general feeling that colonial rule was expensive and would yield a disproportionately low material profit. See Baumgart, 'Das Grössere Frankreich', p. 187. The opposition which, under Clemenceau's leadership, overthrew the Ferry Cabinet in 1885 because of its Indo-China policy, put forward financial- and domestic-policy arguments. See Brötel, *Französischer Imperialismus in Vietnam*, pp. 301, 327–8, 492. For the debates in the Chamber on the budget of the French Sudan (1891–4), see Kanya-Forstner, *The Conquest of the Western Sudan*, pp. 203–5.

288 Brunschwig, *French Colonialism*, pp. 138–9.

289 Ibid., p. 140.

290 For a recent study of him, see Wild, *Baron d'Estournelles de Constant*.

291 Brunschwig, *French Colonialism*, pp. 140–4. See also Ganiage, *L'Expansion coloniale*, pp. 205–6.

292 Dilke, *Problems of Greater Britain*, ii, p. 191.

293 Platt, 'Economic Factors in British Policy', p. 128, footnote 18.

294 Mommsen, 'Nationale und ökonomische Faktoren', p. 629.

295 *Documents diplomatiques français*, le série, xii, p. 117 (No. 68).

296 See Louis, 'The Berlin Congo Conference', pp. 198, 216.

297 See Newbury, 'The Tariff Factor in Anglo-French West African Partition';Newbury, 'The Protectionist Revival in French Colonial Trade'.

298 This aspect has been repeatedly pointed out by Platt in his numerous studies. A critical view is taken, *inter alia*, by Steiner, 'Finance, Trade and Politics', and Eldridge, *England's Mission*, pp. 12–23. A useful general account of the institutional relationship between Britain's foreign policy and her foreign trade is Schädlich, 'Wandlungen in der Aussen-handelsdiplomatie Grossbritanniens'.

299 Platt, 'Economic Factors in British Policy', p. 131.

300 For ensuing remarks, see especially the older books: Feis, *Europe, the World's Banker*; Staley, *War and the Private Investor*; Cairncross, *Home and Foreign Investment*. See also the recent surveys by Segal and Simon, 'British Foreign Capital Issues'; Mommsen, 'Nationale und ökonomische Faktoren'; *The Export of Capital from Britain*.

301 Source material for these figures derives from Staley, *War and the Private Investor*, pp. 523–39; Frankel, *Capital Investment in Africa*, p. 18.

302 See pp. 108–9.

303 Cairncross, *Home and Foreign Investment*, pp. 182–6. Cairncross also discusses the estimates and the bases underlying the calculations, which vary so much in the relevant literature. See also Mommsen, 'Nationale und ökonomische Faktoren', pp. 630, 652–6; Cottrell, *British Overseas Investment*, pp. 27–55.

304 According to Imlah, *Economic Elements*, pp. 72–5, and Mommsen, 'Nationale und ökonomische Faktoren', p. 651; in the latter, the lower turning-point for 1877 and the point for 1899 are inaccurately reproduced. See the charts, which differ partially as to the figures but are essentially the same as to the cycles in Cairncross, *Home and Foreign Investment*, p. 212.

[305] Platt, *Latin America and British Trade*, pp. 279-304.

[306] Frankel, *Capital Investment in Africa*, p. 153.

[307] For ensuing remarks, see Cairncross, *Home and Foreign Investment*, pp. 226-7; Fieldhouse, '"Imperialism": An Historiographical Revision', pp. 198-9.

[308] Dilke, *Problems of Greater Britain*, ii, p. 580.

[309] Cairncross, *Home and Foreign Investment*, pp. 232-3; Saul, *Studies in British Overseas Trade*, e.g. pp. 87, 208, 213. Such reflections, however, were already voiced by political economists of that time, e.g. by Paul Leroy-Beaulieu. See Murphy, *Ideology*, pp. 122-4.

[310] See Mommsen, 'Nationale und ökonomische Faktoren', p. 649.

[311] Ibid., p. 662.

[312] On the 1906 elections, see the recent book by Russell, *Liberal Landslide*.

[313] Brunschwig, *French Colonialism*, p. 76.

[314] For his ideas on colonialism, see above all Murphy, *Ideology*, pp. 103-75.

[315] Leroy-Beaulieu, *De la colonisation*, p. 642. Fieldhouse (*The Theory of Capitalist Imperialism*, p. 73) is in error when he writes that this idea can be found only in the sixth edition of 1908 — probably due to the influence of Hobson's book. It is already expressed in preceding editions.

[316] Lenin, *Collected Works*, xix, p. 162. This statement is basically wrong. See p. 112.

[317] See especially Cameron, *France and the Economic Development of Europe*, in particular pp. 64-88, 204-325; Kindleberger, *Economic Growth*, pp. 36-56 (making extensive use of the controversial literature); Feis, *Europe, the World's Banker*, p. 51; Ziebura, 'Interne Faktoren des französischen Hochimperialismus', pp. 111-18; Michalet, *Les Placements des épargnants français*, pp. 137-50.

[318] See Feis, *Europe, the World's Banker*, p. 51.

[319] Ziebura, 'Interne Faktoren des französischen Hochimperialismus', p. 116.

[320] Brunschwig, 'Politique et économie dans l'empire Français d'Afrique Noire', pp. 408-9.

[321] Ibid., pp. 412-13.

[322] At the turn of the century the forty companies altogether were disposing of capital amounting to 51 million francs. See the detailed account in Coquery-Vidrovitch, *Le Congo*.

[323] See the recent account in Mazenot, *La Likouala-Mossaka*.

[324] See Ziebura, 'Interne Faktoren des französischen Hochimperialismus', p. 118; Kindleberger, *Economic Growth*, p. 59.

[325] Hobson, *Imperialism*, p. 57. The next quote is on p. 59. Other relevant remarks, ibid., pp. 73, 78, 212, 217, 221, 358.

[326] Lenin, *Collected Works*, xix, p. 157.

[327] See Rohe, 'Ursachen und Bedingungen des modernen britischen Imperialismus' (especially p. 69); Medick, 'Anfänge des Organisierten Kapitalismus in Grossbritannien', pp. 72, 73. One of the most thorough recent treatments of the relations between colonial imperialism and the

economic factor is Fieldhouse, *Economics and Empire*. The author, as does also D. C. M. Platt, acknowledges that economic factors played a more important role in late Victorian imperialism than before. The influence of the economic factor (pressure from trade and industry due to the recession of 1873–96, not from finance) in the partition of Africa is stressed by Hynes, *The Economics of Empire*.

[328] Platt, 'The Imperialism of Free Trade', p. 303. On Morier, see the recent biography by Ramm, *Morier*.

[329] This is the much discussed night-watchman's function of the state in the age of *laissez-faire* capitalism, from which it could not help gradually withdrawing in the age of imperialism.

[330] Galbraith, *Mackinnon*, p. 161.

[331] Platt, 'The Imperialism of Free Trade', p. 301. In much the same vein, Salisbury in 1890 placed the interests of investors in South Africa in this perspective: 'On general principles Her Majesty's Government always decline to place the power of the country at the disposal of individual investors to secure investments which they may think fit to make in the territory of another power.' (Robinson and Gallagher, *Africa*, p. 221). A large amount of literature has built up around the role of the capitalists (the Rand mining magnates) in bringing about the incorporation of the Transvaal into British South Africa. It can roughly be divided into two 'schools', one supporting the view, originally put forward by Hobson, that South African politics were decisively influenced by financial interests, the other attacking that view. Some of the most recent participants in the debate are: Mawby, 'Capital, Government and Politics in the Transvaal'; Duminy, *The Capitalists and the Outbreak of the Anglo-Boer War*; Kubicek, *Economic Imperialism*; Porter, *The Origins of the South African War*; Denoon, 'Capital and Capitalists in the Transvaal'.

[332] See Baumgart, 'Das Grössere Frankreich', pp. 189–90. More recently, Cooke, *New French Imperialism*, p. 13.

[333] See Grupp, *Theorie der Kolonialexpansion bei Hanotaux*, pp. 50–3.

[334] Mommsen, 'Nationale und ökonomische Faktoren', p. 660.

[335] Faber, *The Vision and the Need*, p. 69.

[336] Sanderson, *England, Europe and the Upper Nile*, p. 375; see also p. 390. Louis Archinard, former Commandant-Supérieur of the French Sudan, expressed in 1894 his deep distrust of French commercial interests in the following terms: 'One could carefully safeguard the interests of a French trading concern, but we do not rely merely on traders to decide in certain cases whether the interest of the mother country — which has to pay with the blood of her children and her treasure — should be sacrificed to the ambition of founding a colony which will secure for the future a position aspired for among nations.' (Kanya-Forstner, *The Conquest of the Western Sudan*, p. 201, footnote 5.)

[337] Faber, *The Vision and the Need*, p. 71. For the remarks, ibid. p. 121.

[338] Robinson and Gallagher, *Africa*, p. 194.

[339] Böhme, 'Thesen zur Beurteilung des deutschen Imperialismus', p. 41. Manchester was just as little prepared to invest one sixpence in East Africa 'unless the money is safe'. (Galbraith, *Mackinnon*, p. 9).

[340] See p. 111.

[341] Zorn, 'Wirtschaft und Politik im deutschen Imperialismus', p. 349; Fischer, *War of Illusions*, p. 356.

[342] Woolf, *Empire and Commerce in Africa*, pp. 320, 356.

[343] Moon, *Imperialism and World Politics*, p. viii. See also Platt, 'Economic Factors in British Policy', p. 136.

[344] Kemp, *Theories of Imperialism*, pp. 4, 70.

[345] Hallgarten, *Imperialismus vor 1914*. See also the author's more recent account, Hallgarten, 'Der Imperialismus in der historischen Diskussion des Westens'.

[346] Strachey, *The End of the Empire*, pp. 123, 124.

NOTES TO CHAPTER V

[347] For the bibliography on the 'Colonial Reformers', see footnote 229.

[348] Semmel, 'The "Philosophic Radicals"', p. 517.

[349] See p. 6.

[350] See Platt, 'The Imperialism of Free Trade', p. 305, footnote 2; MacDonagh, 'The Anti-Imperialism of Free Trade'.

[351] It is especially Platt who has campaigned against the concept of 'free-trade imperialism'. This idea is based on three premisses: the existence of active state intervention; the drive of British traders towards new markets; and the economic subordination of the backward countries to exports of British industrial goods. Platt points out that the overseas territories which really matter in a debate on free-trade imperialism — the Ottoman Empire, China, and Latin America — lacked basic conditions for implementing imperialism: trade with these countries was hardly a two-way trade since they imported more than they exported; the low purchasing power of the population of these areas meant that there was little prospect of expanding trade; and the markets in these areas were in many respects self-sufficient. British trade therefore sought opportunities for expansion in the established markets — Europe, North America, India, and the other white settlement colonies. See Platt, 'The Imperialism of Free Trade'; and Platt, 'Economic Factors in British Policy'. Platt has met the advocates of the concept of free-trade imperialism halfway in so far as he acknowledges its existence in the decades after 1860. In this context, however, the term 'mid-Victorian' period is limited. See Platt, 'Further Objections'; his basic book, Platt, *Finance, Trade and Politics*; his case-study, Platt, *Latin America and British Trade*; and *Business Imperialism*, a collection of essays which Platt edited (showing that British firms were generally unable to impose their will on the individual South American governments). Other important studies are: Williams, *British Commercial Policy*; Semmel, *The Rise of Free Trade Imperialism* (especially pp. 1–13, 203–29). More recent case-studies: Matthew, 'The Imperialism of Free Trade: Peru' (rejecting the concept for the decades 1820–70); Winn, British

Informal Empire in Uruguay' (supporting it for the nineteenth century throughout); McLean, 'Finance and "Informal Empire"' (equally supporting it in the cases of Turkey, Persia, and China); Hopkins, 'Economic Imperialism in West Africa: Lagos' (agreeing in a limited sense, to its existence in the decades 1880-1900); Harnetty, *Imperialism and Free Trade* (accepting the concept of free-trade imperialism with regard to the interest of the Lancashire cotton industry in India also for the decades prior to 1870); West, 'Theorising about "Imperialism"' (on the difficulties of defining informal and economic imperialism); Knox, 'Reconsidering Mid-Victorian Imperialism' (attempts to mediate between the old concept of anti-imperialism and the new concept of free-trade imperialism); Cain, *Economic Foundations of British Overseas Expansion* (another mediatory attempt).

[352] Hobson, *Imperialism*, pp. 113-52.

[353] Schröder, 'Hobsons Imperialismustheorie', pp. 111-12.

[354] Regarding the term labour aristocracy, see Schröder, *Sozialismus und Imperialismus*, p. 87; Pelling, *Popular Politics*, pp. 37-61. Pelling comes to the conclusion that Lenin's thesis, that the upper parts of the working class have been politically corrupted by imperialism, is demonstrably false (ibid., p. 99). A similar view is to be found in the most recent account on this point, Price, *An Imperial War and the British Working Class*, especially pp. 7-11.

[355] The French Socialist Paul Louis seems to have been the first to point to the corrupting influence of imperialism on the revolutionary consciousness of the workers (in 1899): Louis, 'Le socialisme'. See also Louis, 'La Colonisation'; Schröder, *Sozialistische Imperialismusdeutung*, pp. 65-6, 70-1.

[356] Lenin, *Collected Works*, xix, p. 179.

[357] Wehler, *Bismarck und der Imperialismus*. See my debate with Wehler in Baumgart, 'Zur Theorie des Imperialismus', pp. 5-7, also in *Militärgeschichtliche Mitteilungen*, 10 (1971), pp. 197-207; 12 (1972), pp. 192-202; 14 (1973), pp. 300-3. There was similar controversy between Wehler and Hallgarten in *Geschichte in Wissenschaft und Unterricht*, 22 (1971), pp. 257-65; 23 (1972), p. 226-35; 296-303; 24 (1973), pp. 116-17.

[358] Wehler, *Bismarck und der Imperialismus*, p. 14.

[359] Ibid., p. 25.

[360] *Imperialismus und strukturelle Gewalt*, p. 2.

[361] *Imperialismus*, p. 30.

[362] Rostow, *British Economy*, pp. 7-57.

[363] Rosenberg, *Grosse Depression und Bismarckzeit*, pp. 14-21.

[364] On the difficulties in constructing a model of the growth of the French economy in the second half of the nineteenth century, see Kindleberger, *Economic Growth*, pp. 5-10, 12-13. It is fairly certain that 1867-77 was a period of growth; that 1877-79-82 was a boom period; and 1882-96, without any major interruptions, was a period of stagnation. See however, footnotes 404, 405, and 407; and the most recent surveys in *Histoire économique et sociale de la France*, vol. 3, part 2, pp. 961-1024, vol. 4, part 1, pp. 117-36; *The Cambridge Economic*

History of Europe, vol. 7, part 1, pp. 231–95, 752–4. As for the growth of the German economy see Spree, *Wachstumstrends und Konjunktur-zyklen*, and the survey in the *Handbuch der deutschen Wirtschafts- und Sozialgeschichte*, vol. 2, pp. 204–75.

[365] A brief critical survey of recent research is in Kindleberger, *Economic Growth*, pp. 10–12.

[366] Wehler, *Bismarck und der Imperialismus*, pp. 32–3.

[367] Ibid., p. 23.

[368] Ibid., p. 22.

[369] Ibid., p. 112.

[370] Terms such as 'unevenness' and 'disproportionate growth' of the capitalist economy serve Marxist theorists quite well in explaining economic development which deviates from Marxist dogmas, and thereby preserving the unassailability of these dogmas (even the doctrine of the final collapse of capitalism).

[371] Wehler, *Bismarck und der Imperialismus*, p. 423.

[372] Ibid., p. 454.

[373] Ibid., p. 116.

[374] Ibid., p. 117.

[375] Ziebura, 'Interne Faktoren des französischen Hochimperialismus', p. 96. The quotes are from pp. 116, 124, 125, 126. Wehler characteristically regards Ziebura's essay as confirmation of his thesis of social imperialism. See Baumgart, 'Das Grössere Frankreich', p. 193. Ziebura's conclusions could not have been distorted more thoroughly. They were emphatically reconfirmed by Brötel's analysis of Ferry's policy: 'Sozial-imperialistische Motive, die von der jüngsten deutschen Imperialismus-Forschung — vor allem von Wehler — herausgestellt wurden, gelten für die koloniale Expansion Frankreichs nicht.' ('Social-imperialist motives as they have been emphasized in the most recent German research on imperialism — above all by Wehler — do not apply to France's colonial expansion.') Brötel, *Französischer Imperialismus in Vietnam*, p. 342.

[376] Applying the term social imperialism to the domestic situation in France and ascribing to it a diversionary role after 1885 appears to be particularly absurd. The worse domestic difficulties became, the more colonial activities were paralyzed. Economic difficulties increased also after 1885, as did anticolonialism.

[377] Wehler, *Bismarck und der Imperialismus*, pp. 24, 194.

[378] Ibid., p. 486.

[379] e.g. ibid., pp. 263, 279, 298, 343, 346, 364, 396.

[380] Ibid., p. 279.

[381] It has recently been pointed out that in the case of Bismarck's Samoan policy, economic motives may have played a prominent role, but not social-imperialist ones. Kennedy, 'Bismarck's Imperialism'.

[382] Wehler, *Bismarck und der Imperialismus*, p. 364. The quotations are from pp. 364–6.

[383] Bley, *Kolonialherrschaft und Sozialstruktur in Deutsch-Südwest-afrika*, p. 18.

[384] Wehler, *Bismarck und der Imperialismus*, pp. 315–16.

[385] Ibid., pp. 301–3. The quotations are from p. 279.

[386] Ibid., pp. 336–40.

[387] Ibid., pp. 237, 289, 290–1, 352, 353, 360, 408, 445. The quotation is from p. 305.

[388] Ibid., p. 237.

[389] Ibid., p. 353. The quotation is from p. 289.

[390] Ibid., p. 319.

[391] Ibid., p. 362.

[392] Ibid., p. 362–3.

[393] Ibid., p. 408.

[394] Ibid., p. 410.

[395] Bismarck, *Gesammelte Werke*, viii, p. 646.

[396] Wehler, *Bismarck und der Imperialismus*, pp. 408, 411.

[397] Böhme, 'Thesen zur Beruteilung des deutschen Imperialismus', pp. 52–3.

[398] Ibid., p. 41–2.

[399] Rostow, *Stages*, pp. 4–92. For literature on the debate sparked by Rostow's theory of stages, see Wehler, *Bismarck und der Imperialismus*, p. 40, footnote 3.

[400] On the difficulties in determining a take-off period for the industrialization in France, see Lévy-Leboyer, 'La croissance économique en France'.

[401] Saul, *The Myth of the Great Depression*, pp. 14–15.

[402] Remarks are based on the critical survey by Saul, *The Myth of the Great Depression*. See the bibliography, ibid., pp. 56–62. See also Saul, *Studies in British Overseas Trade*, pp. 90–133; Seaman, *Victorian England*, pp. 262–79.

[403] Unevenness is also a feature of French foreign trade for the years 1873–96. The term stagnation is, generally speaking, not applicable. On the contrary, despite annual fluctuations, there is a considerable increase of almost 100 per cent (index for exports: 1870=60; 1896=104; for imports: 1870=51; 1896=108). See Lévy-Leboyer, 'La croissance économique en France', the table following p. 802.

[404] The index for French industrial production (less the building trades) in five-year intervals is: 1870=63; 1875=81; 1880=88; 1885 =92; 1890=100; 1895=109. It should be noted that France, because of the war and its aftermath, did not experience a boom in 1869–73 as did Britain and Germany. See also ibid., the table following p. 802.

[405] Rosenberg, *Grosse Depression*, p. 47.

[406] In France real wages rose steadily between 1857 and 1905 to double the amount. See Lévy-Leboyer, 'La croissance économique en France', p. 795.

[407] Rostow, *British Economy of the Nineteenth Century*, p. 96. The quotation is from p. 104.

[408] Saul, *The Myth of the Great Depression*, p. 30. The most recent study of unemployment in Britain is Harris, *Unemployment and Politics*. (Statistics are on p. 374).

[409] See pp. 108–9.

[410] See Tetzlaff, *Koloniale Entwicklung*, p. 292.

[411] Brunschwig, *French Colonialism*, p. 191. The English and French

versions of Brunschwig's book (*Mythes et réalités de l'impérialisme colonial français 1871-1914*, Paris, 1960, p. 93) give differenct figures in this respect. For Britain, see Hobson, *Imperialism*, pp. 32-8. A warning against theories propounding a close connection between foreign trade and foreign policy is raised by Birken, '*Das Verhältnis von Aussenhandel und Aussenpolitik*'.

[412] In an essay entitled 'Saving, Investment and Imperialism), Zimmermann and Grumbach have shown by econometric means that imperialism constituted a stabilizing factor for the British economy between 1880 and 1910 with the following logic: when investment at home declined, the export of capital increased; in turn, this entailed an expansion of commodity exports and thereby maintained or raised the level of national income. To prove this sort of mechanism is indeed very important. However, no *cause* of imperialism has been explained; rather, imperialism was seen as a *means* of maintaining the level of national income. This appears to be the assumption of the authors themselves when they write on p. 3: 'that before 1914 capital–export – *made possible* by the imperialistic policy – . . . ' [Italics supplied.] Secondly, when Zimmermann and Grumbach speak of 'foreign investments', no distinction is made between investments in colonies and investments in third countries. The mistake made by Hobson is thus repeated.

[413] Mommsen, 'Nationale und ökonomische Faktoren', p. 642.

[414] Along with the advocates of the measure there were, however, some chambers of commerce that opposed it. See Galbraith, *Mackinnon*, p. 215. The Mombasa railway from the East coast into the interior was primarily built for strategic reasons. It was designed to support the flank of the Dongola expedition pushing ahead, also by rail, from Egypt to the south against the Mahdis, and to transport Indian troops as quickly as possible. Construction of the railway line was justified to the public on humanitarian grounds: it would, for example, eliminate the need for slaves to carry goods from the interior to the coast. See Robinson and Gallagher, *Africa*, pp. 308-10, 350-1. A relevant monograph is Hill, *Permanent Way*.

[415] Semmel, *Imperialism and Social Reform*; Searle, *The Quest for National Efficiency*; Scally, *The Origins of the Lloyd George Coalition*. On the misuse of the term social imperialism by Wehler, see also Ely, 'Defining Social Imperialism'; Ely, 'Social Imperialism in Germany'; Forbes, 'Social Imperialism'.

[416] Hobsbawm, *Industry and Empire*, p. 110.

[417] Searle, *The Quest for National Efficiency*, p. 12. For the remarks in the following paragraph see Hollenberg, *Englisches Interesse am Kaiserreich*; Kennedy, *The Rise of the Anglo-German Antagonism*.

[418] See Anderson, *A Liberal State at War*.

[419] This is the title of the book by Searle.

[420] See pp. 76-77.

[421] Searle, *The Quest for National Efficiency*, pp. 34-53.

[422] Faber, *The Vision and the Need*, p. 70. See also James, *Rosebery*, p. 158.

[423] Semmel, *Imperialism and Social Reform*, p. 62.

[424] Ibid., p. 63. See also Matthew, *The Liberal Imperialists*, p. 141.

[425] Searle, *The Quest for National Efficiency*, p. 114. See also Matthew, *The Liberal Imperialists*, p. 148.

[426] This idea of establishing a national government — there were corresponding concepts in Germany at that time — was expressed by another Liberal Imperialist, Henry H. Fowler, during the Boer War in the following terms: 'We are Englishmen first, and Liberals and Conservatives after.' (Matthew, *The Liberal Imperialists*, p. 178).

[427] James, *Rosebery*, p. 426.

[428] The most recent studies are Matthew, *The Liberal Imperialists*, pp. 79-121; and Scally, *The Origins of the Lloyd George Coalition*, pp. 48-72.

[429] Semmel, *Imperialism and Social Reform*, pp. 72-82; Scally, *The Origins of the Lloyd George Coalition*, pp. 73-95.

[430] Semmel, *Imperialism and Social Reform*, pp. 70-2.

[431] Ibid., p. 73.

[432] Ibid., pp. 222-33. The quotations are from pp. 233 and 229.

[433] Ibid., p. 169.

[434] Ibid., p. 101. The most recent account is Sykes, *Tariff Reform* (especially pp. 55-77).

[435] For the debate between the protectionists under Chamberlain and the advocates of free trade within the Unionists, see the recent account in Rempel, *Unionists Divided*. Chamberlain managed to swing the Unionists over to the idea of protective tariffs in the years up to 1910, but the protectionist debate resulted in a heavy drain on Unionist membership. See also Judd, *Radical Joe*, pp. 238-63; Jay, *Chamberlain*, pp. 285-315, 344-6.

[436] Semmel, *Imperialism and Social Reform*, p. 122. Schröder, *Imperialismus und antidemokratisches Denken*, pp. 57-8, stresses the point that Milner's imperialism was of a genuine and not of a functional type.

[437] Semmel, *Imperialism and Social Reform*, pp. 112, 117.

[438] On the importance of campaigning for protectionism and free trade that preceded the 1906 elections, see the new account in Russell, *Liberal Landslide*, pp. 65-70, 84-91, 172-82.

[439] The most recent accounts are Emy, *Liberals, Radicals and Social Politics*; Searle, *The Quest for National Efficiency*, pp. 142-256; and especially Scally, *The Origins of the Lloyd George Coalition*.

Bibliography

Abrams, L., and Miller, D.J., 'Who were the French Colonialists? A re-assessment of the *parti colonial*, 1890-1914', *The Historical Journal*, 19 (1976) pp. 685-725.

Africa and its Explorers. Motives, Methods and Impact. Ed. by Robert I. Rotberg. Cambridge, Mass., 1970.

Ageron, Charles-Robert, 'Gambetta et la reprise de l'expansion coloniale', *Revue française d'histoire d'outre-mer*, 59 (1972), pp. 165-204.

Ageron, Charles-Robert, *L'Anticolonialisme en France de 1871 à 1914*. [*Documents choisis et présentés par –.*] Paris, 1973.

Ageron, Charles-Robert, *France coloniale ou parti colonial?* Paris, 1978.

Albertini, Rudolf von, *Europäische Kolonialherrschaft 1880-1940*. Zurich, 1976.

Anderson, Olive, *A Liberal State at War. English Politics and Economics during the Crimean War*. London, 1967.

Andrew, Christopher, *Théophile Delcassé and the Making of the Entente Cordiale*. London, 1968.

Andrew, C.M., and Kanya-Forstner, Alexander S., 'French Business and the French Colonialists', *The Historical Journal*, 19 (1976), pp. 981-1000.

Andrew, C.M., and Kanya-Forstner, Alexander S., 'The French "Colonial Party": its composition, aims and influence, 1885-1914', *The Historical Journal*, 14 (1971), pp. 99-128.

Anstey, Roger T., 'Capitalism and Slavery: a critique', *The Economic History Review*, 2nd series, 21 (1968), pp. 307-20.

Anti-Slavery, Religion and Reform. Essays in Memory of Roger Anstey. Ed. by Christine Bolt and Seymour Drescher. Folkestone, 1980.

Arrighi, Giovanni, *The Geometry of Imperialism*. London, 1978. [Transl. from the Italian.]

Asiegbu, Johnson U.J., *Slavery and the Politics of Liberation 1787-1861. A Study of Liberated African Emigration and British Anti-Slavery Policy*. London, 1969.

Axelson, Eric, *Portugal and the Scramble for Africa 1875-1891*. Johannesburg, 1967.

Aziz, Khursheed Kamal, *The British in India. A Study in Imperialism*. Islamabad, 1976.

Bagehot, Walter, *Physics and Politics or Thoughts on the Application of the Principles of 'Natural Selection' and 'Inheritance' to Political Society*. 2nd ed., London, 1873. [1st ed., London 1872.]

Bannister, Robert C., *Social Darwinism. Science and Myth in Anglo-American Social Thought*. Philadelphia, 1979.

Barnaby, Nathaniel, *Naval Development in the Century*. London, 1903.

Baumgart, Winfried, 'Zur Theorie des Imperialismus'. *Aus Politik und Zeitgeschichte. Beilage zur Wochenzeitung 'Das Parlament'*, B 23/71 (5 June 1971), pp. 3–11.

Baumgart, Winfried, *Vom Europäischen Konzert zum Völkerbund. Friedensschlüsse und Friedenssicherung von Wien bis Versailles*. Darmstadt, 1973.

Baumgart, Winfried, '"Das Grössere Frankreich'. Neue Forschungen über den französischen Imperialismus 1880–1914', *Vierteljahrsschrift für Sozial- und Wirtschaftsgeschichte*, 61 (1974), pp. 185–98.

Baumgart, Winfried, *Deutschland im Zeitalter des Imperialismus (1890–1914). Grundkräfte, Thesen und Strukturen*. 3rd ed., Frankfurt/M., 1979. [1st ed., 1972.]

Baumhögger, Goswin, '*Die Geschichte Ostafrikas im Spiegel der neueren Literatur*', *Geschichte in Wissenschaft und Unterricht*, 22 (1971), pp. 678–704, 747–68.

Berger, Heinrich, *Mission und Kolonialpolitik. Die katholische Mission in Kamerun während der deutschen Kolonialzeit*. Immensee, 1978.

Berghahn, Volker R., *Der Tirpitz-Plan. Genesis und Verfall einer innenpolitischen Krisenstrategie unter Wilhelm II*. Düsseldorf, 1971.

Berichte, Stenographische —: see under *Stenographische Berichte*.

Bethel, Leslie, *The Abolition of the Brazilian Slave Trade. Britain, Brazil and the Slave Trade Question 1807–1869*. Cambridge, 1970.

Betts, Raymond F., *The False Dawn. European Imperialism in the Nineteenth Century*. Minneapolis, 1976.

Biddiss, Michael D., 'Racial Ideas and the Politics of Prejudice 1850–1914', *The Historical Journal*, 15 (1972), pp. 570–82.

Biologismus im 19. Jahrhundert. Vorträge eines Symposiums vom 30. bis 31. Oktober 1970 in Frankfurt am Main. Ed. by Gunter Mann. Stuttgart, 1973.

Birken, Andreas, 'Das Verhältnis von Aussenhandel und Aussenpolitik und die Quantifizierung von Aussenbeziehungen. Beobachtungen zum "Zeitalter des Imperialismus" 1880–1913', *Vierteljahrschrift für Sozial- und Wirtschaftsgeschichte*, 66 (1979), pp. 317–61.

Bismarck, Otto von, *Die gesammelten Werke*. Vol. 8. Gespräche. Ed. by Willy Andreas. Berlin, 1926.

Blake, Robert, *Disraeli*. London, 1966.

Bley, Helmut, *Kolonialherrschaft und Sozialstruktur in Deutsch-Südwestafrika 1894–1914*. Hamburg, 1968.

Blinkhorn, Martin, 'Spain: The "Spanish Problem" and the Imperial Myth', *Journal of Contemporary History*, 15 (1980), pp. 5–25.

Böhme, Helmut, 'Thesen zur Beurteilung der gesellschaftlichen, wirtschaftlichen und politischen Ursachen des deutschen Imperialismus', *Der moderne Imperialismus*. Ed. and introd. by Wolfgang J. Mommsen. Stuttgart, 1971, pp. 31–59.

Bolle, Fritz, 'Darwinismus und Zeitgeist', *Das Wilhelminische Zeitalter*. Stuttgart, 1967, pp. 235–87.

Borzunov, B.F., *Transsibirskaja magistral' v mirovoj politike velikich deržav* [The Trans-Siberian Railway in the global policy of the great powers]. Moscow, 1974.

Bouvier, Jean, 'Les traits majeurs de l'impérialisme français avant 1914', Jean Bouvier and René Girault, *L'impérialisme français d'avant 1914. Recueil de textes.* Paris, 1976, pp. 305-33.

Brewer, Anthony, *Marxist Theories of Imperialism. A Critical Survey.* London, 1980.

Brie, Friedrich, *Der Einfluss der Lehren Darwins auf den britischen Imperialismus.* Freiburg i. B., 1927.

Brie, Friedrich, *Imperialistische Strömungen in der englischen Literatur.* 2nd ed., Halle/S., 1928. [1st ed., 1916.]

Brötel, Dieter, *Französischer Imperialismus in Vietnam. Die koloniale Expansion und die Errichtung des Protektorates Annam-Tongking 1880-1885.* Zurich and Freiburg i.B., 1971.

Brown, Michael B., 'A Critique of Marxist Theories of Imperialism', *Studies in the Theory of Imperialism.* Ed. by Roger Owen and Bob Sutcliffe. London, 1972, pp. 35-70.

Brown, Roger G., *Fashoda Reconsidered. The Impact of Domestic Politics on French Policy in Africa 1893-1898.* Baltimore and London, 1970.

Brunschwig, Henri, *L'avènement de l'Afrique noire.* Paris, 1963.

Brunschwig, Henri, *French Colonialism 1871-1914.* London, 1966. [Transl. from the French.]

Brunschwig, Henri, *Brazza explorateur.* [Vol. 1.] *L'Ogooué. 1875-1879.* [Vol. 2.] *Les Traités Makoko. 1880-1882.* Paris and The Hague, 1966-72.

Brunschwig, Henri, 'Politique économique dans l'empire Français d'Afrique Noire 1870-1914', *The Journal of African History,* 11 (1970), pp. 401-17.

Brunschwig, Henri, *Le Partage de l'Afrique noire.* Paris, 1971.

Brunschwig, Henri, 'Anglophobia and French African Policy', *France and Britain in Africa. Imperial Rivalry and Colonial Rule.* Ed. by Prosser Gifford and William R. Louis. New Haven and London, 1971, pp. 3-34.

Brunschwig, Henri, '"Scramble" et "Course au Clocher"', *The Journal of African History,* 12 (1971), pp. 139-41.

Bueb, Volkmar, *Die 'Junge Schule' der französischen Marine. Strategie und Politik 1875-1900.* Boppard, 1971.

[Bülow, Bernhard von], *Fürst Bülows Reden nebst urkundlichen Beiträgen zu seiner Politik . . .* Ed. by Jonannes Penzler. Vol. 1. Berlin, 1907.

Burrow, John W., *Evolution and Society. A Study in Victorian Social Theory.* Cambridge, 1966.

Business Imperialism 1840-1930. An Inquiry based on British Experience in Latin America. Ed. by Desmond C. M. Platt. Oxford, 1977.

Cain, Peter J., 'J. A. Hobson, Cobdenism, and the Radical Theory of Economic Imperialism, 1898-1914', *The Economic History Review,* 2nd series, 31 (1978), pp. 565-84.

Cain, Peter J., *Economic Foundations of British Overseas Expansion 1815-1914.* London, 1980.

Cain, Peter J., and Hopkins, Antony G., 'The Political Economy of

British Expansion Overseas, 1750–1914', *The Economic History Review*, 2nd series, 33 (1980), pp. 463–90.

Cambridge Economic History of Europe, The —. Vol. 7. The Industrial Economics: Capital, Labour, and Enterprise. Part 1. Britain, France, Germany, and Scandinavia. Ed. by Peter Mathias and M. M. Postan. Cambridge, 1978.

Cairncross, Alexander K., *Home and Foreign Investment 1870–1913. Studies in Capital Accumulation*. Cambridge, 1953. [Repr. Clifton, NJ, 1972.]

Cameron, Rondo E., *France and the Economic Development of Europe 1800–1914. Conquests of Peace and Seeds of War*. Princeton, NJ, 1961.

Caplan, Gerald L., 'Barotseland's Scramble for Protection', *The Journal of African History*, 10 (1969), pp. 277–94.

Carr, Raymond, *Spain, 1808–1939*. Oxford, 1966.

Cecil, Lady Gwendolen, *Life of Robert Maquis of Salisbury*. Vol. 4. 1887–1892. London, 1932.

Chamberlain, Joseph, *Speeches*. Ed. by Charles W. Boyd. Vol. 1. London, 1914.

Clark, Grover, *The Balance Sheets of Imperialism. Facts and Figures on Colonies*. New York, 1936.

Colonialism in Africa 1870–1960. Vol. 1. The History and Politics of Colonialism 1870–1914. Ed. by Lewis H. Gann and Peter Duignan. Cambridge, 1969. Vol. 5. A Bibliographical Guide to Colonialism in Sub-Saharan Africa. By Peter Duignan and Lewis H. Gann. Cambridge. 1973.

Concept of Empire. The —. *Burke to Attlee 1774–1947*. Ed. by George Bennet. London, 1953. 2nd ed., 1962.

Conrad, Robert, *The Destruction of Brazilian Slavery 1850–1888*. Berkeley, 1973.

Cooke, James J., *New French Imperialism 1880–1910: The Third Republic and Colonial Expansion*. Newton Abbot· and Hamden, Conn., 1973.

[Coquery-Vidrovitch, Catherine], *Brazza et la prise de possession du Congo. La mission de l'Ouest-Africain 1883–1885*. Introduction et choix de textes par Catherine Coquery-Vidrovitch avec le concours de Otto Gollnhofer [*et alia*]. Paris and The Hague, 1969.

Coquery-Vidrovitch, Catherine, *Le Congo au temps des grandes compagnies concessionnaires 1898–1930*. Paris and The Hague, 1972.

Cottrell, P.L., *British Overseas Investment in the Nineteenth Century*. London, 1975.

Cunningham, Hugh, 'Jingoism and the Working Classes 1877–78', *Bulletin of the Society for the Study of Labour History*, No. 19 (1969), pp. 6–8.

Dachs, Anthony J., 'Missionary Imperialism — the Case of Bechuanaland', *The Journal of African History*, 13 (1972), pp. 647–58.

Darwinismus, Der —. *Die Geschichte einer Theorie*. Ed. by Günter Altner. Darmstadt, 1981.

Denoon, Donald, 'Capital and Capitalists in the Transvaal in the 1890s and 1900s', *The Historical Journal*, 23 (1980), pp. 111–32.

Dike, K. Onwuka, *Trade and Politics in the Niger Delta 1830–1885. An Introduction to the Economic and Political History of Nigeria.* Oxford, 1956.

Dilke, Charles W., *Problems of Greater Britain.* 2 vols., London, 1890.

[Disraeli, Benjamin], *Selected Speeches of . . . the Earl of Beaconsfield.* Arranged and ed. . . . by T. E. Kebbel. Vol. 2. London, 1882.

Documents diplomatiques français (1871–1914). [Ed. by] Ministère des affaires étrangères. Commission de publication des documents relatifs aux origines de la guerre de 1914, 1re série (1871–1900). Paris. – Vol. 3. 1931. – Vol. 11. 1947. – Vol. 12. 1951. – Vol. 13. 1953. – Vol. 14. 1957. – Vol. 16. 1959. – 2me série (1901–1911). Paris. – Vol. 4. 1932.

Drescher, Seymour, *Econocide. British Slavery in the Era of Abolition.* Pittsburgh, 1977.

Düding, Dieter, *Der Nationalsoziale Verein. Der gescheiterte Versuch einer parteipolitischen Synthese von Nationalismus, Sozialismus und Liberalismus.* Munich and Vienna, 1972.

Duignan, Peter, and Gann, Lewis H., *A Bibliographical Guide to Colonialism in Sub-Saharan Africa.* Cambridge, 1973.

Duminy, A.H., *The Capitalists and the Outbreak of the Anglo-Boer War.* Durban, 1977.

Dunmore, John, *French Explorers in the Pacific.* Oxford, 1969.

Dunn, Ross E., *Resistance in the Desert. Moroccan Responses to French Imperialism 1881–1912.* London, 1977.

Eisenbahnen Afrikas, Die –. Grundlagen und Gesichtspunkte für eine koloniale Eisenbahnpolitik in Afrika. Berlin, 1907.

Eldridge, C.C., *England's Mission. The Imperial Idea in the Age of Gladstone and Disraeli 1868–1880.* London, 1973.

Eldridge, C.C., *Victorian Imperialism.* London, 1978.

Ellegård, Alvar, *Darwin and the General Reader. The Reception of Darwin's Theory of Evolution in the British Periodical Press, 1859–1872.* Göteborg, 1958.

Ely, Geoff, 'Defining Social Imperialism: use and abuse of an idea', *Social History,* 1 (1976), pp. 265–90.

Ely, Geoff, 'Social Imperialism in Germany. Reformist synthesis or reactionary sleight of hand?' *Imperialismus im 20. Jahrhundert. Gedenkschrift für George W. F. Hallgarten.* Ed. by Joachim Radkau and Imanuel Geiss. Munich, 1976, pp. 71–86.

Emy, H.V., *Liberals, Radicals and Social Politics 1892–1914.* Cambridge, 1973.

Erusalimskij, Arkadij S., *Kolonial'naja èkspansija kapitalističeskich deržav i osvoboditel'noe dviženie narodov južoj Afriki i Kitaja v XVII–XIX vv.* [The Colonial Expansion of the Capitalist Powers and the Liberation Movement of the Peoples of Southern Africa and China from the Seventeenth to the Nineteenth Centuries.] Moscow, 1974.

Expansion and Reaction. Ed. by H. L. Wesseling. Leiden, 1978.

Export of Capital from Britain 1870–1914. The –. Ed. . . . by Alan R. Hall. London, 1968.

Faber, Richard, *The Vision and the Need. Late Victorian Imperialist Aims.* London, 1966.

Farnie, Douglas A., *East and West of Suez. The Suez Canal in History 1854-1956*. Oxford, 1969.

Fay, Charles R., *Imperial Economy and its Place in the Formation of Economic Doctrine 1600-1932*. Oxford, 1934.

Fay, Charles R., 'The Movement towards Free Trade, 1820-1853', *The Cambridge History of the British Empire*, vol. 2. The Growth of the New Empire 1783-1870. Cambridge, 1940, pp. 388-414.

Feis, Herbert, *Europe, the World's Banker: 1870-1914. An Account of European Foreign Investment and the Connection of World Finance with Diplomacy before the War*. New Haven, 1930. [Repr. New York, 1965.]

Ferry, Jules, *Le Tonkin et la Mère-Patrie. Témoignages et documents*. Paris, 1890.

Fieldhouse, David K., '"Imperialism": an Historiographical Revision', *The Economic History Review*, 2nd series, 14 (1961), pp. 187-209.

Fieldhouse, David K., *The Colonial Empires. A Comparative Survey from the Eighteenth Century*. London, 1966.

Fieldhouse, David K., *The Theory of Capitalist Imperialism*. London, 1967.

Fieldhouse, David K., 'The Economic Exploitation of Africa: Some British and French comparisons', *France and Britain in Africa. Imperial Rivalry and Colonial Rule*. Ed. by Prosser Gifford and William R. Louis. New Haven and London, 1971, pp. 593-662.

Fieldhouse, David K., *Economics and Empire 1830-1914*. London, 1973.

Firth, S.G., 'The New Guinea Company, 1885-1899: A Case of Unprofitable Imperialism', *Historical Studies*, 15 (1972), pp. 361-77.

Fischer, Fritz, *Krieg der Illusionen. Die deutsche Politik von 1911 bis 1914*. Düsseldorf, 1969. — English translation: *War of Illusions: German Policies from 1911 to 1914*. With a foreword by Sir Alan Bullock. Transl. from the German by Marian Jackson. London, 1975.

Forbes, Ian L. D., 'Social Imperialism and Wilhelmine Germany', *The Historical Jouranl*, 22 (1979), pp. 331-49.

Frankel, S. Herbert, *Capital Investment in Africa. Its course and effects*. London, 1938.

Fyfe, Christopher, *A History of Sierra Leone*. London, 1962.

Galbraith, John S., 'The "Turbulent Frontier" as a Factor in British Expansion', *Comparative Studies in Society and History*, 2 (1959-60), pp. 150-68.

Galbraith, John S., *Mackinnon and East Africa 1878-1895. A Study in the 'New Imperialism'*. Cambridge, 1972.

Gallagher, John, and Robinson, Ronald, 'The Imperialism of Free Trade', *The Economic History Review*, 2nd series, 6 (1953), pp. 1-15.

Ganiage, Jean, *Les Origines du protectorat français en Tunisie (1861-1881)*. Paris, 1959.

Ganiage, Jean, *L'Expansion coloniale de la France sous la Troisième République (1871-1914)*. Paris, 1968.

Ganiage, Jean, 'France, England and the Tunisian Affair', *France and Britain in Africa. Imperial Rivalry and Colonial Rule*. Ed. by Prosser

Gifford and William R. Louis. New Haven and London, 1971, pp. 35-72.

Gann, Lewis H., and Duignan, Peter, 'Reflections on Imperialism and the Scramble for Africa', *Colonialism in Africa 1870-1960*, vol. 1. The History and Politics of Colonialism 1870-1914. Ed. by Lewis H. Gann and Peter Duignan. Cambridge, 1969, pp. 100-29.

Garvin, James L., *The Life of Joseph Chamberlain*. Vol. 3. 1894-1900. Empire and World Policy. London, 1934.

Gasman, Daniel, *The Scientific Origins of National Socialism. Social Darwinism in Ernst Haeckel and the German Monist League*. London, 1971.

Geyer, Dietrich, *Der russische Imperialismus. Studien über den Zusammenhang von innerer und auswärtiger Politik 1860-1914*. Göttingen, 1977.

Gillard, David, *The Struggle for Asia 1828-1914. A Study in British and Russian Imperialism*. London, 1977.

Girard, L., '"From Sea to Sea": The era of transcontinentals', *The Cambridge Economic History of Europe*, vol. 6, part 1. Cambridge, 1966, pp. 249-70.

Girardet, Raoul, *Le Nationalisme français 1871-1914. Textes choisis et présentés par —*. 2nd ed., Paris, 1966.

Girardet, Raoul, *L'Idée coloniale en France de 1871 à 1962*. Paris, 1972.

Girault, René, *Emprunts russes et investissements français en Russie 1887-1914. Recherches sur l'investissement international*. Paris, 1973.

Gollwitzer, Heinz, *Europe in the Age of Imperialism 1880-1914*. London, 1969.

Gollwitzer, Heinz, *Geschichte des weltpolitischen Denkens*. Vol. 1. Vom Zeitalter der Entdeckungen bis zum Beginn des Imperialismus. Göttingen, 1972.

Graham, Gerald S., *Tides of Empire. Discursions on the Expansion of Britain Overseas*. Montreal and London, 1972.

Granjel, Luis S., *La Generación literaria del noventa y ocho*. Salamanca, 1966.

Great Britain and the Colonies 1815-1865. Ed. with an introduction by A. G. L. Shaw. London, 1970.

Grenville, John A.S., *Lord Salisbury and Foreign Policy. The Close of the Nineteenth Century*. London, 1964.

Groves, Charles Pelham, 'Missionary and Humanitarian Aspects of Imperialism from 1870 to 1914', *Colonialism in Africa 1870-1960*, vol. 1. The History and Politics of Colonialism 1870-1914. Ed. by Lewis H. Gann and Peter Duignan. Cambridge, 1969, pp. 462-96.

Grupp, Peter, *Theorie der Kolonialexpansion und Methoden der imperialistischen Aussenpolitik bei Gabriel Hanotaux*. Bern and Frankfurt/M., 1972.

Grupp, Peter, *Deutschland, Frankreich und die Kolonien. Der französische 'Parti Colonial' und Deutschland von 1890 bis 1914*. Tübingen, 1980.

Guillen, Pierre, 'The Entente of 1904 as a Colonial Settlement', *France and Britain in Africa. Imperial Rivalry and Colonial Rule*. Ed. by

Prosser Gifford and William R. Louis. New Haven and London, 1971, pp. 333-68.

Hallgarten, George W. F., *Imperialismus vor 1914. Die soziologischen Grundlagen der Aussenpolitik europäischer Grossmächte vor dem ersten Weltkrieg.* 2 Vols. 2nd ed., Munich, 1963. [1st ed., Munich, 1951.]

Hallgarten, George W. F., 'Der Imperialismus in der historischen Diskussion des Westens nach dem Zweiten Weltkriege', *Deutschland in der Weltpolitik des 19. und 20. Jahrhunderts.* Ed. by Imanuel Geiss and Bernd Jürgen Wendt. Düsseldorf, 1973, pp. 419-36.

Halstead, John P., and Porcari, Serafino, *Modern Imperialism. A bibliography of Books and Articles, 1815-1972.* 2 Vols. Boston, 1974.

Hammer, Karl, *Weltmission und Kolonialismus. Sendungsideen des 19. Jahrhunderts im Konflikt.* Munich, 1978.

Hammond, Richard J., 'Economic Imperialism: sidelights on a stereotype', *The Journal of Economic History*, 21 (1961), pp. 528-98.

Hammond, Richard J., *Portugal and Africa, 1815-1910: a Study in Uneconomic Imperialism.* Stanford, Calif., 1966.

Hammond, Richard J., 'Uneconomic Imperialism: Portugal in Africa before 1910', *Colonialism in Africa 1870-1960*, vol. 1. The History and Politics of Colonialism 1870-1914. Ed. by Lewis H. Gann and Peter Duignan. Cambridge, 1969, pp. 352-82.

Hampe, Peter, *Die 'ökonomische Imperialismustheorie'. Kritische Untersuchungen.* Munich, 1976.

Handbuch der deutschen Wirtschafts- und Sozialgeschichte. Ed. by Hermann Aubin and Wolfgang Zorn. Vol. 2. Stuttgart, 1976.

Hanke, Michael, *Das Werk Alfred T. Mahans. Darstellung und Analyse.* Osnabrück, 1974.

Hargreaves, John D., *Prelude to the Partition of West Africa.* London, 1963.

Hargreaves, John D., *West Africa Partitioned.* Vol. 1. The Loaded Pause, 1885-89. London, 1975.

Harnetty, Peter, *Imperialism and Free Trade: Lancashire and India in the Mid-Nineteenth Century.* Manchester, 1972.

Harris, José, *Unemployment and Politics. A Study in English Social Policy 1886-1914.* Oxford, 1972.

Hellberg, Carl J., *Missions on a Colonial Frontier West of Lake Victoria. Evangelical Missions in North-West Tanganyika to 1932.* Lund, 1965.

Helphand, Alexander [pseudonym Parvus], *Marineforderungen, Kolonialpolitik und Arbeiterinteressen.* Dresden, 1898.

Henkin, Leo J., *Darwinism in the English Novel 1860-1910. The Impact of Evolution on Victorian Fiction.* New York, 1963.

Hertslet, Edward, *The Map of Africa by Treaty.* 3 Vols. 3rd ed., London, 1909. [Repr. London, 1967.]

Hildebrand, Klaus, 'Grossbritannien und die deutsche Reichsgründung', *Historische Zeitschrift.* Beiheft 6 (Neue Folge). Europa und die Reichsgründung. Preussen-Deutschland in der Sicht der grossen europäischen Mächte 1860-1880. Ed. by Eberhard Kolb. Munich, 1980, pp. 9-62.

Hill, M.F., *Permanent Way. The Story of the Kenya and Uganda Railway. Being the Official History of the Development of the Transport System in Kenya and Uganda.* Nairobi, 1950 [also London, 1954].

Hirshfield, Claire, *The Diplomacy of Partition. Britain, France and the Creation of Nigeria, 1890-1898.* The Hague, 1979.

Histoire économique et sociale de la France, Ed. by Fernand Braudel and Ernest Labrousse. Vol. 3, part 1; vol. 4, part 1. Paris, 1976-9.

Hobsbawm, Eric J., *Industry and Empire. An Economic History of Britain since 1750.* London, 1968.

Hobson, John A., *Confessions of an Economic Heretic.* London, 1938.

Hobson, John A., *Imperialism. A Study.* 3rd ed., London, 1938. [Repr. 1968. 1st ed., 1902.]

Hodgart, Alan, *The Economics of Imperialism.* London, 1977.

Hoffman, Ross J.S., *Great Britain and the German Trade Rivalry 1875-1914.* Philadelphia, 1933.

Hollenberg, Günter, *Englisches Interesse am Kaiserreich. Die Attraktivität Preussen-Deutschlands für konservative und liberale Kreise in Grossbritannien 1860-1914.* Wiesbaden, 1974.

[Holstein, Friedrich von], *The Holstein Papers.* Ed. by Norman Rich and M.H. Fisher. Vol. 2. Diaries. Cambridge, 1957.

Hopkins, Anthony G., 'Economic Imperialism in West Africa: Lagos, 1880-92', *The Economic History Review,* 2nd series, 21 (1968), pp. 580-606.

Hyam, Ronald, *Britain's Imperial Century 1815-1914. A Study of Empire and Expansion.* London, 1976.

Hynes, William G., *The Economics of Empire: Britain, Africa and the New Imperialism 1870-95.* London, 1979.

Imlah, Albert H., *Economic Elements in the Pax Britannica. Studies in British Foreign Trade in the Nineteenth Century.* Cambridge, Mass., 1958. [Repr. New York 1969.]

Imperialismus. Ed. by Hans-Ulrich Wehler. Cologne and Berlin, 1970. [3rd ed., 1976. Revised repr., 1979.]

Imperialismus und strukturelle Gewalt. Analysen über abhängige Reproduktion. Ed. by Dieter Senghaas. Frankfurt/m., 1972.

Irvin, I., *Obez'jany, angely i viktoriancy. Darvin, Geksli e evoljucija.* [Apes, the English and the Victorians. Darwin, Huxley and evolution.] Moscow, 1973.

James, Robert R., *Rosebery. A Biography of Archibald Philip, Fifth Earl of Rosebery.* London, 1963.

Jay, Richard, *Joseph Chamberlain. A Political Study.* Oxford, 1981.

Jeschke, Hans, Die Generation von 1898 in Spanien. (Versuch einer Wesenbestimmung.) Halle S., 1934. [Span. transl.: La Generacion del 1898 . . . Madrid, 1954.]

Jones, Greta, *Social Darwinism and English Thought. The Interaction between Biological and Social Theory.* Brighton, 1980.

Judd, Denis, *Radical Joe. A Life of Joseph Chamberlain.* London, 1977.

Kanya-Forstner, Alexander S., *The Conquest of the Western Sudan. A Study in French Military Imperialism.* Cambridge, 1969.

Kanya-Forstner, Alexander S., 'Military Expansion in the Western Sudan — French and British style', *France and Britain in Africa. Imperial*

Rivalry and Colonial Rule. Ed. by Prosser Gifford and William R. Louis. New Haven and London, 1971, pp. 409-41.

Kapitalismus, Organisierter —. Voraussetzungen und Anfänge. Mit Beiträgen von Gerald D. Feldman [*et alia*]. Ed. by Heinrich August Winkler. Göttingen, 1974.

Kemp, Tom, *Theories of Imperialism*. London, 1967.

Kendle, John E., *The Colonial and Imperial Conferences 1887-1911. A Study in Imperial Organization*. London, 1967.

Kennedy, Paul M., *The Partition of the Samoan Islands, 1898-1899*. Oxford, 1970.

Kennedy, Paul M., 'Bismarck's Imperialism: the case of Samoa, 1880-1890', *The Historical Journal*, 15 (1972) pp. 261-83.

Kennedy, Paul M., 'Anglo-German Relations in the Pacific and the Partition of Samoa: 1885-1899', *Australian Journal of Politics and History*, 17 (1972/3), pp. 56-72.

Kennedy, Paul M., *The Samoan Tangle: a Study in Anglo-German-American Relations, 1878-1900*. London, 1974.

Kennedy, Paul M., *The Rise of the Anglo-German Antagonism 1860-1914*. London, 1980.

Kettenbach, Hans Werner, *Lenins Theorie des Imperialismus*. Teil 1. Grundlagen und Voraussetzungen. Cologne, 1965.

Kiernan, Vernon G., *Marxism and Imperialism*. New York, 1974.

Kindleberger, Charles P., *Economic Growth in France and Britain 1851-1950*. Cambridge, Mass., 1964.

Klein, Wolfgang, 'Ein zweitrangiger Imperialismus? Zur Herausbildung des französischen Imperialismus vor 1914', *Neue Studien zum Imperialismus vor 1914*. Ed. by Fritz Klein. (East) Berlin, 1980, pp. 165-95.

Knox, B. A., 'Reconsidering Mid-Victorian Imperialism', *The Journal of Imperial and Commonwealth History*, 1 (1972/3), pp. 155-72.

Koebner, Richard, and Schmidt, Helmut D., *Imperialism. The Story and Significance of a Political Word, 1840-1960*. Cambridge, 1964.

Koch, Hannsjoachim W., 'Die Rolle des Sozialdarwinismus als Faktor im Zeitalter des neuen Imperialismus um die Jahrhundertwende', *Zeitschrift für Politik*, 17 (1970), pp. 51-70.

Koch, Hannsjoachim W., *Der Sozialdarwinismus. Seine Genese und sein Einfluss auf das imperialistische Denken*. Munich, 1973.

Krauss, Werner, *Spanien 1900-1965. Beitrag zu einer modernen Ideologiegeschichte*. Unter Mitarbeit von Karlheinz Barck [*et alia*]. Munich and Salzburg, 1972.

Kubicek, Robert V., *Economic Imperialism in Theory and Practice. The Case of South African Gold Mining Finance 1886-1914*. Durham NC, 1979.

Landes, David S., 'Some Thoughts on the Nature of Economic Imperialism', *The Journal of Economic History*, 21 (1961), pp. 496-512.

Langer, William L., *European Alliances and Alignments 1871-1890*. New York, 1931. [Repr. with additional bibliography, 1952.]

Langer, William L., *The Diplomacy of Imperialism 1890-1902*. New York, 1935. [Repr. with additional bibliography, 1951.]

Langer, William L., 'A Critique of Imperialism', in William L. Langer, *Explorations in Crisis. Papers on International History*. Ed. by Carl E. Schorske and Elizabeth Schorske. Cambridge, Mass., 1969, pp. 167–84. [Originally published in *Foreign Affairs*, 14 (1935), pp. 102–19.]

Latour da, Veiga Pinto, Françoise, *Le Portugal et le Congo au XIXe siècle. Etude d'histoire des relations internationales*. Paris, 1972.

Lenin, Vladimir I., *Collected Works*, vol. 19. New York, 1942.

Leroy-Beaulieu, Paul, *De la colonisation chez les peuples modernes*. 2nd ed., Paris 1882. [1st ed., 1874.]

Lévy-Leboyer, Maurice, 'La croissance économique en France au XIXe siècle. Résultats préliminaires', *Annales. Économies – Sociétés – Civilisations*, 23 (1968), pp. 788–807.

Lloyd, Trevor, 'Africa and Hobson's Imperialism', *Past and Present*, No. 55 (1972), pp. 130–53.

Louis, Paul, 'La Colonisation sous la troisième République', *La Revue socialiste*, 13 (1897), pp. 24–38, 155–73.

Louis, Paul, 'Le socialisme et l'expansion coloniale contemporaine', *La Revue socialiste*, 15 (1899), pp. 553–72.

Louis, William R., 'The Berlin Congo Conference', *France and Britain in Africa. Imperial Rivalry and Colonial Rule*. Ed. by Prosser Gifford and William R. Louis. New Haven and London, 1971, pp. 167–220.

Low, Donald A., *Buganda in Modern History*. Berkeley and Los Angeles, 1971.

Lowe, Cedric J., *The Reluctant Imperialists. British Foreign Policy 1878–1902*. 2 Vols. London, 1967.

Lüthy, Herbert, '*Die Kolonisation und die Einheit der Geschichte*', *Imperialismus*. Ed. by Hans-Ulrich Wehler. Cologne and Berlin, 1970, pp. 42–55.

Macdonagh, Oliver, 'The Anti-Imperialism of Free Trade', *The Economic History Review*, 2nd series, 14 (1961–2), pp. 489–501.

McIntyre, William D., *The Imperial Frontier in the Tropics, 1865–75. A Study of British Colonial Policy in West Africa, Malaya and the South Pacific in the Age of Gladstone and Disraeli*. London, 1967.

McLean, David, 'Finance and "Informal Empire" before the First World War', *The Economic History Review*, 2nd series, 29 (1976), pp. 291–305.

Mahan, Alfred T., *The Influence of Sea Power on History 1660–1783*. Cambridge, Mass., 1890.

Malmesbury, James H.H. Earl of, *Memoirs of an Ex-Minister. An Autobiography*, Vol. 2. Leipzig, 1885.

Marcus, Harold G., 'Imperialism and Expansionism in Ethiopia from 1865 to 1900'. *Colonialism in Africa 1870–1960*, vol. 1. The History and Politics of Colonialism 1870–1914. Ed. by Lewis H. Gann and Peter Duignan. Cambridge, 1969, pp. 420–61.

Marcus, Harold G., *The Life and Times of Menelik II: Ethiopia 1844–1913*. London, 1973.

Marlowe, John, *Cecil Rhodes. The Anatomy of Empire*. London, 1972.

Mathew, W.M., 'The Imperialism of Free Trade: Peru, 1820–70', *The Economic History Review*, 2nd series, 21 (1968), pp. 562–79.

Matthew, H. Colin G., *The Liberal Imperialists. The Ideas and Politics of a Post-Gladstonian Élite.* Oxford, 1973.

Mawby, A.A., 'Capital, Government and Politics in the Transvaal, 1900–1907: A Revision and a Reversion', *The Historical Journal,* 17 (1974), pp. 387–415.

Mazenot, Georges, *La Likouala-Mossaka. Histoire de la pénétration du Haut Congo 1878–1920.* Paris and The Hague, 1970.

Medick, Hans, 'Anfänge und Voraussetzungen des Organisierten Kapitalismus in Grossbritannien 1873–1914', *Organisierter Kapitalismus Voraussetzungen und Anfänge.* Ed. by Heinrich August Winkler. Göttingen, 1974, pp. 58–83.

Mejcher, Helmut, 'Die Bagdadbahn als Instrument des deutschen wirtschaftlichen Einflusses im Osmanischen Reich', *Geschichte und Gesellschaft,* 1 (1975), pp. 447–81.

Meyer, Alfred G., 'Lenins Imperialismustheorie', *Imperialismus.* Ed. by Hans-Ulrich Wehler. Cologne and Berlin, 1970, pp. 123–54.

Meyer, Hans, *Die Eisenbahnen im tropischen Afrika. Eine kolonialwirtschaftliche Studie.* Leipzig, 1902.

Michalet, Charles-Albert, *Les Placements des épargnants français de 1815 à nos jours.* Paris, 1968.

Michel, Marc, *La Mission Marchand 1895–1899.* Paris and The Hague, 1972.

Millin, Sarah Gertrude, *Rhodes.* London, 1952. [1st ed., 1933.]

Mogk, Walter, *Paul Rohrbach und das 'Grössere Deutschland'. Ethischer Imperialismus im Wilhelminischen Zeitalter' Ein Beitrag zur Geschichte des Kulturprotestantismus'* Munich, 1972.

Mommsen, Wolfgang J., 'Nationale und ökonomische Faktoren im britischen Imperialismus vor 1914', *Historische Zeitschrift,* 206 (1968), pp. 618–64. Repr. in Wolfgang Mommsen, *Der europäische Imperialismus. Aufsätze und Abhandlungen.* Göttingen, 1979, pp. 12–57.

Mommsen, Wolfgang J., *Imperialismustheorien. Ein Überblick über die neueren Imperialismusinterpretationen.* Göttingen, 1977.

Moon, Parker T., *Imperialism and World Politics.* New York, 1927.

Morison, David, 'Colonial Rule', *Marxism, Communism and Western Society. A Comparative Encyclopedia.* Ed. by C. D. Kernig. Vol. 2. New York, 1972, pp. 48–58.

Murphy, Agnes, *The Ideology of French Imperialism 1871–1881.* Washington, DC, 1948. [Repr. New York, 1968.]

Nersesov, G.A., *Diplomatičeskaja istorija egipetskogo krisisa 1881–1882gg.* [A Diplomatic History of the Egyptian Crisis, 1881–1882.] Moscow, 1979.

Newbury, Colin W., *British Policy towards West Africa. Select Documents.* [Vol. 1.] *1786–1874.* Oxford, 1965. – Vol. 2. *1875–1914. With statistical appendices, 1800–1914.* Oxford, 1971.

Newbury, Colin W., 'The Protectionist Revival in French Colonial Trade: the case of Senegal', *The Economic History Review,* 2nd series, 21 (1968), pp. 337–48.

Newbury, Colin W., and Kanya-Forstner, Alexander S., 'French Policy and the Origins of the Scramble for West Africa', *The Journal of*

African History, 10 (1969), pp. 253-76.

Newbury, Colin W., 'The Tariff Factor in Anglo-French West African Partition', *France and Britain in Africa. Imperial Rivalry and Colonial Rule*. Ed. by Prosser Gifford and William R. Louis. New Haven and London, 1971, pp. 221-59.

Nkrumah, Kwame, *Challenge of the Congo*. New York, 1967.

Novicow [Novikov], Jakov, La Politique internationale. Paris, 1886.

Obichere, Boniface I., *West African States and the European Expansion. The Dahomey-Niger Hinterland, 1885-1898*. New Haven and London, 1971.

Oliver, Roland, *The Missionary Factor in East Africa*. London, 1952.

Organisierter Kapitalismus. Voraussetzungen und Anfänge. Mit Beiträgen von Gerald D. Feldman [*et alia*]. Ed. by Heinrich August Winkler, Göttingen, 1974.

Pearson, Karl, *National Life from the Standpoint of Science. An Address delivered at Newcastle, November 19, 1900*. London, 1901.

Pelling, Henry, 'British Labour and British Imperialism', in Henry Pelling, *Popular Politics and Society in Late Victorian Britain*. London, 1968, pp. 82-100.

Pelling, Henry, *Popular Politics and Society in Late Victorian Britain*. London, 1968.

Perham, Margery, *Lugard*. [Vol. 1.] The Years of Adventure 1858-1898. London, 1956. [Repr. Hamden, Conn., 1968.]

Persell, Stuart M., 'Joseph Chailley-Bert and the Importance of the Union coloniale française', *The Historical Journal*, 17 (1974), pp. 176-84.

Peterson, John, *Province of Freedom. A History of Sierra Leone 1787-1870*. London, 1969.

Platt, Desmond C.M., 'Economic Factors in British Policy during the "New Imperialism"', *Past and Present*, No. 39 (1968), pp. 120-38.

Platt, Desmond C.M., *Finance, Trade, and Politics in British Foreign Policy 1815-1914*. Oxford, 1968. [Repr., 1971.]

Platt, Desmond C.M., 'The Imperialism of Free Trade: some reservations', *The Economic History Review*, 2nd series, 21 (1968), pp. 296-306.

Platt, Desmond C.M., *Latin America and British Trade 1806-1914*. London, 1972.

Platt, Desmond C.M., 'Further Objections to an "Imperialism of Free Trade", 1830-60', *The Economic History Review*, 2nd series, 26 (1973), pp. 77-91.

Poidevin, Raymond, *Les Relations économiques et financières entre la France et l'Allemagne de 1898 à 1914*. Paris, 1969.

Poidevin, Raymond, 'Weltpolitik allemande et capitaux français (1898-1914)', *Deutschland in der Weltpolitik des 19. und 20. Jahrhunderts*. Ed. by Imanuel Geiss and Bernd J. Wendt. Düsseldorf, 1973, pp. 237-49.

Porter, A.N., *The Origins of the South African War. Joseph Chamberlain and the Diplomacy of Imperialism 1895-99*. Manchester, 1980.

Porter, Bernard, *Critics of Empire. British Radical Attitudes to Col-*

onialism in Africa 1895-1914. London, 1968.
Price, Richard, *An Imperial War and the British Working Class. Working-class Attitudes and Reactions to the Boer War 1899-1902*. London and Toronto, 1972.
Problems in the History of Colonial Africa 1860-1960. Ed. by Robert O. Collins. Englewood Cliffs, NJ, 1970.
Prompt, Victor, 'Soudan nilotique', *Bulletin de l'Institut Égyptien*, 3me série, No. 4 (January 1893), pp. 71-116.
Ramm, Agatha, 'Great Britain and France in Egypt 1876-1882', *France and Britain in Africa. Imperial Rivalry and Colonial Rule*. Ed. by Prosser Gifford and William R. Louis. New Haven and London, 1971, pp. 73-119.
Ramm, Agatha, *Sir Robert Morier. Envoy and Ambassador in the Age of Imperialism 1876-1893*. Oxford, 1973.
Ramsden, Herbert, *The 1898 Movement in Spain. Towards a Reinterpretation*. Manchester, 1974.
Raskin, Jonah, 'Imperialism: Conrad's Heart of Darkness', *The Journal of Contemporary History*, 2 (1967), No. 2, pp. 113-31.
Reese, Trevor R., *The History of the Royal Commonwealth Society. 1868-1968*. London, 1968.
Rempel, Richard A., *Unionists Divided. Arthur Balfour, Joseph Chamberlain and the Unionist Free Traders*. Newton Abbot, 1972.
Renault, François, *Lavigerie, L'esclavage africain et l'Europe 1868-1892*. Vol. 1. Afrique Centrale. Vol. 2. Campagne anti-esclavagiste. Paris, 1971.
Renault, François, *L'abolition de l'esclavage au Sénégal. L'attitude de l'administration française 1848-1905*. Paris, 1972.
Renty, Ernest-Amédée de, *Les chemins de fer coloniaux en Afrique. 1re partie. Chemins de fer des colonies allemandes, italiennes et portugaises*. Paris, 1903.
Reuter, Peter W., *Die Balkanpolitik des französischen Imperialismus 1911-1914*. Frankfurt/M., 1979.
Robinson, Ronald, and Gallagher, John, with Alice Denny, *Africa and the Victorians. The Official Mind of Imperialism*. London, 1961.
Robinson, Ronald, and Gallagher, John, 'The Partition of Africa', *The New Cambridge Modern History*, vol. 11. Material Progress and World-Wide Problems 1870-1898. Cambridge, 1962 [reprint, 1970], pp. 593-640.
Robinson and Gallagher Controversy. The — . Ed. with an introduction by William Roger Louis. New York and London, 1976.
Rohe, Karl, 'Ursachen und Bedingungen des modernen britischen Imperialismus vor 1914', *Der moderne Imperialismus*. Ed. by Wolfgang J. Mommsen. Stuttgart, 1971, pp. 60-84.
Rosenbaum, Jürgen, *Frankreich in Tunesien. Die Anfänge des Protektorates 1881-1886*. Zurich and Freiburg i.B., 1971.
Rosenberg, Hans, *Grosse Depression und Bismarckzeit. Wirtschaftsablauf, Gesellschaft und Politik in Mitteleuropa*. Berlin, 1967.
Rostow, Walt W., *British Economy of the Nineteenth Century. Essays*. Oxford, 1948.

Rostow, Walt W., *The Stages of Economic Growth. A non-Communist manifesto.* 2nd ed., Cambridge, 1971. [1st ed., 1960.]

Roumens, Étienne-Clément-Victor, *L'impérialisme français et les chemins de fer transafricains.* Paris, 1914.

Rubenson, Sven, *The Survival of Ethiopian Independence.* London, 1976.

Rumpler, Helmut, 'Zum gegenwärtigen Stand der Imperialismusdebatte', *Geschichte in Wissenschaft und Unterricht*, 25 (1974), pp. 257–71.

Russell, A.K., *Liberal Landslide. The General Election of 1906.* Newton Abbot and Hamden, Conn., 1973.

Sanderson, George N., *England, Europe and the Upper Nile 1882–1899. A Study in the Partition of Africa.* Edinburgh, 1965.

Sanderson, George N., 'The Origins and Significance of the Anglo-French Confrontation at Fashoda, 1898', *France and Britain in Africa. Imperial Rivalry and Colonial Rule.* Ed. by Prosser Gifford and William R. Louis. New Haven and London, 1971, pp. 285–331.

Sanderson, George N., 'The European Partition of Africa: coincidence or conjuncture?,', *European Imperialism and the Partition of Africa.* Ed. by E. F. Penrose. London, 1975, pp. 1–54.

Saul, Samuel B., *Studies in British Overseas Trade 1870–1914.* Liverpool, 1960.

Saul, Samuel B., *The Myth of the Great Depression, 1873–1896. London, 1969.*

Scally, Robert J., *The Origins of the Lloyd George Coalition. The Policies of Social-Imperialism, 1900–1918.* Princeton, NJ, 1975.

Schädlich, Karlheinz, 'Wandlungen in der Aussenhandelsdiplomatie Grossbritanniens (1885–1910)', *Neue Studien zum Imperialismus vor 1914.* Ed. by Fritz Klein. (East) Berlin, 1980, pp. 135–63.

Schäfer, Hans-Bernd, *Imperialismusthesen und Handelsgewinne. Zur Theorie der Wirtschaftsbeziehungen zwischen Industrie- und Entwicklungsländern.* Düsseldorf, 1972.

Schieder, Wolfgang, 'Aspekte des italienischen Imperialismus vor 1914', *Der moderne Imperialismus.* Ed. by Wolfgang J. Mommsen. Stuttgart, 1971, pp. 140–71.

Schmidt, Helmut D., and Mommsen, Wolfgang J., 'Imperialism', *Marxism, Communism and Western Society. A Comparative Encyclopedia.* Ed. by C. D. Kernig. Vol. 4. New York, 1972, pp. 211–29.

Schmitt, Karl, *Der Begriff des Politischen. Text von 1932 . . .* Berlin, 1963.

Schölch, Alexander, *Ägypten den Ägyptern! Die politische und gesellschaftliche Krise der Jahre 1878–1882 in Ägypten.* Zurich und Freiburg i.B. [1973?].

Schreuder, Deryck M., *The Scramble for Southern Africa, 1877–1895. The Politics of Partition Reappraised.* Cambridge, 1980.

Schröder, Hans-Christoph, *Sozialismus und Imperialismus. Die Auseinandersetzung der deutschen Sozialdemokratie mit dem Imperialismusproblem und der 'Weltpolitik' vor 1914.* Teil 1. Hanover, 1968.

Schröder, Hans-Christoph, 'Hobsons Imperialismustheorie', *Imperialismus.* Ed. by Hans-Ulrich Wehler. Cologne and Berlin, 1970, pp. 104–22.

Schröder, Hans-Christoph, *Sozialistische Imperialismusdeutung. Studien zu ihrer Geschichte.* Göttingen, 1973.

Schröder, Hans-Christoph, *Imperialistisches und antidemokratisches Denken. Alfred Milners Kritik am politischen System Englands.* Wiesbaden, 1978.

Schumpeter, Joseph, 'The Sociology of Imperialism', in Joseph Schumpeter, *Imperialism. Social Classes. Two Essays.* Introduction by Bert Hoselitz. Transl. by Heinz Norden. New York, 1955, p. 3–98.

Seaman, Lewis C.B., *Victorian England. Aspects of English and Imperial History 1837–1901.* London, 1973.

Searle, G.R., *The Quest for National Efficiency. A Study in British Politics and Political Thought, 1899–1914.* Berkeley and Los Angeles, 1971.

Searle, G.R., *Eugenics and Politics in Britain, 1900–1914.* Leyden, 1976.

Sébillot, Amédée, *Le Transafricain, les grandes lignes commerciales de la Méditerranée au golfe de Guinée et à l'océan Indien* . . . Paris, 1893.

Sée, Henri, *Histoire économique de la France.* Vol. 2. Les Temps modernes 1789–1914. Paris, 1942.

Seeley, John R., *The Expansion of England.* Ed. . . . by John Gross. Chicago and London, 1971. [1st ed., London, 1883.]

Segal, Harvey H., and Simon, Matthew, 'British Foreign Capital Issues, 1865–1894', *The Journal of Economic History*, 21 (1961), pp. 566–81.

Seidler, Eduard, 'Evolutionismus in Frankreich', *Sudhoffs Archiv*, 53 (1969), pp. 362–77.

Seidler, Eduard, and Nagel, Günter, 'Georges Vacher de Lapouge (1854–1936) und der Sozialdarwinismus in Frankreich', *Biologismus im 19. Jahrhundert* . . . Ed. by Gunter Mann. Stuttgart, 1973, pp. 94–107.

Semmel, Bernard, *Imperialism and Social Reform. English Social-Imperial Thought 1895–1914.* London, 1960.

Semmel, Bernard, 'The Philosophical Radicals and Colonialism', *The Journal of Economic History*, 21 (1961), pp. 513–25.

Shick, Tom W., 'A Quantitative Analysis of Liberian Colonization from 1820 to 1843 with Special Reference to Mortality', *The Journal of African History*, 12·(1970), pp. 45–59.

Sieberg, Herward, *Eugène Étienne und die französische Kolonialpolitik (1887–1904).* Cologne and Opladen, 1968.

Smith, Iain R., *The Emin Pasha Relief Expedition 1886–1890.* Oxford, 1972.

Smith, Michael S., *Tariff Reform in France, 1860–1900. The Politics of Economic Interest.* Ithaca, 1980.

Smith, Paul, *Disraelian Conservatism and Social Reform.* London and Toronto, 1967.

Soleillet, Paul, *Voyage à Ségou 1878–1879.* Rédigé d'après les notes et journaux de voyage de Soleillet par Gabriel Gravier. Paris, 1887.

Sombart, Werner, *Der moderne Kapitalismus. Historisch-systematische Darstellung des gesamten Wirtschaftslebens von seinen Anfängen bis zur Gegenwart.* Vol. 3. Das Wirtschaftsleben im Zeitalter des Hochkapitalismus. Part 1. Die Grundlagen — Der Aufbau. Munich and Leipzig, 1927.

Spree, Reinhard, *Wachstumstrends und Konjunkturzyklen in der deutschen Wirtschaft von 1820 bis 1913. Quantitativer Rahmen für eine Konjunkturgeschichte des 19. Jahrhunderts.* Göttingen, 1978.

Staley, Eugene, *War and the Private Investor. A Study in the Relations of International Private Investment.* Garden City, NY, 1935. [Repr. New York, 1967.]

Steiner, Zara S., 'The Last Years of the Old Foreign Office 1898-1905', *The Historical Journal*, 6 (1963), pp. 59-90.

Steiner, Zara S., *The Foreign Office and Foreign Policy, 1898-1914.* Cambridge, 1969.

Steiner, Zara S., 'Finance, Trade and Politics in British Foreign Policy, 1815-1914', *The Historical Journal*, 13 (1970), pp. 545-52.

Stembridge, Stanley R., 'Disraeli and the Millstones', *The Journal of British Studies*, 5 (1965), pp. 122-39.

Stengers, Jean, 'L'impérialisme colonial de la fin du XIXe siècle: mythe ou réalité?', *The Journal of African History*, 3 (1962), pp. 469-91.

Stengers, Jean, 'King Leopold and the Anglo-French Rivalry 1882-1884', *France and Britain in Africa. Imperial Rivalry and Colonial Rule.* Ed. by Prosser Gifford and William R. Louis. New Haven and London, 1971, pp. 121-66.

Stenographische Berichte über die Verhandlungen des Reichstags. VIII. Legislaturperiode. I. Session 1890/91. Vol. 1. Berlin, 1890.

Stokes, Eric, 'Late Nineteenth-Century Colonial Expansion and the Attack on the Theory of Economic Imperialism: a case of mistaken identity?', *The Historical Journal*, 12 (1969), pp. 285-301.

Strachey, John, *The End of Empire.* London, 1959.

Studies in the Theory of Imperialism. Ed. by Roger Owen and Bob Sutcliffe. London, 1972.

Sykes, Alan, *Tariff Reform in British Policy 1903-1913.* New York and London, 1979.

Temperley, Howard, *British Antislavery 1833-1870.* London, 1972.

Tetzlaff, Rainer, *Koloniale Entwicklung und Ausbeutung. Wirtschafts- und Sozialgeschichte Deutsch-Ostafrikas 1885-1914.* Berlin, 1970.

Thobie, Jacques, *Intérêts et impérialisme français dans l'empire ottoman (1895-1914).* Paris, 1977.

Thomas, William, *The Philosophic Radicals. Nine Studies in Theory and Practice, 1817-1841.* Oxford, 1979.

Touval, Saadia, 'Treaties, Borders, and the Partition of Africa', *The Journal of African History*, 7 (1966), pp. 279-93.

Treue, Wolfgang, *Die Jaluit-Gesellschaft auf den Marshall-Inseln 1887-1914. Ein Beitrag zur Kolonial- und Verwaltungsgeschichte in der Epoche des deutschen Kaiserreiches.* Berlin, 1976.

Uzoigwe, Godfrey N., *Britain and the Conquest of Africa. The Age of Salisbury.* Ann Arbor, 1974.

[Victoria, Queen], *The Letters of Queen Victoria.* Third series. A selection from Her Majesty's correspondence and journal between the years 1886 and 1901. Ed. by George Earle Buckle. Vol. 1. 1886-

1890. London, 1890.

Vinogradov, K.B., and Naumenkov, O.A., 'Sovremennaja buržuaznaja istoriografija razdela Afriki'. [Present-day bourgeois historiography on the partition of Africa.] *Voprosy istorii* (May 1972), pp. 188–97.

Vogüé, Eugène-Melchior de, *Le Maitre de la mer*. 49th ed., Paris, 1924. [1st ed., not dated, about 1903.]

Walker, James St. G., *The Black Loyalists. The Search for a Promised Land in Nova Scotia and Sierra Leone 1783–1870*. New York, 1976.

Walker, John W., 'The "Comité de l'Afrique française." (1890–1895): a French Colonial Pressure Group'. *Ph.D., University of California, Berkeley, 1977*.

Wallach, Jehuda L., *Kriegstheorien. Ihre Entwicklung im 19. und 20. Jahrhundert*. Frankfurt/M., 1972.

Ward, William E. F., *The Royal Navy and the Slavers: the Suppression of the Atlantic Slave Trade*. London, 1969.

Wehler, Hans-Ulrich, *Bismarck und der Imperialismus*. Cologne and Berlin, 1969. [3rd ed., 1972.]

Wehler, Hans-Ulrich 'Sozialdarwinismus im expandierenden Industriestaat', *Deutschland in der Weltpolitik des 19. und 20. Jahrhunderts*. Ed. by Imanuel Geiss and Bernd J. Wendt. Düsseldorf, 1973, pp. 133–42.

Wehler, Hans-Ulrich, *Bibliographie zum Imperialismus*. Göttingen, 1977.

Wernecke, Klaus, *Der Wille zur Weltgeltung. Aussenpolitik und Öffentlichkeit im Kaiserreich am Vorabend des Ersten Weltkrieges*. Düsseldorf, 1969.

West, Katherine, 'Theorising about "Imperialism": a methodological note', *The Journal of Imperial and Commonwealth History*, 1 (1972–73), pp. 148–54.

Wild, Adolf, *Baron d'Estournelles de Constant (1852–1924). Das Wirken eines Friedensnobelpreisträgers für die deutsch-französische Verständigung und europäische Einigung*. Ph.D. Mainz, 1973.

Williams, Eric, *Capitalism and Slavery*. Chapel Hill, 1944. [Paperback ed., New York, 1966.]

Williams, Judith B., *British Commercial Policy and Trade Expansion 1750–1850*. Oxford, 1972.

Wilson, Charles, 'The Economic Role and Mainsprings of Imperialism', *Colonialism in Africa 1870–1960*. Vol. 4. The Economics of Colonialism. Ed. by Peter Duignan and L. H. Gann. Cambridge, 1975, pp. 68–91.

Winn, Peter, 'British Informal Empire in Uruguay in the Nineteenth Century', *Past and Present*, No. 73 (1976), pp. 100–26.

Wirz, Albert, *Vom Sklavenhandel zum kolonialen Handel. Wirtschaftsräume und Wirtschaftsformen in Kamerun vor 1914*. Zurich and Freiburg i.B., 1972.

Witt, Peter-Christian, *Die Finanzpolitik des Deutschen Reiches von 1903 bis 1913. Eine Studie zur Innenpolitik des Wilhelminischen Deutschland*. Lübeck and Hamburg, 1970.

Woodruff, William, *Impact of Western Man. A Study of Europe's Role in the World Economy 1750–1960*. London, 1966.

Woolf, Leonard, *Empire and Commerce in Africa. A Study in Economic*
Wrigley, C.C., 'Neo-Mercantile Policies and the New Imperialism', *The Imperial Impact. Studies in the Economic History of Africa and India.* Ed. by Clive Dewey and A. G. Hopkins. London, 1978, pp. 20–34.
Wyatt, Harold F., 'God's Test by War', *The Nineteenth Century and After*, No. 411 (April 1911), pp. 591–606.
Young, Leonard K., *British Policy in China 1895–1902.* Oxford, 1970.
Zaghi, Carlo, *L'Europa davanti all'Africa.* Vol. 1. La via del Nilo. Naples, 1971.
Zaghi, Carlo, *I Russi in Etiopia.* Vol. 1. Il protettorato italiano nell' Etiopia. Vol. 2. Menelik e la battaglia di Adua. Naples, 1972.
Ziebura, Gilbert, 'Interne Faktoren des französischen Hochimperialismus 1871–1914', *Der moderne Imperialismus.* Ed. by Wolfgang J. Mommsen. Stuttgart, 1971, pp. 85–139.
Zimmermann, Louis J., and Grumbach, Franz, 'Saving, Investment and Imperialism. A reconsideration of the theory of imperialism', *Weltwirtschaftliches Archiv*, 71 (1953), p. 1–21.
Zmarzlik, Hans-Günter, 'Der Sozialdarwinismus in Deutschland als geschichtliches Problem', in Hans-Günter Zmarzlik, *Wieviel Zunkunft hat unsere Vergangenheit? Aufsätze und Überlegungen eines Historikers vom Jahrgang 1922.* Munich, 1970, pp. 56–85.
Zmarzlik, Hans-Günter, 'Sozialdarwinismus', *Sowjetsystem und demokratische Gesellschaft. Eine vergleichende Enzyklopädie.* Vol. 5. Freiburg i.B., 1972, pp. 905–10.
Zorn, Wolfgang, 'Wirtschaft und Politik im deutschen Imperialismus', *Wirtschaft, Geschichte und Wirtschaftsgeschichte. Festschrift zum 65. Geburtstag von Friedrich Lütge.* Ed. by Wilhelm Abel [*et alia*]. Stuttgart, 1966, pp. 340–54.

Index

Abyssinia, 42, 44–5, 169
Administrative Reform Association, 168
Africa: *passim*
Ahlefeld, Hunold von, 88
Alis, Harry, 78
Ammon, Otto, 85
Anderson, H. Percy, 39, 40, 133
Anglophobia, in France, 39, 55–6
Anti-slavery, 11–13, 14, 179, 187–8 n.21
Arabi Pasha, 44
Archinard, Louis, 18, 64, 206 n.336
Asquith, Herbert H., 166, 171, 176, 182

Bagehot, Walter, 84
Baghdad Railway, 27, 111, 133
Baker, Sir Samuel, 24, 25
Balance of power, 32–9, 48, 69, 166, 172, 180, 181
Balta-Liman, treaty of, 138
Barnaby, Nathaniel, 88
Barotseland, 16
Bébin, 57
Belgium: cf. *Leopold II*
Benoît, G.-C., 64
Berlin Congo Conference (1885), 3, 16, 37, 41, 121, 180, 193 n.110
Berlin Congress (1878), 34–5, 131, 180, 181, 191 n.78
Berlin Evangelical Missionary Society, 15
Bernstein, Eduard, 101
Binger, Louis G., 18
Bismarck, Herbert Fürst von, 148, 151
Bismarck, Otto Fürst von, Eastern question, 35, 36; France, 37, 41, 59; German colonies, 63, 133, 146–53; imperialist associations, 81; social imperialism, 140, 142, 144–5, 164, 177
Blake, Robert, 23
Blatchford, Robert, 172–3
Bleichröder, Gerson, 133

Boehme, Helmut, 154
Boer War, 51, 55, 86, 94, 124, 126, 160, 168, 169, 170, 171, 176, 182, 195 n.133
Bonghi, Ruggiero, 45
Borgnis-Desbordes, Gustave, 29
Bosnia, 35
Brazza, Pierre Savorgnan de, 19, 37, 41, 60–1, 179, 181
Brazza-Makoko treaty (1882), 3, 19, 59–62, 181
Brière de l'Isle, Louis-A.-E.-G., 28
Britain, export of capital, 2, 6, 96, 97–9, 109–11, 123–6, 163, 173; anti-slavery, 11–13, 179; West Africa, 14–15; East Africa, 46; Uganda, 16, 46, 179, 188 n.32; Suez Canal, 22–3; Egypt, 25, 35, 44, 108–9, 113, 114, 148, 162, 179, 180, 181; Portugal, 36–7, 41; France, 39, 41, 63–8, 181–2; jingoism, 49–55; imperialist pressure-groups, 76–7, 81; Germany, 87, 148–9, 166–7; foreign trade, 113–14, 115, 116, 126, 138, 162; protectionist agitation, 119–22; China, 122, 138; Turkey, 138; business cycles, 142; social imperialism, 145, 165–77, 185; Russia, 148; economic development in the 19th century, 157–64, 166–7
British Empire, 49, 50, 51, 73, 77, 98, 113, 120, 124, 125, 137, 165, 166, 168, 169, 170, 172, 173, 174–5, 177, 184; pride in, 52, 89, 181
Brötel, Dieter, 209 n.375
Brunschwig, 14, 15, 19, 79, 118, 119
Bukharin, Nikolaj I., 107
Bülow, Bernhard von, 50
Business cycles, 142, 155–64
Buxton, Thomas F., 14

Cairncross, Alexander K., 124, 125
Cameron, Rondo E., 127
Campbell-Bannerman, Sir Henry, 175